Using IXP2400/2800 Development Tools

A Hands-on Approach to Network Processor Software Design

Donald F. Hooper

INTEL PRESS

ISBN 0-9743649-4-0

This book is printed on acid-free paper. ∞

Publisher: Richard Bowles
Managing Editor: David B. Spencer
Assistant Editor: Lynn Putnam
Text Design & Composition: Wasser Studios
Graphic Art: Wasser Studios (illustrations), Ted Cyrek Designs (cover)

Library of Congress Cataloging in Publication Data:

Printed in the United States of America

10 9 8 7 6 5 4 3 2 1

First Printing, August 2004

To my wife Sandy, who doesn't have a clue as to what I do for a living

Contents

Foreword

The network is getting smarter. Intricate access control rules govern use and misuse. Classification techniques establish complex flow definitions. Advanced traffic engineering and quality-of-service requirements with detailed statistical monitoring and anomaly detection are applied to the serviced network traffic. TCP termination or proxy with security functions such as IPSec or secure sockets layer (SSL) are layered on top of network traffic. Intelligent services, such as virtualization and advanced file management mechanisms, are found in the storage area.

Network processors provide the foundation for these advanced capabilities. Highly parallel, arrayed, multithreaded network instruction, focused processors are being deployed to address the smart network.

To unleash the promise of network processors, effective software design, coding, debugging, and test tools are required. Intel has developed the IXP2XXX product line of flexible network processors. To exploit these processors' flexibility, Intel has also developed a rich set of system development tools.

It is with great pleasure that I introduce you to Don Hooper's *Using IXP2400/2800 Development Tools*. I have had the honor of working with Don for many years. He is a mentor and a gentleman, as well as an amazing engineer. In his early days, Don was a hardware designer. He developed complex instruction units for high-end VAX processors, and then he developed logic synthesis tools to help design teams operate more efficiently. He then moved on to artificial intelligence. Later, Don developed video server software and chaired an MPEG-2 transport committee. I asked Don to rejoin me to drive software architecture for this new thing—network processors—and was very pleased when he accepted. Since that point, Don and I have visited many customers together. Without exception, customers are won over by Don's gentle and understated, yet authoritative, approach. I have watched as the "light has gone on" for customers, after Don has explained very complex concepts in a simple manner.

When Don suggested this book, I was very curious about what the tone and style would be. I am delighted that Don carries out in writing his simple verbal style and respectful approach; I am sure the reader will be pleased. In this book, Don introduces and guides you through a real-world design of an IPv4 and IPv6 router and teaches you best-practice coding and design, which he successfully employed to develop the initial Intel 10 gigabit Packet over Sonet reference design. He involves you in a thoughtful and engaging manner.

This book targets five classes of readers: managers, software architects, assembly language programmers, C programmers, and test engineers. Don describes a systems approach to developing a software solution on Intel IXP2XXX network processors using the six key Intel® Internet Exchange Architecture (Intel® IXA) tools:

1. *The Architecture Tool*—used for establishing the software architecture and mapping to a highly parallel processor, the IXP2XXX network processor

2. *The Developers Workbench*—used to code and debug the example IPv4, IPv6 router project

3. *The optimizing Assembler*—used to assemble Intel IXA uBlocks demonstrated in the example project

4. *The explicitly parallel C compiler and the autopartitioning C compiler*—used in the router project

5. *The packet generator*—configured to exercise the router project

6. *The packet profiler*—used to analyze the router output to verify that the project accomplishes its objective

Don walks us through the router project, demonstrating expert best practices including how to:

■ Reassemble segmented incoming packets

■ Determine the layer 3 protocol

■ Classify and translate the protocol

■ Determine the destination

■ Enqueue to the correct queue

■ Schedule a packet for transmission

■ Dequeue the packet and transmit to a CSIX fabric

Don accomplishes all this instruction by using the appropriate tool at the appropriate time in the design cycle. His experience in this arena, coupled with his clear approach, offers the reader a rare insight into network design.

I thoroughly enjoyed this book. Intel has developed many labor-conserving tools to unleash the IXP2XXX network processor potential. Don pulls all of these tools together in a coherent fashion. Managers will understand the design flow and tradeoffs. Architects will gain insight to structure and resource allocation tools. Programmers will learn how to get started, how to employ the correct tool, and how to use advanced features. Programmers and test engineers will learn the simulation and network traffic generator tools available to debug, analyze, and exercise their designs. Finally, Don explains how to use the profiler to unravel the transmitted data so analysis of correctness may be performed.

The reader will find Don's style engaging and elegant, and the reader will, in short order, understand how all the different Intel IXA tools and documents are leveraged. My only dissatisfaction is that the reader will obtain only a glimpse of the gentle software giant Don Hooper is.

Matthew Adiletta
Intel Fellow

Director Communications Processor Architecture

Preface

Be nice to nerds. Chances are you'll end up working for one.

—Bill Gates

Before Intel acquired us, the Hudson Massachusetts network engineering group at Digital Equipment Corporation (DEC) was like a little outpost on the frontier of some unwanted planet. Our offices were nestled in a vast sea of empty cubicles, but we had no lack of enthusiasm. We had Matthew Adiletta, Gil Wolrich, Bill Wheeler, myself, and a few other hardware engineers. Matt would pump up anyone in earshot with the glories of this new technology. Gil (who really does have ten thumbs, when it comes to operating a computer) would describe in great detail performance calculations and pipe stage timing as if he had it all written on an imaginary screen approximately two feet behind the listener's head. Bring a problem to Gil, and instantly a group would gather in the hallway discussing five possible solutions. The white boards of meeting rooms had bits and parts of microengines all over them, A and B registers, pipe stages, transfer registers, microstore… And the microcode! What was this? Bill had just cranked out a high-level simulation model of the first microengine and converted an Assembler from a previous project to generate instructions. We had alu instructions and branches (with bugs), and SRAM instructions would be ready any day now. Matthew was on fire. He was rallying the troops (who were not there yet!) with daily meetings. "Come on guys! It takes guts and desire," he would say.

I was the first software engineer on this new project. The goal was to develop a programmable processor that could act as an Ethernet bridge. I would be making the transition from distributed network development to chip-based software development. Previously I had started and led the design of a distributed system of up 100 DEC Alpha servers streaming video-on-demand to homes. When DEC pulled the plug, we had over 30 telco customers conducting trials in various locations throughout the world, but the problem was that it was just too costly to route 1.5 million bits per second to millions of homes. So I decided network engineering was where I wanted to be.

I talked to Matt about his new project. This chip could replace application-specific integrated circuits (ASICs)! It could compete with ASICs because of hardware multi-threading and multiple microengines. It could be used for Ethernet, ATM, and other protocols. Being programmable, this chip could be used for many other purposes. My first thought was to make this into a programmable layer 3 router as well.

My second thought was to get some software engineers on board. We picked up Jim Guilford for the Assembler (allowing Bill to finish the memory controller simulation) and Rich Muratori for the graphics user interface (GUI). Jim loves mathematical puzzles, and I hear he has an evil twin with whom he tackles increasingly complex problems. Rich did the GUI for Matt's previous project, which was an MPEG processor for set-top boxes. I brought in Desmond Johnson for the Linker. We were set for tools, Simulator, Assembler, GUI, and Linker!

From these small beginnings we hired more engineers, managers, and marketing representatives. I wish I could name them all in this short space, but this is a book about tools. I'll try to give acknowledgements later in this section, but if I forget your name, remember I will be thinking of you more often because of it.

First Customers

We had a room with two well-used white boards. Customers would come in for the day. Matt would spend the morning describing the hardware. After a nice lunch, it was my turn.

Matt had filled the white boards, so I had to erase as I went. With a software on top of hardware theme, I would draw what came to be known as a day in the life of a packet, as it entered the processor through the FBI, transferred to DRAM and microengines, was classified and modified by the microcode, queued and transmitted. By the end of the day, the board was filled, along with the customers' swelled heads.

Presenting the tools involved an overhead projector showing a DOS window and command line. Bill or I would walk through a few pages of code, assemble it, start the simulator and count the packets received. The first example forwarding design moved packets into a giant dram array, and then moved them back out, first-in, first-out. I used a watch command to display all the PCs of every thread (24 in all) and see whether the microengines were keeping busy. Watching the scrolling PCs was quite mesmerizing, a far cry from the Developer Workbench we now have.

Intel

DEC sold the Hudson semiconductor plant to Intel in early 1998. At the time, both DEC and Intel had little appreciation for the extra baggage that came along with the deal—a small, fledgling programmable network processor engineering group and a Intel® StrongARM* processor engineering group.

We went to Intel Oregon to present our design. Now here was a company that knew what they had! They were running the numbers the first day. They told us they would support us for the long haul. We knew now we had first-class management and marketing to help us succeed.

Our processor became known as a network processor. Instead of a basement-engineering project, we were now developing the Internet Exchange Processor (IXP). Our tool suite was labeled the Developer Workbench, and our software framework was called the Intel® Internet Exchange Architecture (Intel® IXA). This was sounding good!

Acknowledgements

Much of this book describes the GUI that has been integrated into the Developer Workbench. Myles Wilde, Rich Muratori and I worked out the concepts of the thread history window (US Patent 6,611,276) and simulation debug windows. At first I thought Myles was from the government, investigating us because we had a unit named the FBI, but I now know he is just another brilliant member of our cast. To avoid further suspicions, the FBI unit was renamed to media switch fabric (MSF). Ron Rocheleau, Eric Walker, and Dennis Rivard worked tirelessly on GUI enhancements and new packet simulation features. Filling the pages with screenshots made this book much easier to write. Phil Young, Steve Doyle, and Brian Will developed the new Packet Generator.

Myles also started the development of the Architecture Tool. Ron Rocheleau did the initial GUI. A team in Ireland, led by Brian Keating and John Griffin, is now responsible for this development.

Raj Yavatkar is the overall software architect for Intel Network Products. The first time I met him, I said, "We need to develop building block libraries." Little did I know that he would run with this, bringing in exceptional talent in Prashant Chandra, Larry Huston, Uday Naik, Alok Kumar, Erik J. Johnson, and Aaron Kunze. Later Raghu Makaram, who worked closely with customers on technical issues, would join the software architecture group. This group was instrumental in establishing the software framework that is a perfect complement to the new direction of packet-aware tools.

Uday Naik is most responsible for the implementation of Intel IXA microblocks. He has kept the focus on plug-and-play and leads a team of exceptional developers in creating example applications.

I interviewed Bob Kushlis for the microengine C Compiler on the most miserable, cold, sleet-filled day in February. I could not understand why he would want to move from the warm West Coast to Massachusetts, but he said he loved the snow. I think Matt instilled the fire in him.

I would like to thank Prashant Chandra for providing code samples to run on the new autopartitioning C Compiler. He has been the key architect driving the user interface and strategic direction for this compiler. Luddy Harrison is architect of the compiler and has a worldwide team working on it. Needless to say, his team looks up to him in more ways than one (he is also a very tall person).

Jim Guilford and Mariano Fernandez have steadily improved the Assembler over the last 6 years to the point where it optimizes, moves code around, and inserts code. In short, it now behaves like a compiler.

Desmond Johnson is the Linker and runtime debug library man. It is amazing how he keeps up with all of the types of IXP2XXX processors.

Lai-Wah Hui is the software manager for the tools. She has been a tremendous force in driving releases of quality tool products on schedule.

Mark Rosenbluth is the lead hardware engineer. Together, Mark and I developed the proposals for packet-centric debugging tools.

I had many volunteers offering to review this book; it was a bit overwhelming to get so much encouragement. I would like to thank David Spencer, Raj Yavatkar, Bill Carlson, Erik J. Johnson, Eric Heaton, James Guilford, Ihab Bishara, Mike Selissen, Tom Clancy, Prashant Chandra, Uday Naik, Luddy Harrison, Bob Kushlis, Andrew Hsieh, Eric Walker, Rich Muratori, and John Griffin for helping me with this book.

I could fill half the book with peoples' names. To hundreds of others in engineering, field technical support, marketing, and management, thanks for your support.

Most of all, thanks to Matthew Adiletta, without whom none of this would have happened.

■ Let's Do It!

During many customer visits, I have presented the IXP2XXX Product Line tool suite and software examples. Each time, there is some new feature that is particularly exciting. Collectively, the Developer Workbench and its tools are impressive indeed. I have stepped customers through tool features, code and simulation, and watched the "light bulb" go on. They got it!

It is my sincere hope that I can convey this same experience to you. As you go through the design examples in this book, using new tools at every step, you will discover better, faster ways to design and debug your network processor application.

Don Hooper

Chapter 1

What's In It for Me?

Morons...I have morons on my team.

—Dave Letterman

Not really! You've assembled the greatest team ever! They are like a herd ready to stampede. You just need to point them in the right direction—a goal. That goal, which coincidentally is the hypothetical development project used throughout this book, is to design a 4-gigabit IPV4/IPV6 tunneling router with additional fabric header processing. This book walks you through the design of this project using all of the tools in the Intel® Internet Exchange Architecture (Intel® IXA) Software Development Toolkit (SDK). Not only will you learn the basics of each tool, but also the advanced features to really put you in high gear. In the end, you will be an expert on IXP2XXX Product Line tools.

What Hat Do You Wear?

What hat do you wear? Are you a jack of all hats? This book has five sections, one for each member of your team. However, as in any team project, it is good to know what the others are doing so that later, during system integration, the pieces play together correctly. So you should at least look at the pretty pictures in other sections. Most importantly, refer to Figure 1.1 as a substitute for any other illustration in the book.

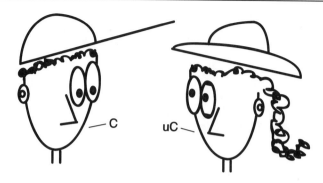

Figure 1.1   Your Team

The roles of your team members are as follows:

- *The Manager.* The manager needs to know the development tasks, how complex the tasks are, how to get tasks done on or ahead of schedule, and how to ensure the design is maintainable and portable forward to the next design. Part I gives you the "2800 foot tour" of the IXP2XXX Product Line characteristics—the tools and strategies for fast project development. Only software project development is covered in the manager's section. The introductions to the other sections of the book give you an overview of the tasks and how the tools are used.

- *The Architect.* The architect needs to understand the complete system; how the design fits in the network; the demands of the design on the memory and I/O subsystems; the coding tasks to be done, the partitioning of code to processing units such as microengines, the Intel XScale® core, and host; how performance goals can be achieved; and the technical assignments of the programmers. Part II focuses on the Architecture Tool and the Developer Workbench basics of setting up a project.

- *The Microcode Programmer.* The driver programmer reaches out and touches the hardware, writing microcode—a language that symbolically represents the microengine instruction. When packets are coming in every 70–150 cycles, according to the architect's calculation, you can't afford to waste any cycles. You must hand-tune and write code for the receive and transmit media switch fabric (MSF) interfaces. Part III presents the assembler and the nuances of microcode.

■ *The C Programmer*. The high-level language programmer is responsible for packet processing, including lookups, classification, packet modification, and queueing. For this section, I assume that readers have a background in network stack code development. Part IV covers the C Compiler with two modes: auto-partitioning and explicit-partitioning.

■ *The Test Engineer*. Everybody needs to be a test engineer at some point in his or her life. The test engineer creates the test harness that drives packets into the chip and validates the transmitted packets coming out. During debug, the test engineer follows code flow and packet data in thread list view, sets watches, tracks packet status, and finds the cause of dropped and erroneous packets. Part V covers packet-centric debugging and real-life debug scenarios.

Choosing a Network Processor

While your initial design will be a 4-gigabit router, you may later have the requirement to convert it to a 10-gigabit router. To forward packets at 10 gigabits per second, what do you need? Lots of parallelism! Here's why: Let's say you need to work on each packet for 3,000 cycles, and each cycle is .7142 nanosecond. That's about 2 microseconds per packet. If you are handling these one at a time, you are running at 500 thousand packets per second. For Ethernet at 10 gigabits per second, you must run at 15 million packets per second. Your serial performance is only one-thirtieth of your goal. What are the solutions?

■ *More processing engines running in parallel*. But if you put 30 processors in a chip, that would be a very hot chip indeed.

■ *Multithreading*. Each thread works on a packet. However, when thread contexts change, isn't there a penalty for swapping in the new local variables?

■ *Using cache to reduce the 3,000 cycles of packet processing*. This stopgap wouldn't work either because the packet data is always changing, so a packet data cache does you no good.

■ *Using asynchronous I/O so threads don't block on memory references*. Now this processor isn't a normal processor.

The IXP2XXX network processors offer a combination of all four solutions. The network processor's microengine is a compact processing core with explicit hardware support for multithreading. Each thread has its own general-purpose registers so that when contexts swap, the system incurs no penalty for setting up the new context. Each thread also has its own set of transfer registers that can hold read and write data while asynchronous I/O is pending. Each thread can control as many as 15 independent asynchronous events, with signaling for each. Local memory and content-addressable memory (CAM) in the microengine can be used to cache control information, such as live TCP/IP connection state, in the event back-to-back packets need to access the same memory location. Finally, up to 16 microengines, each having eight threads, provide up to 128 threads working in parallel. Now you can get to 10 gigabits per second!

Figure 1.2 shows the internal structure of the Intel® IXP2800 Network Processor.

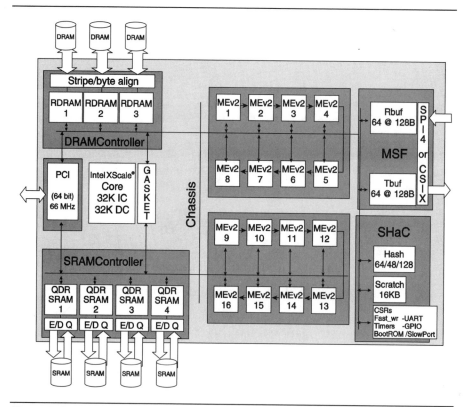

Figure 1.2   Internal Architecture of the Intel® IXP2800 Network Processor

The unit contains a media switch fabric (MSF) interface for the buffering of received and transmitted packets data, 16 microengines with eight threads each, a scratch memory unit for common on-chip storage of transient state information, a hash unit, four SRAM controllers, three DRAM controllers, an Intel XScale core with Intel® StrongARM* technology, and a PCI interface. The Intel IXP2800 network processor's microengines run at 1,400 megahertz.

The Intel® IXP2850 Network Processor is the same as the Intel IXP2800 Network Processor, except that it also includes a cryptography unit that performs DES, 3DES, AES, and SHA-1 algorithms.

The Intel® IXP2400 Network Processor is similar to the Intel IXP2800 Network Processor, with eight microengines instead of 16. All variations of the IXP2XXX Product Line use the same microengine design. The Intel IXP2400 network processor's microengines run at 800 megahertz.

Figure 1.3 shows the structure of the microengine.

The microengine at first appears to be a normal execution unit datapath. You can see how it would be very programmable, unlike ASICs or state machines. In addition, key features help you to achieve high performance:

■ Transfer registers hold read and write data for asynchronous I/O and memory operations, allowing the execution to continue without stalling.

■ Next neighbor registers allow you to quickly pass data to an adjacent microengine.

■ Local memory and CAM can be used as a smart cache. You control what gets prefetched and what gets evicted.

■ CRC (cyclic redundancy check) can be used for ATM SAR calculations and for hash index calculations.

■ General-purpose registers can be dedicated to each thread or individually shared among all threads.

If you want more than a cursory description of the hardware architecture, you can find a complete description in the Internet exchange architecture and applications (Carlson 2003) and in the respective processor's hardware reference manual (Intel 2004).

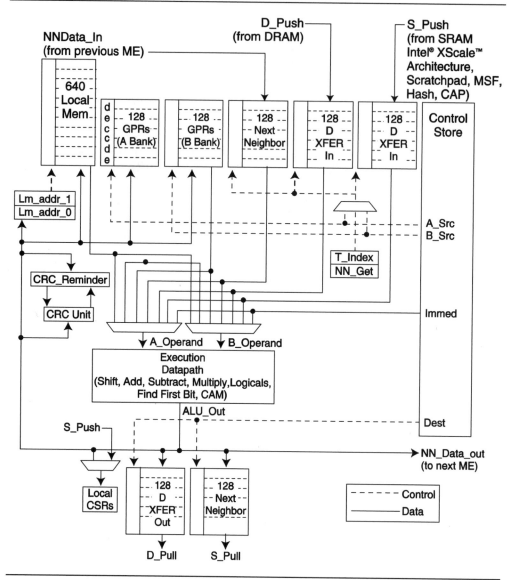

Figure 1.3   Intel® IXP2400 Network Processor Microengine Detail

What Tools Do You Need?

With up to 128 threads doing work in parallel, each controlling up to 15 asynchronous events, you need tools that can help you make sense of all that is occurring. You must be able to partition your design, verify up front that it fits within memory bandwidth and performance cycle limitations, get your team working in parallel on different code tasks, debug complex interactions of packets and their descriptors, and manage all of these tasks as a project. You need the IXP2XXX Product Line Developer Workbench!

Partitioning and Feasibility

The biggest problems you'll probably encounter are the early feasibility study and partitioning of your design, which require that you answer the following questions:

- Does the application code fit in the microengine?
- What partitioning is most likely to meet the line rate requirements?
- Do the memory accesses per packet fit within the I/O and internal bus bandwidths supported by the chip?
- How much memory is needed to support the data structure sizes?
- How many microengines are needed to support the desired line rate?
- Can I reuse some proven code blocks and add my new code?
- Can I do a top-level partitioning with code task flow and hand the partitioning off to programmers for implementation?

Figure 1.4 shows the IXP2XXX Product Line Architecture Tool. Using this tool, you can enter and analyze your software design in a top-down fashion.

Part II of this book shows you how to use the Architecture Tool to enter the IPV4 router design as follows:

1. Partition the code blocks, reusing microblocks from the Intel IXA Software Framework.
2. Add task flow diagrams, I/O references, and data structures.
3. Run the analysis, obtaining performance, bandwidth utilization, and size calculations.

After successful analysis, create a skeletal Developer Workbench project. You may then compile this Developer Workbench project and run it in the simulator. The simulator models the memory references you defined in the Architecture Tool. However, the non-I/O code is represented as no-op instructions. Later, your programmers will replace these no-op instructions during the implementation phase of the project.

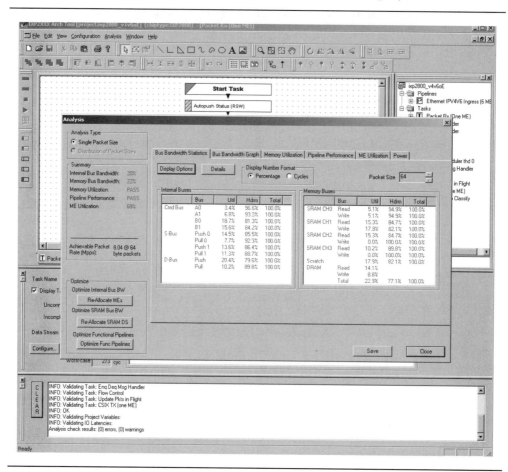

Figure 1.4   IXP2XXX Product Line Architecture Tool

Putting the Project Together

Figure 1.5 shows one of the screens in the Developer Workbench. The architect configures the project for the programmers to begin their implementation. Some microengines are assigned to packet processing code blocks. Part III of this book takes you through the use of the assembler and IXP2XXX Product Line Assembly Language—also known as microcode—covering the basics needed to write receive and transmit driver blocks. To prepare you for the implementation of packet processing in C, Part IV of this book discusses the C compiler choices you have regarding design issues and programming in explicit-partitioning and autopartitioning modes.

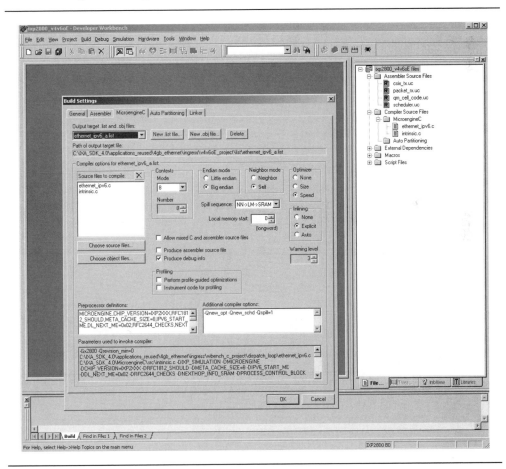

Figure 1.5   Workbench Build

Simulating

As soon as the receive code blocks have been entered, that is, when the application contains code to recognize arriving packet data, you can begin debugging the design in the simulator. As the design is filled in with more and more code, you can step deeper and deeper into the handling of the packets. You can verify the first cases by stepping through thread list and thread history views. Figure 1.6 shows the Developer Workbench in simulation mode. Part V of this book shows you how to generate packets, run simulation, and debug the design.

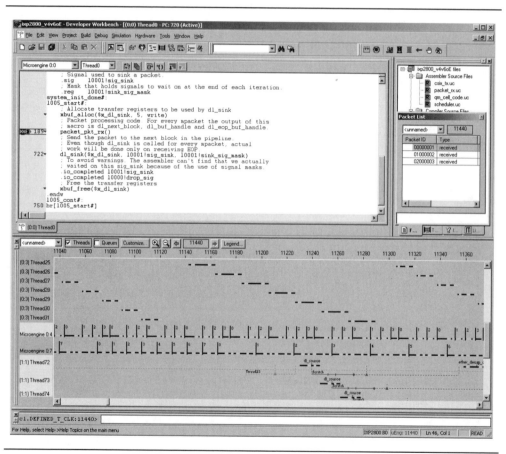

Figure 1.6 Developer Workbench Simulation

Packet-Centric Debugging

When you have a lot going on in simulation—remember, up to 128 threads and all those asynchronous events—you need faster ways to sift through all the information that is available in the simulator. You need to know which transmitted packets are bad; for those in error, you must trace back to the cause quickly.

Figure 1.7 shows the packet list and event list views. The packet list shows you at a glance which packets are suspect. The event list provides a detailed list of packet and memory reference events. You can highlight the packet of interest and go directly to the source code related to the event.

Packet List

Packet ID	Type	Status	Disposition	Generator/Validator attributes
1	received	validated	ok	
2	received	validated	Payload error	
3	received	transmitted	---	
4	received	dropped	QoS error	
5	derived	transmitted	---	
6	received	active	---	
7	received	active	---	

Event List

<unnamed>   Filtering...   1   15954

Cycle	Thread	Type	SubType	Attributes
11660	(0:0) Thread1	Packet	Received	Packet ID=0x00000001, Rx Device=0, Rx Port=0
11660	(0:0) Thread1	Packet	AssociateThreadWithPacket	Packet ID=0x00000001, Thread=1
11660	(0:0) Thread1	Packet	ProcessingStarted	Packet ID=0x00000001
11689	(0:0) Thread1	Packet	AssociateMemory	Packet ID=0x00000001, Region=Dram, Address=0x00001188, L...
11869	(0:0) Thread0	Packet	Received	Packet ID=0x01000002, Rx Device=0, Rx Port=1
11869	(0:0) Thread0	Packet	AssociateThreadWithPacket	Packet ID=0x01000002, Thread=0
11869	(0:0) Thread0	Packet	ProcessingStarted	Packet ID=0x01000002
11898	(0:0) Thread0	Packet	AssociateMemory	Packet ID=0x01000002, Region=Dram, Address=0x00000988, L...
11944	(0:0) Thread1	Packet	Received	Packet ID=0x02000003, Rx Device=0, Rx Port=2
11944	(0:0) Thread1	Packet	AssociateThreadWithPacket	Packet ID=0x02000003, Thread=1
11944	(0:0) Thread1	Packet	ProcessingStarted	Packet ID=0x02000003
11973	(0:0) Thread1	Packet	AssociateMemory	Packet ID=0x02000003, Region=Dram, Address=0x00004988, L...
12157	(0:0) Thread0	Packet	Received	Packet ID=0x03000004, Rx Device=0, Rx Port=3
12157	(0:0) Thread0	Packet	AssociateThreadWithPacket	Packet ID=0x03000004, Thread=0
12157	(0:0) Thread0	Packet	ProcessingStarted	Packet ID=0x03000004
12186	(0:0) Thread0	Packet	AssociateMemory	Packet ID=0x03000004, Region=Dram, Address=0x00005188, L...
12603	(0:0) Thread1	Packet	Received	Packet ID=0x00000005, Rx Device=0, Rx Port=0
12603	(0:0) Thread1	Packet	AssociateThreadWithPacket	Packet ID=0x00000005, Thread=1
12603	(0:0) Thread1	Packet	ProcessingStarted	Packet ID=0x00000005
12632	(0:0) Thread1	Packet	AssociateMemory	Packet ID=0x00000005, Region=Dram, Address=0x00005988, L...
12815	(0:0) Thread0	Packet	Received	Packet ID=0x01000006, Rx Device=0, Rx Port=1
12815	(0:0) Thread0	Packet	AssociateThreadWithPacket	Packet ID=0x01000006, Thread=0
12815	(0:0) Thread0	Packet	ProcessingStarted	Packet ID=0x01000006

Figure 1.7 Packet List and Event List Views

Figure 1.8 shows the concept of the packet dataflow view. After selecting a "packet of interest," this view shows you the code blocks and data operated on for that packet. As you can see, this information is similar to the partitions and data structures you entered in the Architecture Tool, but uses actual data from simulation. From here you can zoom into the code blocks and, using the operand trace feature, quickly trace back the cause of a failure.

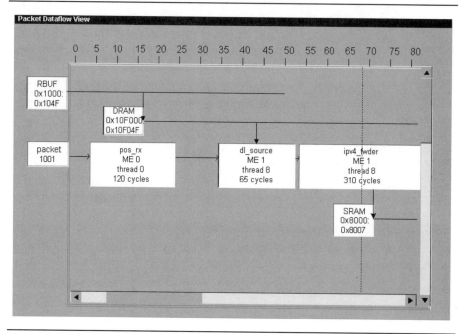

Figure 1.8   Packet Dataflow View

Understanding the Examples

This book operates on a design by example basis. The vehicle for instruction is a network processor project, which you and your team members follow from conception, through design, to testing and debug. You are encouraged to switch hats and play the role of each team member as you go. However, each section provides an overview, a quick run-through of key features, and summary, so feel free to read the short run-throughs and dig into a section in detail when you really *need to know it*!

You can find the example project source files plus pointers to the Intel IXA Software Development Toolkit and Intel IXA Software Framework on this book's Intel Press Web site, listed in "References."

To help you correlate the code in the book to the proper file on the Web, the code examples are located in the directory of the project under discussion. The screen shots are from the actual project.

The file and project names are provided in the examples. Lengthy code examples have line numbers to make it easy to refer to individual code segments in the text. The line numbers correspond to the same lines in the source file.

You'll find a complete list of other books about Intel network processors, in "References" in the back of this book.

Many acronyms are used in this book. You can find their definitions in the "Glossary."

Finally, Appendix A provides a compact summary of the microcode instruction set, and Appendix B contains a brief description of what's next in tool features.

Part I
The Manager:
The "2800 Foot" Tour

Chapter 2

Why You Need New Tools

When the only tool you own is a hammer, every problem begins to resemble a nail.

—Abraham Maslow

You've heard it said, "The old tools were OK. Why do I need new ones?" Or maybe, "I don't need no stinking GUI!" These are common sentiments. While change is sometimes painful, in the end, it'll be worth it. Just imagine a command-line interface displaying the status of 128 threads running in parallel and thousands of packets being classified and queued for transmit. You could create a command-line watch that captures simulation state—printing PCs; printing a list of threads have pending memory references; printing a list of threads that are active; printing packet data as it is received, stored in DRAM, and transmitted; and printing packet descriptor and queueing information. This situation was life with the IXP2XXX network processor simulator before the Developer Workbench came along.

The problem is, simply, how do you make the tools do something and present to you the resulting information? That is what a GUI does. It gives control over the functionality and information organized so you see what you need to know, when you need to know it. Even with a GUI, you will feel more comfortable doing some things from the command line, such as a quick memory examination, or a "go 100" (run the simulator 100 cycles) command. With the Developer Workbench, you can do all of these operations from either the GUI or command line, plus you can assign shortcut keys for operations you do most frequently.

The way programs run on the IXP2XXX network processors differs from traditional processors. Popular tool suites give you a compiler, an assembler, and a debugger, each of which makes no assumptions about the application. However, with network processors, the objective is clear. The application is working on packets or cells, forwarding data in a network environment. With this in mind, the tools can be made more application-friendly and debugging can be more *packet-centric*.

In this chapter, you learn key aspects of high-performance IXP2XXX network processor applications, such as common design partitioning and sequencing techniques that call for a new network-application-friendly tool suite. For each design or debug problem, you will discover the need for a corresponding tool to accelerate the development process.

Parallel Processing

High-performance packet-forwarding applications must be partitioned in a way that provides maximum throughput from packet receive to packet transmit. You label the top-level partitions and list the sequence—receive to transmit—as something like this:

- Packet Segment Receive
- Reassembly
- Lookup
- Classification
- Modification
- Policing
- Statistics Update
- Queue for Transmit
- Schedule Transmit
- Packet Transmit

You need a tool to draw and connect these partitions, then attach key metrics to them, such as what tasks each performs, throughput, and memory bandwidths used, to capture the design at the top level. The tool must be flexible so that you can easily move the tasks from one partition to another as you balance the performance when assigning tasks to processing units. This tool is the IXP2XXX Product Line Architecture Tool, which is discussed in Chapters 4 and 5.

Some tasks are simple, and can be performed in just a few cycles. For example, in IXP2XXX network processors, most of the work of receiving packet data from the network is done by the media switch fabric (MSF), so all Packet Segment Receive has to do is notify the MSF that it can take more data, get the status—that is, which receive buffer, how many bytes, and so on—when the data arrives, then verify the status. The next step, reassembly, involves much more work. Reassembly must get a buffer location in DRAM, and copy the packet segment from RBUF to DRAM. Fortunately, the IXP2XXX network processor architecture has hardware-supported linked lists, so getting a buffer pointer is a single instruction. Also, since copying data from RBUF to DRAM is a single instruction, reassembly isn't too difficult. Packet data can come in on more than one MAC device port interface, so you must store the buffer location and other reassembly states while a series of data segments are being received for a packet. The buffer location must be updated by adding the size of each segment as it is received. There aren't that many ports, and this is Ethernet, which means successive segments of a packet come back-to-back on a port. Microengine local memory can be used to hold this information. Packet reassembly state can be stored in a local memory array and indexed by port. If the receive port is a cell-based protocol, such as CSIX or ATM, the reassembly state can be kept in SRAM, indexed by a protocol-specific connection identifier. Now the receive/reassembly partition receives, looks up, and updates port information and reassembles the packet in DRAM.

You need a tool that reports the number of packets received; whether there was an error, such as a missing start of packet indicator, with which you can capture the reassembled packet data and look at it later; and where you can watch the port information as it is updated in local memory.

You calculate that the packet segments arrive every 70 cycles. You also know that the next stages need to get the packet header, hold onto it, and perform many operations. This segment is a good place for a partition. The first stage reassembles packets and dispatches them to the next stages, which work on the header. The first stage can keep up with the arrival rate, and many parallel MEs can run the header processing stages. Figure 2.1 shows this arrangement. Packet Receive dispatches assignments through scratch rings to packet processing threads, which run on many microengines.

 You need a tool that can show the partitioning of code to MEs and execution of many threads running in parallel. You need to know when threads are idle and, when busy, what packets they are working on.

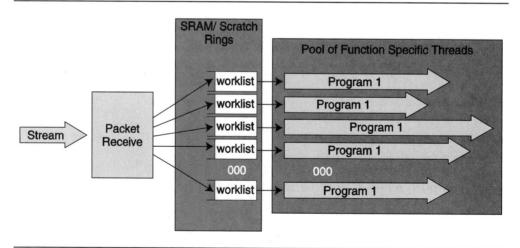

Figure 2.1   Partitioning of Packet Receive and Packet Processing

When packet processing is completed and the packet is modified, the packet is then queued for transmission, or forwarding. Scheduling, queuing, dequeueing, and transmitting are simpler operations that do not require a lot of packet data. Therefore, the pipe can narrow again for these stages, with each running at the transmit rate; for example, one enqueue/dequeue per 70 cycles, one schedule per 70 cycles, and one transmit per 70 cycles.

> You need a tool that can watch queue status and show whether queues are backed up and causing stalls. You need to see packets being segmented and transmitted, and transmit rate. You need to report packets that are modified incorrectly, dropped, or transmitted to the wrong output interface.

Asynchronous Events

Packet data being worked on in a network device is always transient, moving through at a high rate. In fact, throughput for given functionality is the primary consideration. Traditional processors use a cache to accelerate their programs. In a cache, the likelihood of reusing data is very high for most single-user programs. A cache close to the execution datapath of a processor usually speeds up the time it takes to access data. However, if the data is always changing, the cache could spend all of its time evicting old data and reading in new data from off-chip memory. Such is the case with the network processor.

Except for the Intel XScale® core, the network processor does not use a cache, causing the microengines to be greatly reduced in size. Extra space is given to general-purpose registers dedicated to each thread. A thread runs for a while, issues a memory I/O request, and swaps out. That thread is available to run again when the memory operation completes and sends a signal back to the microengine. Also, as it swaps out, another thread can immediately swap in and run, because its general purpose registers are *live* and dedicated. Figure 2.2 shows eight threads executing on the same microengine.

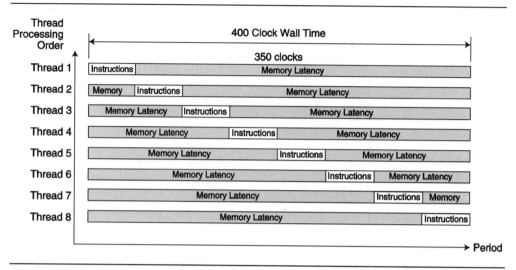

Figure 2.2   Hardware-Supported Multithreading

Ideally, the eight threads of a microengine would run at maximum efficiency by swapping out often enough to allow others to run and not so often as to be stalled waiting for I/O operations to complete.

 You need a tool that can show threads as lines in time, executing and swapping out, issuing memory requests, and receiving event signals. The tool should mark places on the thread execution line that are significant code milestones, such as starting a packet processing stage. During simulation, you should be able to scroll back in simulation history to see execution during any cycle.

Packets

Following parallel execution of threads and their memory references is not enough. The network processor application is all about packets. So why not show them? In many places, a packet can be checked as it goes through the processing stages. You need to observe packet data, packet-derived information, and network connection state. During debug, you might want to ask the following questions:

■ What TCP/IP or ATM connection is this packet associated with? What is the rate for this connection?

- Was all of the packet data received by the network processor correctly?

- Was there an error, such as a parity error, on the received data?

- At what rate were packets received for a port?

- Was the packet reassembled correctly in DRAM?

- Was the header verified correctly in the packet-processing microengine?

- Was the correct output port obtained by the router lookup?

- Was the IP time-to-live field updated correctly?

- Was the correct Ethernet address pre-pended to the IP header?

- Was the descriptive information, such as buffer pointer and size, correct?

- Was the packet enqueued for transmit?

- Was the scheduler fair in assigning a queue to be transmitted?

- Did transmit get the right packet buffer?

- Was the packet segmented and transmitted in the right order?

- What was the transmit rate for the connection?

- What was the transmit rate for the port?

These questions are just a few of the ones that, if answered quickly, can greatly reduce your debug time. Figure 2.3 shows the concept of a scrolling history view that presents the events of selected packets.

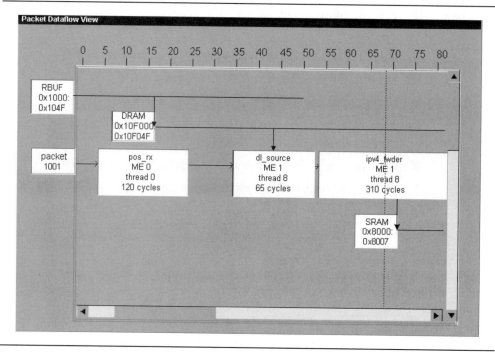

Figure 2.3   Packet Dataflow View

This window shows the top-level stages and tasks, and important packet-related data as it is read or written.

 You need a tool that traces packets and displays all events related to selected packets, including code partitions as they execute packet-related data. From a high-level diagram of the packet's actual execution, you should be able to zoom to code from any point in the diagram and trace quickly back to the cause of a failure.

Conceptually, you have come full circle, where the top-level partitioning and debugger actually agree!

Chapter 3

Project Development Strategies

Lack of planning on your part does not constitute an emergency on my part.

—Epigram

When did you say you wanted it? Yesterday! This chapter is for the project manager. However, if you are a designer, you might want to know what your manager is going to ask you to do, so read on. This chapter discusses ways to use the tools that can give you the fastest development with the least risk. For example, your architect should do high-level partitioning and feasibility analysis before committing the team to work in parallel on code development and test generation. In this chapter you will learn the names of the tools and their features, the proper order of using them, which programming languages are supported, and how to reuse code from previous working designs.

The Project Phases

The project, which could be any typical network processor project, proceeds in phases, as shown in Figure 3.1. To help you learn the tools, you will run small test examples for each phase, primarily to grease the skids. The more small, quick examples your team does, the more comfortable they will be with the tools. However, if you skip a phase, you are on your own.

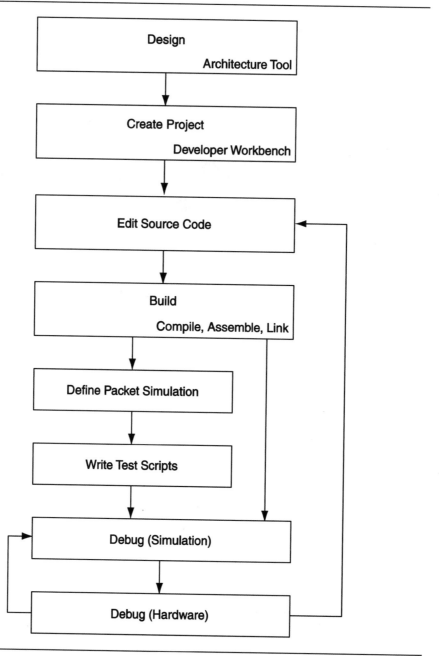

Figure 3.1 The Order in Which to Use the Tools in the Intel® Internet Exchange Architecture (Intel® IXA) SDK

Design It

First, you must design the application. The architectural design can be entered and verified using the Architecture Tool. This tool has a graphics entry that lets you drag and drop packet-processing stages into the design, enter flow diagrams for each stage, and enter key data elements. The tool then verifies that the design fits within the bandwidth constraints of the processor and performance constraints of your application. Chapters 4 and 5 discuss the use of the Architecture Tool for high-level partitioning, data and task flow definitions, and analysis.

Create the Project

Knowing your design works, you can then create the development project using the Developer Workbench. Your architect can extract the skeletal design, creating the initial Developer Workbench project using the Architecture Tool. Your architect can fill in the project with additional shared project data, such as configuration of media switch fabric (MSF) ports, any new common include-file paths, and linker settings. Chapter 6 discusses the creation of the Developer Workbench project. Your architect can attend to some of the system-level aspects of the product as the developers implement the design.

Edit the Source Code

Once the project is set up, each programmer can get a copy, enabling parallel code development. Ideally, you want each programmer to have a sandbox to play in without too much interference. That sandbox is the microengine. One programmer might write in microcode, the assembly language, while developing the network interface drivers; another programmer might write in C, to develop the network stack processing layers. Chapters 7 through 10 cover the programming languages, compilers, and assembler used in microengine development. For doing the development work for the Intel XScale® core, you can use one of the many Intel® StrongARM* technology tools that are readily available. VxWorks† and Linux tools are the most popular; you can find projects using these applications on this book's Intel Press Web site, listed in "References."

Build It

If the linker settings are right—that is, if they identify what microengine must have the top-level root code on it—you can run the compilation, assembly, and linking processes. This entire process is called the build. Each developer can perform a separate build to ensure no syntax errors, uninitialized variables, variables set without being used, or other local microengine coding violations. Each developer then checks the code into your source control system. Now each developer can get the latest modules for the whole project and build the entire design. Any linking errors, such as mismatched global variables between microengines, are discovered at this time. You learn how to build your project in Chapter 6. Just repeat: click the build icon and fix those mistakes. Your engineers will appreciate being able to fix errors before anyone else has a chance to see them—so will everybody else.

Define Packet Simulation

What is packet simulation? Well, just about everything is a simulation these days. Running a simulation before the concrete is poured, before you commit the big bucks, is always best. To test the design, a set of packets must be created and streamed into the processor. To be sure you are testing the corner cases of your design, the streams must be controlled, meaning you must insert specific protocol headers and specific field values into the protocol headers. You should try various packet sizes. If the software does one thing for minimum-size packets and another for maximum-size packets, you need to test the boundary conditions. Much more detail can be seen in simulation, so you will likely go back and forth between running the design simulation for simple stepping and detailed debugging and hardware-based debugging. Construct the test cases with this division in mind.

Create Control Scripts

GUI is great. However, when you have done something a thousand times, it can get tedious even if it is easy. Command line scripts let you repeat tasks performed during simulation or while running the design. The Developer Workbench lets you extract the script that initializes processor, device, and packet simulation. It can also include any startup scripts needed to set up data, such as lookup tables, for the debug test suite. The simulation command line accepts two forms of interpretive or file script, Ind and Tcl. Ind is a C-interpretive script language that also supports some basic simulator commands such as `go`, `examine`, `deposit`. If your C coding skills are a little rusty, do a few `for` loops or `printfs` interactively in the simulator. You'll be programming in no time. Tcl is a standard `Tcl` shell that can be entered from the `ind` command line or script file and does everything that `Ind` does, but with `Tcl` syntax.

Debug in Simulation

Put simply, you can see everything in the simulator, or count millions of packets per second in the hardware. Simulation can save you a lot of time. Each of your programmers should step through key code paths to make sure the basic packet processing and forwarding is working. The packet profiler makes it easy to follow packets from generation, through the processor, to validation. The profiler GUI can display the packet-processing steps, what microengines or threads are working on the packet for each code block, and key data that tells your programmer instantly if something is suspicious or in error. Although the simulator is slow, processing only 200 to 400 cycles per second, depending on your PC, four packets per second translates to 14,400 packets per hour; 230,400 in a 16-hour overnight run; or 1 million packets over 2.5 days. However, you can just set a machine aside and let it run. If the simulation hits an error, you can follow back through simulation history, checking what code paths were followed, what instructions were executed, even what the data was at any given cycle in the history window. You can debug without a lengthy simulation rerun.

Debug in Hardware

By now you probably realize that you need to run the same packet tests on real hardware, which is likely to be on a prototype card or network switch blade you have developed. To do so, the Developer Workbench can connect to your card through an Ethernet or serial network interface to the Intel XScale core on the IXP2XXX network processors. Running at full line speed can uncover system-level problems such as device underflow or overflow. Your test engineer can set breakpoints and view variables and memory data at specific program lines. Program stepping runs several cycles for each step, from thread swap to thread swap—called hopping. Your Developer Workbench top debug menu has a checkbox for either simulation or hardware. Switching back and forth between simulation and real hardware debug is easy. You can see everything, or count millions of packets per second. Use each to its best advantage.

The Tools

This section is an overview of the tools your team will use in developing the microengine code for your network processor.

The Architecture Tool

When deciding which processor to use, or even which IXP2XXX (the Intel® IXP2400 or the IXP2800) processor to use for a network processor-based system, you must consider many issues. Will the application code fit in the microengine? What processing stage partitioning will likely meet the line rate requirements? Will the desired memory accesses per packet fit within the bandwidths supported by the processor? How many microengines will be needed to support the desired line rate?

Using the Architecture Tool, you can draw the partitioning of the design, specify data structures and task flow, and finally run analysis to determine whether the design fits. With it, you can determine the feasibility of a design before embarking on the full-blown project. With the major partitioning done, programmers can be assigned to work on coding the various blocks in parallel. With the Architecture Tool's views of code partitioning and data structures, you can easily determine where you can reuse previous code, such as microblocks from the Intel® Internet Exchange Architecture (Intel® IXA) Software Framework, and where you must write new code.

Once feasibility has been proven, you can use the Architecture Tool to create a skeletal Developer Workbench project that can be opened, built, and simulated.

The Developer WorkBench

The Developer Workbench is the graphical user interface of the Intel IXA microengine (ME) tools suite. With it you can create an IXP2XXX network processor software development environment. In this environment, you can create and edit source code; assemble, compile, and link the code; configure and then run the simulation system; generate packets; debug, load, and run software on an IXP2XXX network processor hardware platform; and debug on hardware.

The Developer Workbench lets you choose the appropriate programming language for the task at hand. Depending on the need, you can select from the following a language to run on each microengine:

- *Autopartitioning C* is high-level C programming in which the compiler allocates your code to microengines and packet-processing code blocks and inserts signal events for you.

- *Explicit-partitioning C*—known as Microengine C—is mid-to-low-level C programming. In this mode, you can write most of the code in pure C, and use intrinsics or assembly language where needed to access hardware-specific features.

- *Assembly* or microcode is low-level symbolic programming in which you use the specific instructions to be executed. The format is simplified through the use of symbolic names for operands and results.

The Packet Generator

The packet generator, included with the Developer Workbench, provides the capability to source and validate packets continually according to the specification of plug-in protocol modules. These modules define protocol types and a traffic specification of packet grouping into flows. The flows correspond to connections in ATM or TCP/IP. The headers can be layered for a flow in any order, and flows can be bundled within other flows. Sequencing algorithms include round robin, token bucket, and random order. You have many choices for setting the rate on a flow, from simple peak rate to the detailed parameters of a flow specification based on ATM TM4.1.

The Packet Profiler

The packet profiler, included with the Developer Workbench, provides a packet-centric view of debugging. That is, you select packets of interest and display only those simulation events related to them. Starting with packet status, you can trace a suspect packet by displaying all major code and memory access events; filter by packet, memory type, or microengine; scan back through simulation history while displaying code block execution and data variable values; create your own packet events; and trace quickly through cause-effect in the instruction execution history.

Jump Start with Code Reuse

The Intel IXA Software Framework provides a selection of code blocks, called *microblocks*, that can be used in your designs to reduce development time. A microblock is a code block that can be added to a design to implement a given function, such as IPV4 forwarding or network address translation (NAT). With each release, more microblocks are added and more example applications are demonstrated (see this book's Intel Press Web site, listed in "References"). Here are some of the microblocks you can use:

- **rx* is a driver microblock that receives packet segments from the MSF interface and re-assembles them in DRAM. Several types of rx microblocks are provided, each used for a specific physical network interface.

- *dl_sink* is a packet-processing microblock used to send a packet to a queue or the next stage of packet processing.

- *dl_source* is a packet-processing microblock used to get a packet.

- *ether_decap_classify* is a packet-processing microblock used to remove the Ethernet header and set the next header type.

- *v6v4_natpt_translate* is a packet-processing microblock used to translate from IPV6 to IPV4 or vice-versa.

- *v6v4_tunnel_decap* is a packet-processing microblock used to remove the outer IPV4 header if it is tunneling an IPV6 packet.

- *ipv4_forwarder* is a packet-processing microblock used to verify and classify packets based on their IPV4 headers.

- *ipv6_forwarder* is a packet-processing microblock used to verify and classify packets based on their IPV6 headers.

- *statistics* is a driver microblock used to perform atomic 64-bit statistics counter update.

- *dl_qm_sink* is a packet-processing microblock used to send a packet to the queue manager for transmit enqueueing.

- *queue_manager* is a driver microblock used to queue and dequeue packets.

- **tx* is a driver microblock that segments packets and transmits them via the MSF interface. The Intel IXA Software Framework provides several types of tx microblocks, each used for a specific physical network interface.

As a starting point for your application, the microblocks can be placed in dispatch loops. Alternatively, you can take an existing example design and add or replace microblocks. Either way, you can quickly set up an application and begin to set up a simulation environment in which you can see immediately what happens as you make modifications.

Each microblock has an associated Intel XScale core component, also provided with the Intel IXA Software Framework. The Intel XScale core components are responsible for initialization, table maintenance, and handling of exception code paths.

Also, when you design your program in microblocks, you can use them in future designs, combining them with other microblocks to be provided in future releases. You will also have portability forward to future generations of processors. Due to the granularity of the microblocks, new releases of the microblocks can take advantage of new hardware features, making more microengines available for new application functionality and increasing the performance of your application.

Summary

As a manager, you want to ensure that your projects produce quality products on schedule. You want a minimum of surprises, and you want your developers' time to be spent in the most efficient way possible. This section has outlined the important issues of network application design styles, tool selection, and project development strategies, and has set the stage for your team to build a successful product.

Part II
The Architect

## Chapter 4

The Architecture Tool—The Basics

> *Walking on water and developing software from a specification are easy if both are frozen.*
>
> —Edward V. Berard

You have a team. They are waiting to begin designing. Or maybe you don't have a team, and you have nothing else to do until they are hired. Or maybe you *are* the architect *and* the team. Whatever the case, this section is for you!

The next two chapters introduce you to the IXP2XXX Product Line Architecture Tool and demonstrate how to use this tool for the high-level design of your IPV4/IPV6 router application. These chapters do not cover every detail of the tool, but you will hopefully learn enough to get you going. For further information, refer to the user's guide for the tool (Intel 2004). Refer to Figure 4.1 when your project is late and your team is out to lunch.

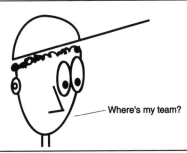

Where's my team?

Figure 4.1   You, the Architect

The Design Requirements

This is your mission, should you choose to accept it: Design the packet classification and forwarding software for an IPV4/IPV6 router, as shown in Figure 4.2.

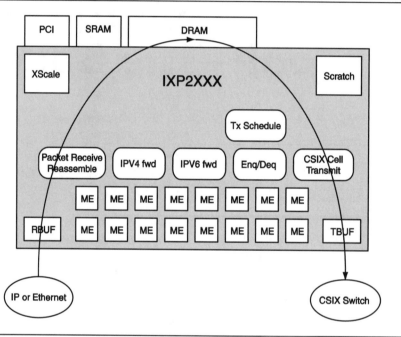

Figure 4.2   The IPV4/IPV6 Router Project

As you see, it is all about *microengines* (it is all about MEs). This area of design is where the performance and flexibility of the IXP2XXX network processors become evident. The MEs are used for the packet-forwarding path, also known as the *fast path*. The Intel XScale® microarchitecture is used for exception and control/management. The decision is simple. In the case of the IXP2800 network processor, the MEs outnumber the Intel XScale microarchitecture 16 processor cores to one. In addition, the MEs have 128 threads with individual, or local, general-purpose registers and asynchronous I/O transfer registers and instant process swap with no stack overhead when execution changes from thread to thread, This combination makes for some very fast packet processing: for example, 25 million packets per second for a POS OC192 design forwarding 49-byte packets.

However, your design is conservative, with headroom for added functionality. The IPV4/V6 router has the following characteristics:

■ The initial network interfaces will be Ethernet and CSIX fabric.

    − Keep the receive and transmit drivers for the network interface in separate software modules. Having separate modules enables you to easily change the design to accommodate other interfaces.

■ Partition the design as a software pipeline, making sure that packets are handled in the order received.

■ Reassemble the packet in DRAM and assign the packet-to-packet processing.

■ In the packet-processing stage, decapsulate the Ethernet header; determine the layer 3 protocol; then perform layer 3 verification, translation, classification, and queue for transmit.

    − If IPV4 or IPV6 tunnel, get the inner layer 3 header and process it.

    − Perform NAT translation, if necessary.

    − Encapsulate the header with the output header determined by route lookup.

■ Enqueue and dequeue the packets in high-performance transmit queues.

■ Schedule packets for CSIX transmit.

■ Segment the packet into CSIX cells and transmit.

■ Use an IXP28XX network processor to provide plenty of room for expanding functionality, adding new protocols, and so on. Initially, design the ingress path.

■ Design for 4 gigabits per direction, using four 1-gigabit Ethernet ports. One direction, called *ingress*, takes Ethernet in and forwards to the CSIX fabric. The other direction, called *egress*, takes CSIX and forwards to Ethernet. Minimum-size packets will therefore be received every 150 cycles.

In this book, you will design the IPV4/IPV6 router fast path for ingress from Ethernet to CSIX. In the course of creating this design, you use all of the tools in the Intel® IXA Software Development Toolkit. As an architect, you naturally believe in properly structured design techniques, starting with the big picture, defining the problem, partitioning the design, and performing feasibility analysis. Just remember, no matter how deep you get into the details, you can always step back and reground yourself in the big picture.

A Quick Tour of the Architecture Tool

Figure 4.3 shows three key views of the Architecture Tool: pipeline drawing, task drawing, and analysis.

The top level is the software pipeline drawing. In this drawing, you partition packet processing into stages. Each stage represents a major partition; in fact, the top-level partitioning of the design. The partitioning boundary between stages is typically a message ring, allowing the stages to run autonomously, receiving requests or assignments from the previous stage, and handing requests or assignments to the succeeding stage.

You use task drawings to define all code blocks and I/O operations and to show the dependency relationships of the code blocks and I/O references. Here you specify parallel I/O running while code is executing. The task drawing is the next lower partition. The partition boundary should be chosen to give you maximum flexibility in extending your application capabilities. For example, each network protocol can be defined by a separate task drawing, such as IPV4 and IPV6.

You insert task drawing blocks in the stages of the pipeline drawing, define the source of the packet stream, and illustrate the flow from packet stream through the stages. If you put the appropriate ring get-and-put I/O references in the task drawings, connecting them in the pipeline drawing is easy.

I/O references are key to understanding the bus bandwidth utilization of your design. Therefore, you must define your major data structures, refer to them in the I/O references, and specify the data size of each I/O reference.

Having done all of this, you can perform allocation and analysis. Allocation is done for:

■ *Memory*. Balancing the data structures across multiple memory banks is critical to achieving best performance. You can specify the bank for a data structure, or let the tool do it for you.

■ *Microengines*. The tool needs a sample allocation to perform the analysis. Here again, you can specify the ME allocation or let the tool do it for you. You can use this allocation if you are planning to code in assembly language or the explicit-partitioning mode of the C compiler. If you are using the autopartitioning mode of the C compiler, actual ME allocation is done for you when the C compiler is run.

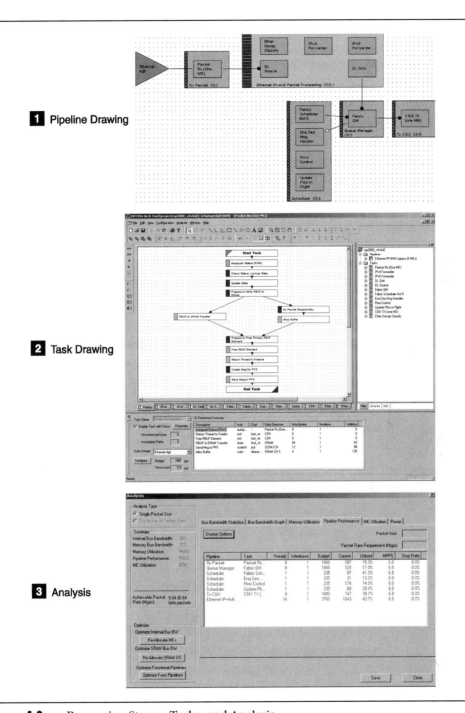

1 Pipeline Drawing

2 Task Drawing

3 Analysis

Figure 4.3   Processing Stages, Tasks, and Analysis

Finally, you can run the analysis portion of the Architecture Tool, which shows the utilization of the chip's resources, headroom, and ultimately whether your design is feasible. Analysis provides the following information:

- *Pipeline performance* shows execution time versus budget for each stage.

- *Memory utilization* provides capacity utilization for each memory bank.

- *Bus bandwidth* provides a view of bus utilization for internal buses and memory controller interfaces. Remember, microengines are arranged in clusters, with separate internal buses for each cluster.

- *ME utilization* is an indicator of processor execution headroom available in each ME.

As you can see, you can drag and drop task drawings of Intel IXA software framework microblocks into your pipeline stages to quickly create a design using the Architecture Tool. In most cases, more than 80 percent of your design can be quickly constructed from existing microblocks. After establishing the functionality, you must answer two questions:

- Will it fit?

- Will it achieve the performance goals?

Viewing the existing task drawings is a very good way to get a handle on code sizes for various application functions. The typical microblock ranges in size from 20 instructions for a layer 2 decapsulation to 200–400 instructions for a layer-forwarding protocol. You must sometimes trade off functionality for performance because the execution latency divided by the number of threads for a given function is the performance.

Creating the Project

In the File menu, select New Project. The New Project dialog appears, as shown in Figure 4.4. The project name is important to distinguish this project from others later on. For example, you may run a similar design on two different processors, and you might have slight variations in protocol. Your design might run on half-duplex ingress or egress, full-duplex supporting two pipelines, or receive and transmit on different network interfaces.

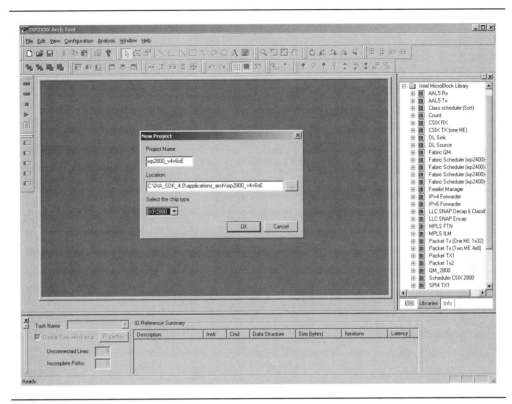

Figure 4.4   New Project

This particular project is identified by chip type and receive-side protocol, Intel® IXP2800 Network Processor IPV4 and IPV6 over Ethernet. Thus, you call the file ixp2800_v4v6oE. In the New Project dialog, enter the name and the directory for the project files and select the appropriate type of chip.

The Chip Configuration dialog displays next, as shown in Figure 4.5. Take a look at the tabs:

- *SRAM*. The Intel IXP2800 Network Processor has four SRAM channels. Based on your system configuration, you can set size, bus frequency, and efficiency.

- *DRAM*. The Intel IXP2800 Network Processor has three DRAM channels.

- *Clocks*. Clocks for microengines, the Intel XScale core, and external buses can be changed. Set these for your particular system configuration.

■ *Memory Addresses.* From the microengines, addresses for each memory type start from zero. However, from the Intel XScale core, the addresses of each memory type are mapped into one big address space.

■ *MSF.* The MSF, or media switch fabric, provides the network receive and transmit interface. On this interface, up to 256 bytes transfer into or out of the processor for each bus transaction. The transfer size can be set to 64 bytes, 128 bytes, or 256 bytes. Large packets are segmented into RBUF/TBUF element sizes. For receive, each transfer adds bytes to an RBUF element. When the element is full, the status for that element is pushed to a receive thread, enabling it to process the data. The reverse is true for transmit. A TBUF element is filled and validated by a transmit thread. Then the MSF interface drains the element.

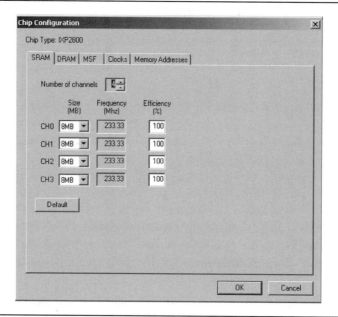

Figure 4.5   New Project Chip Configuration

The MSF chip configuration settings are shown in Figure 4.6. You should now configure the following three settings:

■ *Protocol.* The elements are allocated to partitions. The RBUF receive-side and TBUF transmit-side are configured for SPI-4 or CSIX. SPI-4 requires one partition. CSIX requires two partitions.

■ *Half duplex versus full duplex*. RBUF and TBUF may be configured either half duplex or full duplex. Half duplex means the interface is one direction—one interface is receiving and the other interface is transmitting. Full duplex means an interface is both receiving and transmitting. In the full-duplex configuration, two partitions are used if the MSF supports SPI-4 in both directions, or all three partitions are used if the MSF supports both SPI-4 and CSIX.

■ *Element size*. This setting requires a key tradeoff. A smaller element size results in more active RBUF/TBUF elements. The reassembly code owns the element for a longer period of time before the code has to move the element out and free the element. A larger element size enables a higher data rate. For example, if the receive code can reassemble one element per 80 cycles, then reassembling a 128-byte element per 80 cycles requires two times the rate of reassembling a 64-byte element per 80 cycles.

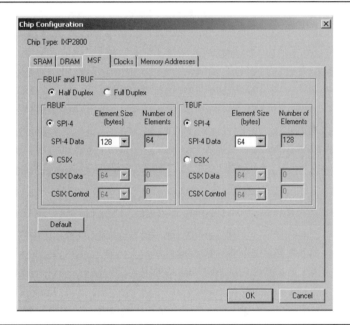

Figure 4.6   Media Switch Fabric Settings

The size of RBUF/TBUF is 8,000 bytes. So, depending on element size, you will have:

- Size: 64 bytes = 128 elements
- Size: 128 bytes = 64 elements
- Size: 256 bytes = 32 elements

Table 4.1 shows the element counts for each partition, based on element size, protocol, and half-duplex or full-duplex settings.

Table 4.1   RBUF/TBUF Partitioned Element Counts, Size = 64B/ 128B/ 256B

Configuration	Partition 1	Partition 2	Partition 3
Half-duplex SPI-4	128/ 64/ 32	Not used	Not used
Half-duplex CSIX	CSIX Data 96/ 48/ 24	CSIX Control 32/ 16/ 8	Not used
Full-duplex SPI-4, CSIX	CSIX Data ½ total size 64/ 32/ 16	SPI-4 3/8 total size 48/ 24/ 12	CSIX Control 1/8 total size 16/ 8/ 4

Initially, click OK to choose the other defaults. You can always go back and change the chip configuration later. When configuring the receive data stream in the pipeline drawing, you can set numbers of ports, rates, and packet sizes with the help of a calculation feature based on protocol.

Defining Processing Stages and Tasks

The top-level drawing consists of stages, starting with the receive-side network interface and going through a pipeline of five major steps:

1. *Receive.* This stage receives the packet and reassembles the packet in DRAM.

2. *Validate, classify, modify, bend, fold, and mutilate; in short, everything you want to do to the packet.* This stage typically comprises a number of microblocks; for example, one per protocol.

3. *Enqueue and dequeue atomic operations.* In the IXP2XXX network processor, dedicated threads are needed to add and remove packets on transmit queues.

4. *Schedule for transmit.* If there are a lot of queues, you must decide which one gets selected for each transmit. The algorithm can be very simple, such as round-robin distribution, or very

complex, such as TM4.1 shaping. There are microblocks for both kinds of algorithm.

5. *Transmit.* This stage segments and sends the packet to the network.

To create the top-level drawing, click New Pipeline in the File menu. Figure 4.7 shows the top-level stage drawing window. The vertical tool bar on the left provides the top-level drawing objects. Click the desired object in the toolbar, then move the cursor over the drawing and click again. Name the object in the dialog.

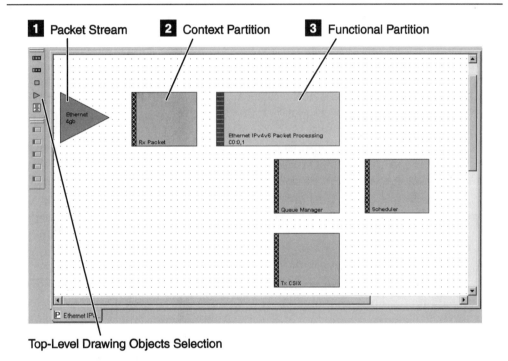

1 Packet Stream **2** Context Partition **3** Functional Partition

Top-Level Drawing Objects Selection

Figure 4.7 Initial-Stage Drawing

- ■ *Packet, or Data, Stream.* Because the data stream is used to define the packet source, you should create the data stream first.

- ■ *Context Partition, or context pipeline stage.* A context block is a sequential function that performs its operations at the rate of the input data stream. For example, if a new packet arrives every 150 cycles, the context stage performs its tasks for that packet within the 150-cycle budget. The threads run in round-robin order. Often a CAM is needed to support caching of shared data. The context pipeline stage executes within one microengine.

■ *Functional Partition, or functional pipeline stage.* In a functional block, there is typically a large amount of metadata that must be kept around until all of the required functions have been performed. Therefore, a functional pipeline stage can have many task blocks. Many threads on many microengines can be assigned to a functional stage. This stage typically has very long execution latency.

■ *Task Block, or Pipe Stage.* A task block represents an execution and I/O reference flow. Task blocks are inserted in the context and functional partitions. For the Intel IXA Framework Library, the task blocks are the microblocks.

Click the stream symbol, the triangle, to create the packet stream source first. Then move the cursor over the drawing and click again. The Data Stream Properties dialog appears, as shown in Figure 4.8.

At a minimum, you must enter name **1** and packet size **4**. The name appears on the stream symbol in the drawing. Packet size is the size of the packet that enters the processor—after the MAC device has stripped off preamble and trailer. For individual protocols, you can specify layer 2 sizes in Protocol Settings **1**. For IPV4 and IPV6 over Ethernet, the portion of the packet entering the network processor includes the Ethernet header, which contains the source address, destination address, and protocol/length. Minimum size should therefore be 64 bytes; maximum size is 1,500 kilobytes up to 64 kilobytes, depending on whether you are handling jumbo-size packets.

For Ethernet, specify SPI-4 as the MSF bus protocol **2**. RBUF Element Size was set earlier in the Chip Configuration dialog using the MSF tab. Max payload size in RBUF should be set to RBUF Element Size.

The Architecture Tool calculates data rate **3** one of two ways:

■ *By port type and port wire rate.* For example 4 x 1-gigabit ports can set a 4-gigabit rate.

■ *By packet size* **4** *and rate.* For Ethernet, the interpacket gap, preamble, and trailer affect the packet rate. For a 64-byte packet, this overhead is the equivalent of 20 extra bytes.

The execution path **5** must be checked to enable performance analysis for the data stream. The execution path determines what pipeline partitions get executed for the data stream. Later, after you have entered all of your pipeline stages, you need to come back to this dialog, click Execution Path, and click—or enable—the pipeline stage boxes.

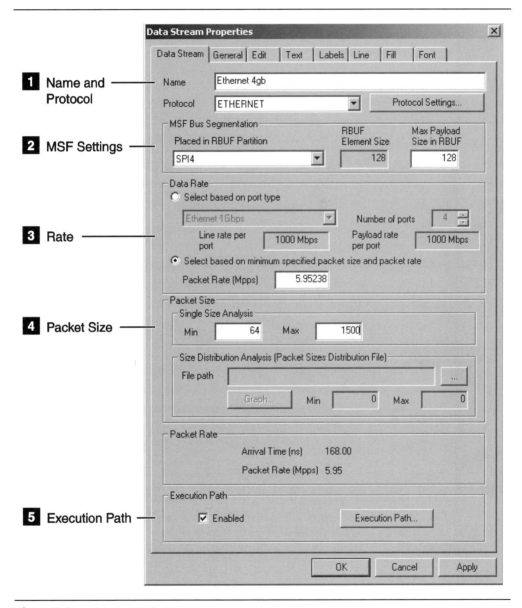

1 Name and Protocol

2 MSF Settings

3 Rate

4 Packet Size

5 Execution Path

Figure 4.8   Defining the Data Stream

Create the pipeline stages for your design by clicking the appropriate stage symbol **1**, then clicking where you want the stages in the drawing **2**:

- ■ *rx packet*. Context stage for receiving packets.

- ■ *Ethernet IPV4 v6 packet processing*. Functional stage for processing packet headers.

- ■ *Queue manager*. Context stage for enqueueing and dequeueing transmit queues.

- ■ *Scheduler*. Context stage for scheduling transmit dequeues.

- ■ *tx CSIX*. Context stage for transmitting packets.

Now you are ready to specify your code execution, as shown in Figure 4.9.

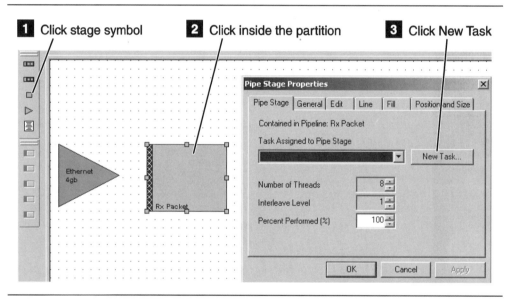

Figure 4.9 Inserting a Pipe Stage Task in the rx Pipeline Partition

Clicking New Task makes the New Task dialog appear **3**, shown in Figure 4.10. The name for the task should be consistent with other task names, so choose it wisely. You can, however, rename your tasks later by right-clicking the tasks in the Files view of the project workspace window. When you export the task block as a library object, you can use it in other projects.

Figure 4.10 Naming the New Task

Click OK. The task block appears in the pipeline partition, shown in Figure 4.11. Drag it and center it to taste.

Packet Rx in Context Partition

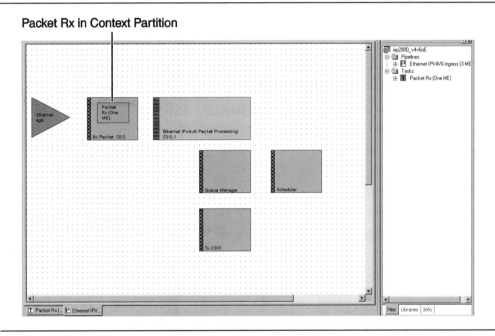

Figure 4.11 Pipe Stage Task in the Pipeline Partition

At this time, continue on at the top level, partitioning, naming, and inserting the task blocks. The Intel IXA microblocks library has many task blocks that you can use with free license to copy, modify, and distribute. So why not plug them in and get something running quickly? At a minimum, you can get a feel for how an application on a real IXP2XXX network processor behaves. You might even impress your boss! To see the library, activate the Libraries tab in the project workspace window.

After packets have been received and reassembled by rx packet, the packet must be validated, classified, and modified. You can pull in the microblocks for Ethernet decapsulation, IPV4, and IPV6 from the microblock library. As shown in Figure 4.12, right-click the IPV4 forwarder microblock **1** and choose Import Task from the menu. You are then notified that data structures are being imported **2**. These imported structures can be table structures, queues, buffer pools, and rings. For example, the DL source microblock is used to get packet metadata from a scratch ring. The packet rx writes packet metadata to that ring. Later in this chapter, you match up these ring names, so you can successfully connect the pipeline stages. In the next chapter, you fill in the data structure details.

Become acquainted with data structures as they are being imported with the microblock. For a complete specification of each microblock, refer to the software building blocks developer's manual (Intel 2004).

2 Data structures are imported　　　　　　　　**1** Right-click the microblock

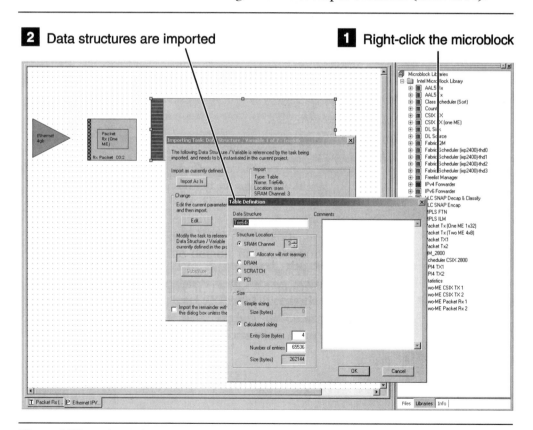

Figure 4.12　Check the Data Structures

You can change the definition of each data structure right now, if you know what you're doing, but let's assume you don't. So click Import As Is for each data structure. You can make a mental note of each data structure as it is added to the project. To get the data structure definition, refer to the software building blocks applications design guide (Intel 2004). If you have done this before, you can just check the box at the bottom left of the import dialog to automatically import all data structures. The project variables used by these microblocks are then imported. Creation of data structures and project variables are described in Chapter 5.

After the data structures and variables have been imported, you get a summary, as shown in Figure 4.13. Click OK and you've got it.

Figure 4.13   Data Structures for IPV4 Imported

The high-level objects are listed in the Files tab of your project workspace window, as shown in Figure 4.14. The objects are pipeline drawings and tasks. You can easily drag **1** and drop **2** tasks from the Files tab into the desired partition of a pipeline drawing.

As you import tasks, you are also importing task drawings. The task drawing is a flowchart showing the dependency of code blocks and I/O operations. The drawing window now has tabs across the bottom for each imported task. Remember, the new task "Packet Rx (One ME)" has an empty drawing. You learn about task drawings later in this chapter after you have completed the top-level pipeline drawing.

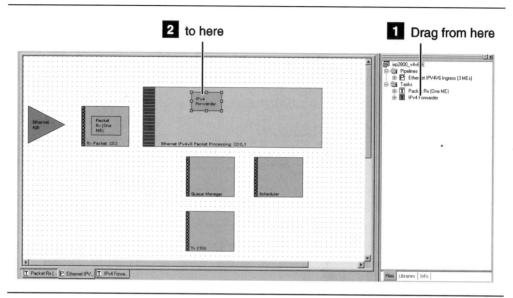

Figure 4.14   The IPV4 Task Imported

For IPV4 and IPV6 over Ethernet, you need the following task blocks:

■ *DL source.* Get a packet.

■ *Ether decap classify.* Remove the layer 2 header and decide what should be done next; for example, work on layer 3.

■ *IPV4 forwarder.* Validate the IPV4 header and perform longest prefix match route lookup. Modify the header.

■ *IPV6 forwarder.* Validate the IPV6 header and perform longest prefix match route lookup. Modify the header.

■ *DL sink.* Send the packet to be enqueued for transmit.

You can add other task blocks later to the Ethernet Ipv4v6 packet processing stage to complete the header processing.

Standard queue manager, scheduler, and CSIX transmit blocks for less than 5-gigabit rates are then added. Remember, you have to import the transmit blocks first, then drag and drop them from the File tab to stages in the pipeline drawing. There are different blocks for running at 10 gigabits or OC192 rates. The pipeline drawing with all tasks added is shown in Figure 4.15.

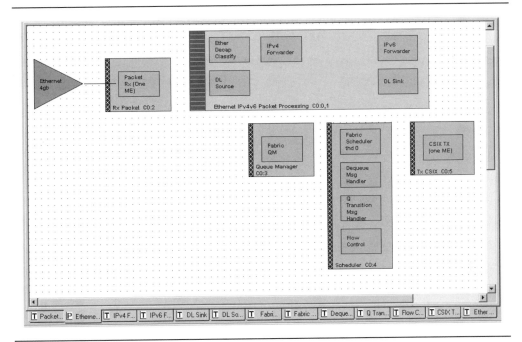

Figure 4.15 Tasks Added

  At this time, you can connect the Ethernet 4 gigabits data stream to the packet rx task block. To do this, click the Link button at the top toolbar, and then click the source and destination of the link.

Defining the Tasks of the Stage

Now you have all of the task blocks in. Most of them are imported, thus already defined. However, you must still define what the rx packet task block does.

Along the bottom of the drawing window are tabs for the pipeline and all tasks in the project. To display the task drawing, click the Packet Rx tab. Start with grouping operations that the receive code must perform. Here is what you know—or don't know:

■ The receive thread places itself on the MSF (media switch fabric) thread freelist to be eligible for a status autopush when data arrives. After the first autopush, the receive thread takes ownership of an RBUF element. The receive thread must free the RBUF element when finished with it.

- The receive thread allocates in advance a buffer in DRAM for packet data and a corresponding buffer in SRAM for packet descriptor.

- The receive thread gets the autopush, with information about the received data in RBUF. The receive thread checks the autopush status for errors. If the data is part of a packet, the receive thread looks up the state for that packet, such as packet buffer, and offsets into the buffer.

- The receive thread transfers the packet data from the RBUF element to the correct offset in the DRAM packet buffer.

- The receive thread assembles a packet metadata assignment to be sent to a scratch ring for packet header processing threads to pick up.

As shown in Figure 4.16, the task drawing symbols are at the left of the drawing and include, in order:

- *Start Task* is where the execution iteration begins.

- *End Task* is where the execution iteration ends. If this task is in a context pipeline stage, or if this task is the only task in a functional pipeline stage, the thread goes to Start Task to process the next packet.

- *I/O Reference* is a request to a unit outside the microengine.

- *Code Block* represents a number of cycles performing a computation inside the microengine.

- *Next Neighbor* is a write to or read from a next neighbor register bank. The next-neighbor register bank is a special hardware mechanism for efficient communication from a microengine to the next microengine (ME number +1).

Click and drop these symbols in the same way you did for the pipeline drawing symbols. For each one, a dialog appears asking you, at a minimum, to name the task object.

For code blocks, enter name and size. The size is the number of cycles this code block is expected to take, including cycles for the execution of all instructions, plus aborted-execution, defer-shadow cycles. Aborted cycles occur for branches taken and context-swaps if the *defer shadow* is not filled with other instructions. You may have to come back and update this block after you see what the assembler or compiler has done to optimize these defer shadows. Also, looking at other task drawings can give you a feel for the cycle counts.

Task Drawing Symbol Toolbar

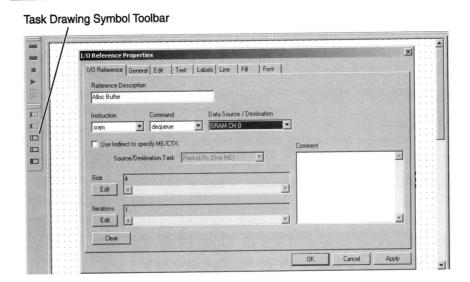

Figure 4.16   Adding an I/O Reference

For an I/O reference, name the reference, and then enter the following:

■ *Instruction*—typically, the name of the target unit, such as SRAM

■ *Command*—the read, write, or other command to the target unit

■ *Data Source/ Destination*—the memory or data structure where data will be read/written

■ *Size*—the number of bytes transferred in the reference

This dialog is also accessible by double-clicking a symbol on the drawing or by selecting a symbol and then choosing Properties from the Edit menu.

Figure 4.17 shows the initial grouping of task objects. You are actually grouping subtasks that perform different functions. You later connect the subtasks together to complete the task drawing. Use the arrow connector in the top toolbar to connect one task object to the next.

You may want to manually add information such as cycle counts and byte counts for I/O references to help you decide how to arrange the subtasks. Simply add text boxes from the top toolbar and move them into place.

Note   The connections are dependency arrows; that is, one task object executes when task-dependent objects have executed. You can therefore indicate parallel task execution by drawing parallel dependency paths.

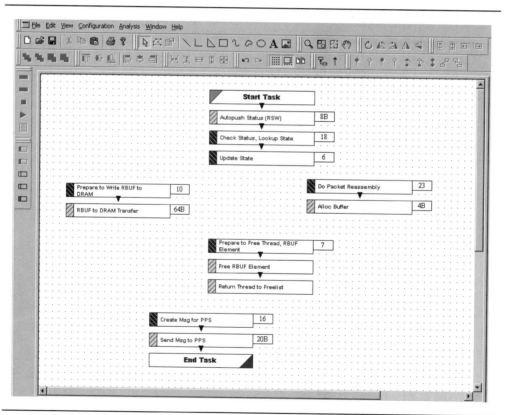

Figure 4.17   Grouping the Tasks

To get best performance, you need to take advantage of asynchronous I/O. For example, many cycles are wasted if the thread swaps out after every I/O reference. The microengine is largely idle, waiting for the I/O to complete. Even other threads may not fill the idle cycles. Looking at the task groups, it looks like the RBUF to DRAM transfer and the next Alloc Buffer could run in parallel. When both have completed, the thread can resume execution. As shown in Figure 4.18, the parallelism is shown by running parallel paths for the I/O, while keeping the code blocks in just one path. The task drawing therefore depicts the dependency relationship of the task objects.

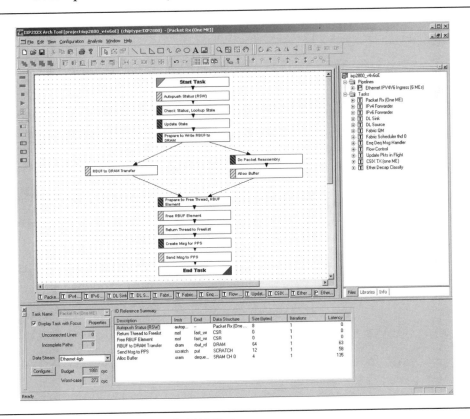

Figure 4.18 Arranging the Parallel I/O References

> **Note** You could have code blocks in parallel paths. The dependency chart would still be valid. However, the drawing would be misleading because the microengine cannot execute both paths at the same time. You don't want to confuse your programmers if you can avoid it.

Keeping the task drawing up to date is very important. For example, later on, when you actually write the code, and even later, when you run simulation, the numbers for the cycle counts associated with each code block will be more accurate if the task drawing is kept current.

Connecting Stages

The pipeline drawing is not yet complete. The stages must be connected. The connection represents the communication, or handoff, between stages in the packet-processing sequence. The most portable methods for this handoff are:

- A message in a scratch ring
- A message in the next neighbor ring

When you imported the DL source microblock, you also imported a scratch ring data structure for it. The "Send Msg to PPS" I/O reference in packet rx should actually be putting the message that DL source gets. A quick click on the DL source task drawing tab lists that scratch get operation in the I/O reference summary of the task definition window. Now go back to packet rx task drawing. As shown in Figure 4.19, right-click the "Send Msg to PPS" I/O reference and select Properties to bring up the properties dialog.

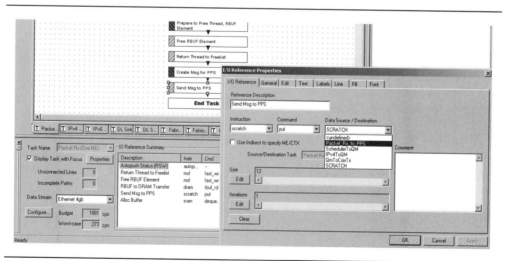

Figure 4.19   Identifying the Scratch Ring

Under Data Source/Destination, select Packet Rx to PPS. DL source uses this scratch ring. Click OK, and you've got a match.

A matching data structure is all that is needed to enable the connection between stages. Now, click the Scratch Ring button from the top tool bar to connect packet rx with the DL source, as shown in Figure 4.20.

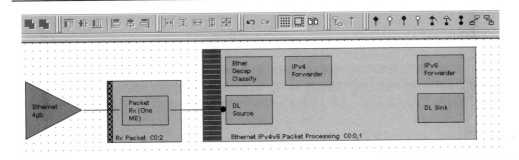

Figure 4.20   Rx to PPS Scratch Ring Connected

Continuing with scratch ring and next-neighbor ring connections, the pipeline stage connections can be completed. When using imported microblocks, look for matching names in I/O Reference Summaries to determine the type of communication; for example, scratch or next neighbor. The finished top-level design is shown in Figure 4.21.

Note   When importing microblocks, if a microblock imports a data structure that already exists in the project—for example, the data structure came in with a previous microblock, any references to the data structure are automatically updated to use the existing data structure. In this way, importing two microblocks that communicate via a shared data structure shouldn't require user intervention to update the tasks.

Note   The connections between stages are actually cosmetic and do not affect the final analysis. The analysis is performed on the blocks you check for the Execution Path in the Data Stream Properties dialog; click the Ethernet 4gb symbol.

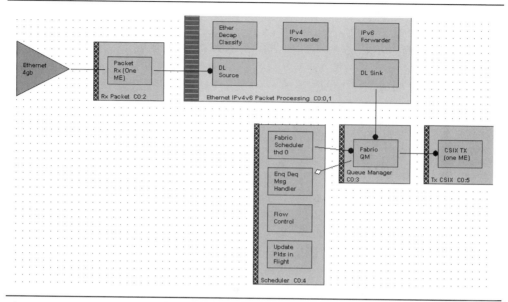

Figure 4.21 The Connected Design

Summary

In this chapter you have learned how to create a top-down design for the microengines, with all associated memory I/O references and memory data structure allocations. This is the big picture. If you become confused at any time while reading the book, you can come back to this picture, and feel secure that there was a purpose, after all.

In this chapter, you have accomplished much. You have done the following—or at least you have read about doing it:

- Created a pipeline drawing
- Defined the pipeline stage partitions
- Defined a task drawing with the code flow and parallel I/O references
- Imported microblocks
- Dragged and dropped microblocks in the pipeline drawing
- Specified the communication between pipeline stages
- Set the stage for the rest of the book

Chapter 5

The Architecture Tool—More Details

There are two ways of constructing a software design. One way is to make it so simple that there are obviously *no deficiencies. And the other way is to make it so complicated that there are no* obvious *deficiencies.*

—Charles Hoare

The devil is always in the details. In Chapter 4 you learned the basic features of the Architecture Tool. You partitioned your design into processing stages. You believe the instruction counts and I/O parallelism of your design perform at the desired rate and that each pipeline stage has enough threads to keep up with the data stream. But you still have two burning questions—only two, I say?—"How much memory is needed to hold the data structures?" and "Will the memory accesses exceed the I/O bandwidths of internal and external buses?" To answer the size question, you must name and declare the sizes of the data structures. To answer the bandwidth question, you must specify all memory references in their proper processing stage, associate the memory references with data structures, and associate the data structures with memory channels. To specify name, size, and channel, you must edit the data structures themselves. To associate a memory reference with a processing stage, edit the task flow diagram for each processing stage and account for all memory references and their associated data structures.

This chapter shows you how to enter and modify this information in your IPV4/IPV6 router project using the Architecture Tool. You also run the analysis to get your pipeline performance, microengine utilization, memory usage, and bus bandwidth utilization. Finally, you export the new rx packet (One ME) microblock and the skeletal Developer Workbench project for the new design.

Defining Data Structures

Data structures should be defined for the project. In addition to program code flow, the data structures provide a way of organizing a packet-related state. But of course! You learned this in Computer Programming 101. The data structures are used for:

- *Memory utilization.* How much space is taken in each memory?

- *I/O references.* The I/O references in the task flow read and write data structures in memory. When running at the data stream packet rate, what is the utilization of internal buses and external memory bus interfaces?

Enter the data structures dialog from the top configuration menu, as shown in Figure 5.1.

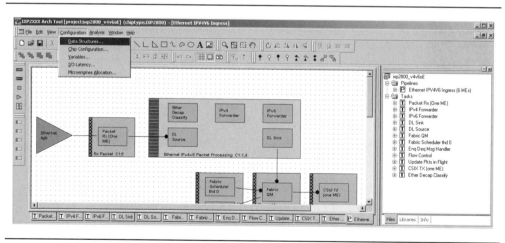

Figure 5.1   Configuration Menu, Selecting Data Structures

The data structures are organized into four categories:

■ *Queues*. Queue structures are dependent on the processor-specific hardware Q array in the SRAM controller.

■ *Generic*. Generic structures are fixed memory blocks and arrays of structures. There are no hardware dependencies.

■ *Buffer pools*. Buffer pools are unique structures that specify places for packet data, packet descriptor, and link-list pointer for use in the buffer freelist.

■ *Rings*. The hardware supports a limited number of rings. Location, scratch or SRAM, and size are specified.

As you have seen, when you import microblocks, you also import the data structures that they use. The names are probably fine, but you may want to adjust some of the sizes; for example, to support more routes, or more stored packets. Now is the time to make the adjustment.

Queue Data Structures

Figure 5.2 shows the dialog for editing queue data structures. The Q array hardware requires three 32-bit words, or 12 bytes, for the head, tail, and count of each queue. User data can be specified for each queue entry. For example, for transmit queue, user data can include WRED parameters or sequence number. This state should be valid only when the item is on the queue.

After the queue set has been created, you can select it when editing task drawing I/O references for queue commands such as enqueue and dequeue. In the I/O references, the following extensions are added to your queue set name:

■ Queue array: _QARR

■ User data: _USR

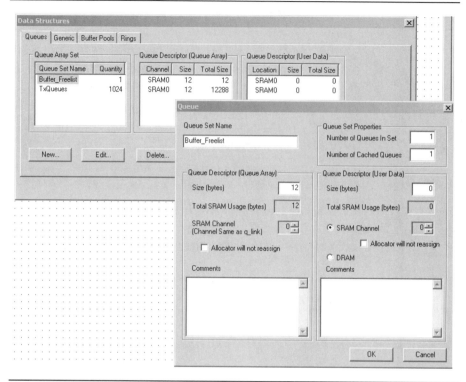

Figure 5.2   Queue Data Structures

Generic Data Structures

Figure 5.3 shows the dialog for editing generic data structures. There are two types of sizing:

- *Simple*. Size in bytes is specified.

- *Calculated*. This is effectively an array. Element size and number of elements are specified.

Rather than specify a memory type and location in the task drawing I/O reference, it is better to define the data structure separately and refer to it by name in the I/O reference. If you need to move the structure to another memory or channel, you can then do it once for the data structure—as opposed to making the change in each I/O reference.

Note The technique of moving a data structure to another memory also applies to queues, buffer pools and rings, in addition to generic data structures. If a data structure is moved to a different memory type, for example from SRAM to DRAM, the I/O reference in the task drawing must be changed; that is, the instruction changes from SRAM to DRAM I/O.

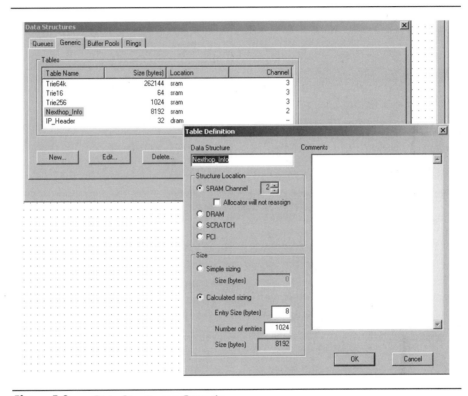

Figure 5.3   Data Structures Generic

Buffer Pool Structures

Figure 5.4 shows the dialog for editing buffer pool data structures. The buffer pool entry represents three kinds of information:

- *The packet itself.* The packet is typically placed in one or more DRAM buffers. For example, you could size the buffer to hold up to 2,048 bytes. If the packet size exceeds that amount, the buffers are chained together. If there are a lot of minimum-size packets in the mix, you might size the buffer at 256 or 512 bytes.

■ *The packet descriptor.* The packet descriptor is a term for packet-related information, or packet metadata. Making this information fast-access, so threads can quickly access it with short memory latency, is desirable. The packet descriptor is typically placed in SRAM.

■ *The link-list pointer.* When the buffer is not in use, a pointer to the buffer is kept on a freelist. The link-list pointer is also in SRAM for fast access. Keeping it in SRAM requires a single pointer per buffer. If you are counting every byte, you should have a related queue data structure in the same SRAM channel to hold the 12 bytes of the Q array for the freelist.

In the I/O references, the following extensions are added to your buffer pool name:

■ Data buffer: Packet Buffer_DBUF

■ Buffer descriptor: Packet_Buffer_BDSC

■ Q link: Packet_Buffer_QLNK

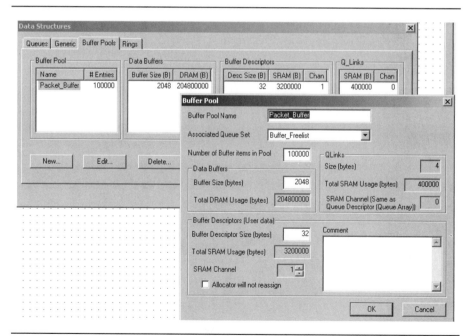

Figure 5.4   Buffer Pool Data Structures

Ring Structures

Figure 5.5 shows the dialog for editing ring data structures. The in and out pointers for the rings are maintained in the hardware. Therefore, you only need to specify memory type—SRAM or Scratch, and size. Scratch rings are always preferred for on-chip messages because external memory bandwidth is not consumed for these operations. During analysis, you may discover that memory bus bandwidth is a precious commodity.

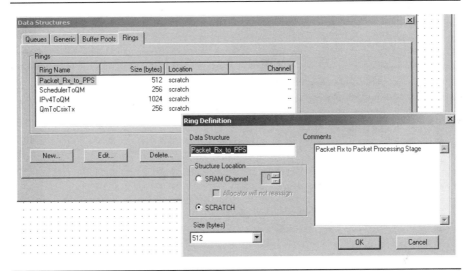

Figure 5.5   Ring Data Structures

Using the Data Structures

To get an idea of the complete use of data structures in the task drawing, take a look at the CSIX tx task drawing. As shown in Figure 5.6, an I/O reference summary is displayed just below the drawing in the task definitions window. Every time this task block is executed, these references are invoked.

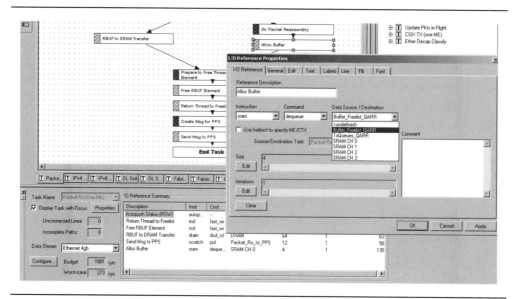

Figure 5.6 CSIX Tx Data Structures

Now is the time to update the packet rx I/O references. Click the Packet Rx tab to display the task drawing. Right-click the Alloc Buffer reference and choose Properties, as shown in Figure 5.7.

Figure 5.7 Updating Rx Buffer Pool

Alloc buffer is performing a dequeue from the packet buffer pool freelist. Therefore, replace SRAM CH0 with Buffer_freelist_QARR because this packet is being accessed for a buffer freelist dequeue or enqueue.

Do the same for the transfer of the packet data to DRAM. This I/O reference writes packet data to the packet buffer, as shown in Figure 5.8.

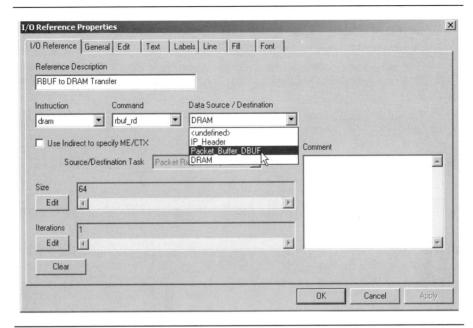

Figure 5.8   Updating Rx DRAM

The I/O reference update is now complete. Everything should now match up. Figure 5.9 shows the completed I/O reference summary for packet rx.

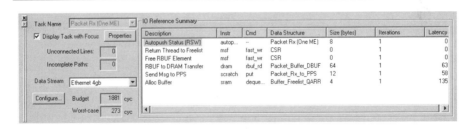

Figure 5.9   Updated Rx Data Structures

Defining Variables

Using variables instead of magic numbers in your project is good practice. These variables are *not* application variables in the implementation code; they are variables used for the project performance analysis that you can use as fixed values or in calculations. For example, a given I/O reference may not happen 100 percent of the time. While editing the I/O reference, you can enter a calculation for the frequency of execution. The Architecture Tool provides some defaults that are used by the Data Stream objects. To get the set of variables used in the current project, in the Configuration menu click Variables, as shown in Figure 5.10. Note that some variables were imported with the microblocks.

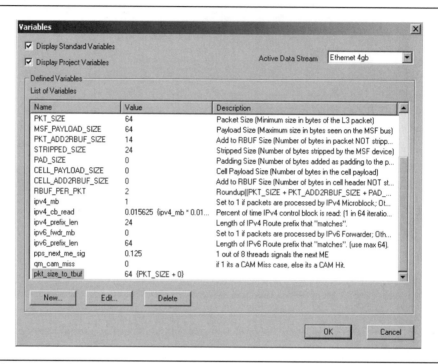

Figure 5.10   Standard and Project Variables

Note   You cannot modify the default variables in this view. However, you can change them by editing the data stream configuration. You do this through the properties dialog of the data stream object.

The IPV4 forwarder has an I/O reference called Port Enable Check. This reference is an occasional read of port status in scratch to see if a port has been disabled. In this design, the Intel XScale® microarchitecture is responsible for updating port status if it gets a management message to disable a port. Here is a perfect place for a variable to be used in a calculation of the frequency of this reference, as shown in Figure 5.11.

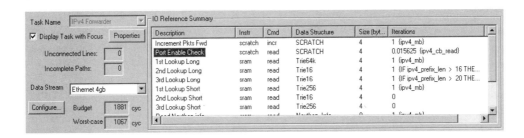

Figure 5.11   Use of Variable in the I/O Reference

The Port Enable Check uses the ipv4_cb_read variable. To display the variables list from the configuration menu, highlight ipv4_cb_read and click Edit. Use the Variable Properties dialog, shown in Figure 5.12, to enter an equation for the calculation of the value.

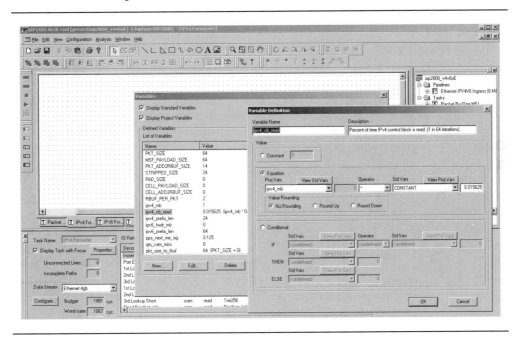

Figure 5.12   Variable Properties Dialog

Analysis

You have entered the top-level stage drawing, the task flow, and the data structures. Now you can analyze your design. The analysis menu has several choices:

- *Project Validation.* Validate all tasks are complete and fully connected from start through end blocks. Validate I/O references and variables for consistency.

- *Analyze Single Size.* Analyze using the range of minimum to maximum packet sizes, specified in the Data Streams Properties page.

- *Analyze Size Distribution.* Analyze using packet sizes and frequency for each size, specified in the Data Streams Properties page.

- *Allocate MEs and Analyze.* Perform a sample ME allocation and analyze.

- *Optimization Setting.* Specify optimization heuristics to guide the tool during the allocation of SRAM and MEs.

For a complete description of Architecture Tool analysis features, refer to the Architecture Tool user's guide (Intel 2004).

The analysis reports the following results:

- *Bus bandwidth statistics.* These statistics are a comprehensive evaluation of bus utilization. Each cluster of microengines has its own data buses, called push/pull buses, and command buses. Each memory controller has buses to external memories.

- *Bus bandwidth graph.* This bar graph shows bus utilization by packet size.

- *Memory utilization.* This summary shows how memory is allocated, adding up all of your data structure sizes.

- *Pipeline performance.* This statistic gives you an idea of how much headroom your software design has. How busy are your threads? Can the design keep up with the data rate or does it drop packets?

- *ME utilization.* This summary shows instruction counts, local memory usage, and whether the CAM is used.

- *Power.* This calculation is steady-state power usage, based on bus utilization, ME utilization, and other chip power usage.

Figure 5.13 shows the pipeline performance analysis results. This table shows the relationship between the number of threads working on a stage to the budget utilization. If the analysis results are green, your pipeline design is promising. Check the other analysis views. If you see any red analysis results in the views for bus bandwidth, memory utilization, pipeline performance, or ME performance, you are not making budget. You can correct the problem by introducing more parallelism in your I/O references or splitting tasks into more stages. If the stage is a functional partition, or if the stage is a context partition running fewer than eight threads, more threads may solve the problem.

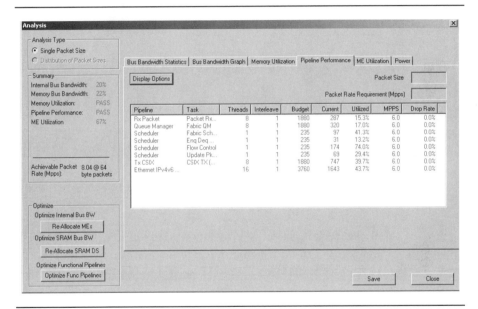

Figure 5.13   Analysis: Pipeline Performance

A common problem is unbalanced utilization of the buses. For example, if all of your I/O references go to data structures in SRAM channel 0, you will likely exceed that channel's capacity. Figure 5.14 shows the memory utilization analysis for the IPV4/IPV6 over Ethernet design.

You can elect to have the tool re-allocate the SRAM data structures to balance the I/O references. Click Re-Allocate SRAM DS. If you have done a good job by hand, the tool terminates the re-allocation and informs you that no improvements could be made. Otherwise you will notice data structures have moved from one channel to another.

Note | The tool tries to balance both memory store utilization and bus bandwidth utilization. You can weight memory or bandwidth to guide the balancing tradeoff.

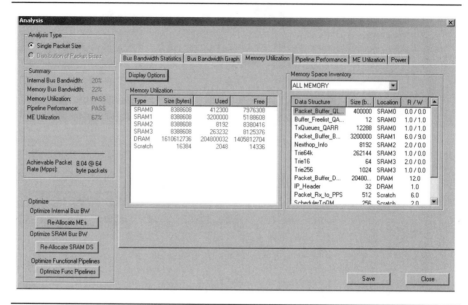

Figure 5.14   Analysis: Memory Utilization

You can perform analysis for single packet sizes or for a distribution of packet sizes. You can adjust packet sizes and frequencies in the Data Stream Properties dialog.

Exporting a Microblock

Most of the work in specifying the design is in the task drawing. The task drawing has the code flow, the I/O references, and the data structures; it is your primary reusable building block. You can export the task block to a library, so it can be imported in other designs. As you have seen, importing microblocks is the fastest way to assemble a design.

While in any task drawing, click Properties in the lower-left corner of the window. Enter the characteristics of your new microblock, as shown in Figure 5.15.

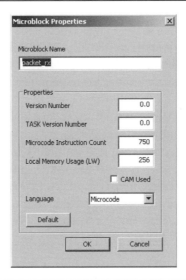

Figure 5.15   Microblock Properties Dialog

From the File menu, you can elect to export a single task or all tasks. This selection creates a file with a .tsl extension for each task.

Creating a Workbench Project

You have not only proven feasibility, but you have created the top-level specification for your design. You can also generate the initial workbench project. Under the project File menu, choose Generate Workbench Project. The Microblock Properties dialog shown in Figure 5.16 appears. Enter the project name and choose a location for the project.

Figure 5.16   Generate Workbench Project Dialog

Summary

In this chapter, you have proven the feasibility of your design. You have created the top-level partitioning, defined task flows, data structures, and performed the analysis that your manager is waiting for. Now it's almost time to get your team rolling.

For the specifics about the Architecture Tool, refer to the Architecture Tool user's guide (Intel 2004).

The Architecture Tool is continually being improved. Future releases will include support for the autopartitioning (AP) C compiler. The top-level stage partitions will optionally be packet-processing stages (PPSs). There will be a new event-based analysis as well as increased interoperability between the Architecture Tool and the Developer Workbench tools. Stay tuned.

Chapter 6

The Developer Workbench

Never trust a computer you can't throw out a window.

—Steve Wozniak

Let's see that forefinger perspire! Move that mouse! You are about to see a lot of windows! The Developer Workbench is the platform for the Intel® Internet Exchange Architecture (Intel® IXA) tools suite. As you recall, the Architecture Tool created a skeletal workbench project for you, but you still have some configuring to do to prepare the project for your programmers.

This chapter covers the basic operation of the Developer Workbench and leads you through the steps necessary to set up and run two projects:

1. A fast project for learning and experimentation.

2. The IPV4/IPV6 router design, including standard libraries in the build and configuring the system-level simulation.

The Quick Tour: One Minute to a Heartbeat

The sections that follow present the fastest way to go from creating a project to running your code. Although taking shortcuts is possible, going through these steps often, such as when trying out a new language feature, is recommended. You might even want to create several test projects for trying out what you are learning. With a test project, you can test new code snippets even faster: open project, modify code, run.

You have installed the Intel IXA SDK and started the Developer Workbench. You would like to create a simple design, called "heartbeat." It makes a microengine periodically increment a global scratch memory counter, indicating that the design is still running.

The major steps to create and run this project are:

1. Create the project

2. Create, edit, and insert the source file or files

3. Create and assign the list file or files

4. Run simulation

Create the Project

From the File menu, select New Project **1**. The New Project dialog appears, as shown in Figure 6.1.

In this dialog, you must enter a project name **2** and select a chip version **3**. IXP2800 B0, or the latest revision, is a fine choice. You may want to relocate your project to a specific parent directory. To relocate the project, modify the Location box. The actual directory name in the parent directory is the project name **4**. You can also name the chip if you are creating a multiprocessor project. Click OK, and you're ready to put something in the project.

1 From File menu, choose New Project   **2** Name the Project

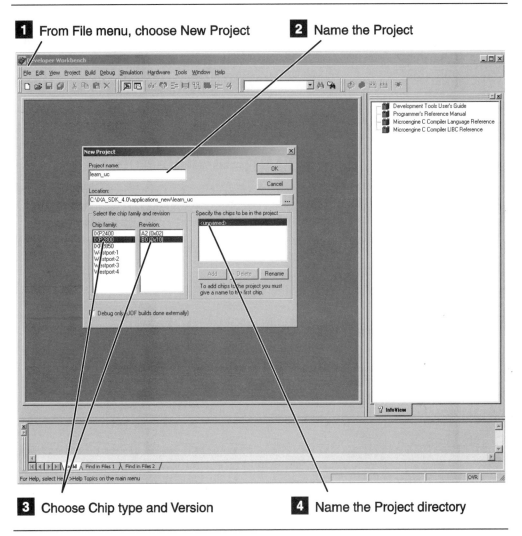

3 Choose Chip type and Version   **4** Name the Project directory

Figure 6.1   Create a Project

Create, Edit, and Insert the Source File

Next, you must create a source file. This source file is a microcode file that runs a few instructions to initialize, then goes into the heartbeat loop. Microcode files have the .uc file suffix.

The next few pages walk you through the steps shown in Figure 6.2.

1 From File menu, choose New, the select Source File

2 Enter code in editor

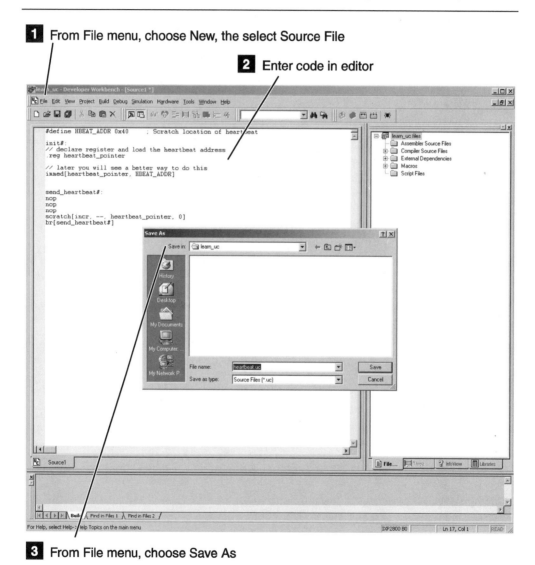

3 From File menu, choose Save As

Figure 6.2   Create, Edit, and Save a Source File

A dialog box appears, giving you a choice of several types of files. Because you are writing microcode, highlight the selection Source File **1** and click OK. Enter your code in the editor window **2**. Microcode on an IXP2XXX network processor is very straightforward. Each microcode instruction represents exactly one instruction in the microengine—no more, no less. The operands of the instruction are symbolic names that you choose. A few commonly used instructions are:

- *alu*— has two input arguments and one result

- *immed*— used to load constants into registers

- *branch*— used as the notorious assembly language goto function

- *sram, dram, scratch*— used for memory I/O access

To get an idea of what microcode on an IXP2XXX network processor is like, create the sample program.

Heartbeat Program Example

```
1    #define HBEAT_ADDR 0x40    ; Scratch location of heartbeat
2
3    init#:
4    // declare register and load the heartbeat address
5    .reg heartbeat_pointer
6
7    // later you will see a better way to do this
8    immed[heartbeat_pointer, HBEAT_ADDR]
9
10
11   send_heartbeat#:
12   nop
13   nop
14   nop
15   scratch[incr, --, heartbeat_pointer, 0]
16   br[send_heartbeat#]
```

Line 1

Define the address (HBEAT) of the heartbeat in scratch memory. The preprocessor command #define is used to define constants. A semicolon or double slash starts a comment. In a real design, you would place this in a separate .uc or .h file, and use #include <filename> to bring it in.

Lines 3–8

The init# label is declared using the *label_name*#: syntax. Labels can be used to mark key milestones in the code. Declare the symbolic name heartbeat_pointer, for assignment to a general-purpose register. Load the constant using the immed instruction. Instead of an immed instruction, you could have used a .init declaration. With this directive, you instruct the microcode loader to initialize the register.

Lines 11–16

Enter the loop, executing three non-operation cycles (nop), a scratch increment, and a branch back to the label send_heartbeat#.

Saving It and Putting It in the Project

Let's give the code sequence a filename, say heartbeat.uc. To do this, choose Save As in the File menu and enter the file name in the dialog box **3**.

Finally, the file must be added to the project. As shown in Figure 6.3, choose Insert Assembler Source Files **4** from the Project Menu. A list of all source files in the project directory is shown; in this case, there is just one. Highlight heartbeat.uc and click Insert.

4 From Project menu, choose Insert Assembler Source Files

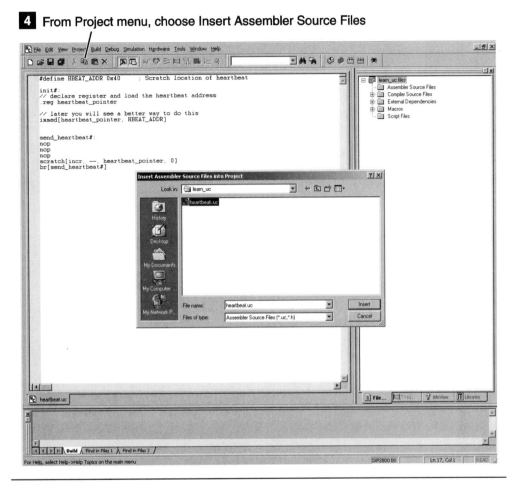

Figure 6.3 Insert Source File in Project

Create and Assign the List File

The next step is to name and assign the list file. The list file is the output of the Assembler—the .uc goes in, and the .list comes out. In the Intel® IXP2800 Network Processor, there are 16 microengines. Therefore, you can have up to 16 list files. Each list file has an associated root file, which is the main microcode that includes all others to be loaded for a given microengine.

As shown in Figure 6.4, choose Settings in the Build menu **1**. Then select the Assembler tab of the Build Settings dialog. There are a number of optimization choices, but ignore those for now. Beside Output to Target List File, click New **2** to bring up the Insert New List File dialog box. In the file name box, type *h*. A list of files in your local directory is displayed. In fact, the filename heartbeat.uc appears in the File name box. Merely change the suffix to .list **3** and click OK.

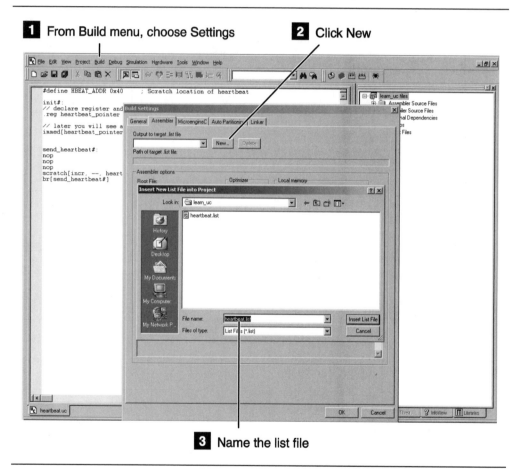

1 From Build menu, choose Settings   **2** Click New

3 Name the list file

Figure 6.4   Create List File

The list file that you now have needs to be associated with two things: a root microcode file and a microengine. As shown in Figure 6.5, click the down arrow under Root File and choose heartbeat.uc **1**.

1 Make heartbeat.uc the root file for heartbeat.list

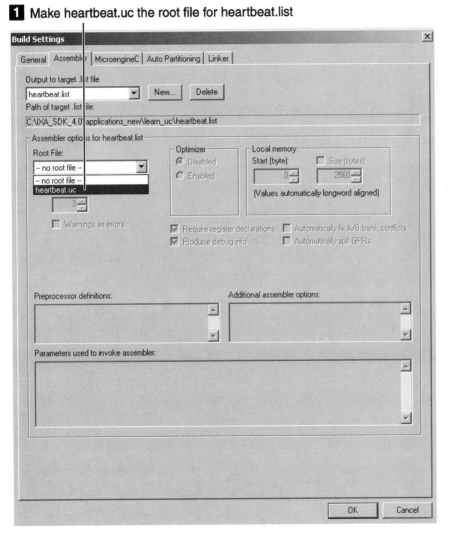

Figure 6.5   Assign List File to Root File

The Assembler settings are now completed. Now you can configure the Linker. While still in the Build Settings dialog, select the Linker tab, shown in Figure 6.6. The Linker takes as input the .list file, and produces a .uof file. The .uof is the binary format that is loaded into the microengines.

For learning microcode or microengine C notation or for initial experimentation with various pieces of the application, you usually run just one microengine. In this test program, we don't want too many heartbeats! Click the down arrow at the box next to Microengine 0:0, and select heartbeat.list **1**. Click OK, and you have completed your design.

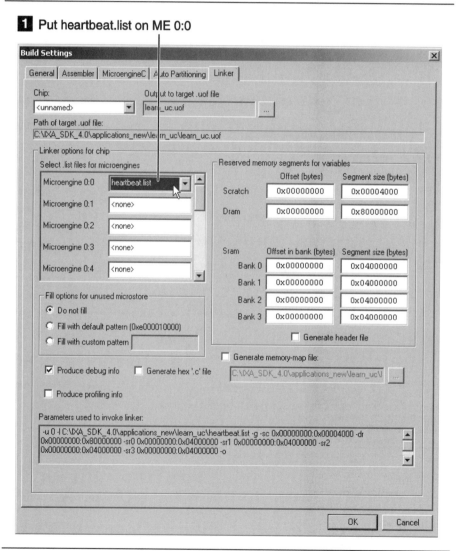

Figure 6.6   Assign List File to Microengine

Run Simulation

You're probably thinking, "How can I run simulation when I haven't even assembled it?" When you try to start up simulation, the Workbench detects whether any of the source files are newer than their related list files and forces a build for those microengines that need it. Figure 6.7 shows the simulation view that is displayed when you click the Simulation Start—the bug—button **1**. Notice the Build menu is no longer present.

The simulator runs a few hundred cycles, performing various initializations in the processor's functional units. Following this, from the View menu, choose Debug Windows. A toggle menu appears allowing you to display or hide many different views of the simulation in progress. For example, selecting Thread Status brings up a dialog box showing the status of all active threads **2**. This view initially presents the list of microengines that have list files; that is, code to run. Double-click Microengine 0:0; the following appears for each thread **3**:

■ *Program counter* (PC) is the current instruction being executed.

■ *Condition codes* are flags for the last time an instruction set condition codes: = zero, negative, carryout, overflow.

■ *Signalled events* are events the thread is waiting on.

■ *Wakeup events* identify those events that have completed.

The thread debug list view is opened by double-clicking on any given thread status line **3**. This view shows the instructions that have been loaded in the microengine, with PC to the left of each one. In the heartbeat case, six instructions appear in blue. In fact, all eight threads of microengine 0 are at PC 0, ready to execute these instructions.

Note

Docking. The thread status and other windows can be docked or undocked to the main Developer Workbench window. This window shows the thread status window undocked, which means you can move it freely around your top windows workspace. When docked, it takes up tile space vertically or horizontally in the Developer Workbench. To turn docking on and off, right-click the double bars on the left of the window and select or deselect Allow Docking.

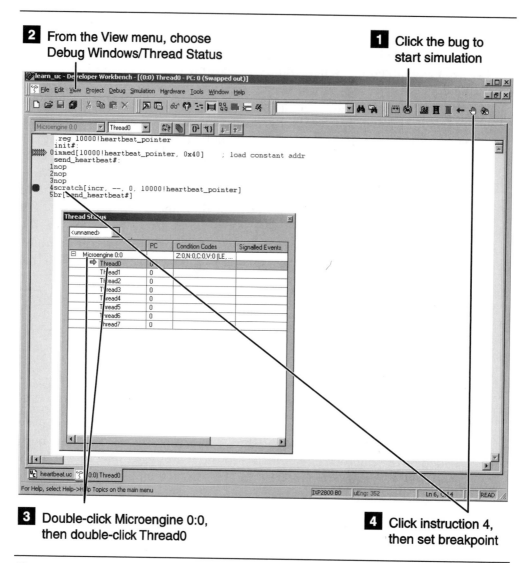

2 From the View menu, choose
Debug Windows/Thread Status

1 Click the bug to
start simulation

3 Double-click Microengine 0:0,
then double-click Thread0

4 Click instruction 4,
then set breakpoint

Figure 6.7   Run Simulation

A real program has many more instructions. The first thing to do is run the program to some significant milestone in the code and stop there. In this example, the program stops when the thread issues the increment to the heartbeat counter and checks to see if the address is correct.

4   You can follow this procedure by first setting a breakpoint. Right-click on instruction 4, the `scratch incr` instruction, and select Insert/Remove Breakpoint.

Or click instruction 4, and then click the Breakpoint button. A red dot appears to the left of the instruction, indicating an un-conditional—always stop—breakpoint.

Second, click the Simulation Stop/Go button. Note that the button is green when simulation is stopped. The simulation runs until the breakpoint occurs. Move your cursor over the operand `10000!heartbeat_pointer` in instruction 4. The value of the register displays. Check to make sure it is correct.

Now let's remove the Breakpoint and run for few seconds. You can remove all breakpoints by clicking the No Breakpoint button.

Click Simulation Stop/Go. The button changes from green to red while simulation is running.

Wait a few seconds, and then click Simulation Stop/Go again; the button changes back to green when simulation is stopped. From the View menu, choose Debug Windows, and select History.

As shown in Figure 6.8, the History screen displays the activity of threads and their memory references. In the heartbeat example, only one thread is running. Do you know why? The reason is that the thread never swapped out.

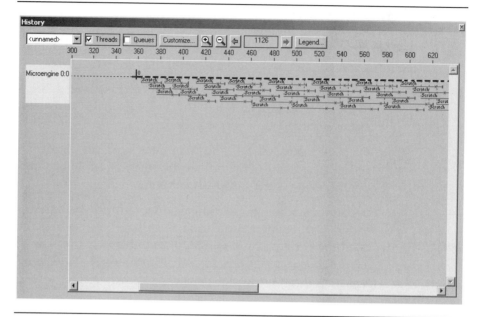

Figure 6.8   Run Simulation

You can simulate much more. For example, you can open the Memory Watch View and select Set Break On Change for the scratch address 0x40. Then run simulation. When that scratch location changes in value, simulation stops and then displays the value. The resulting memory watch display is shown in Figure 6.9. Notice that the value of location 0x40 is 0x5a5a5a…. This result occurs because that location wasn't initialized at the start of the program. But at least that location's value is incrementing. To get an actual count of heartbeats, you must deposit 0 into that location before the program begins incrementing the value. Chapter 12 covers many more simulation views and options.

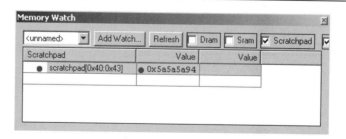

Figure 6.9   Memory Watch on the Heartbeat

Your programmers can now experiment with microcode. For more details about microcode development, see Chapter 7. All microengine programmers should learn the instruction set, which provides an essential foundation for debugging difficult problems.

To program in C, follow almost the same project creation procedure: Choose C Source File when creating the source file, select the compiler tab in build settings, and assign the list file to a C source file. Starting and running the simulation is the same. For details of C development for microengines, see Chapters 8 through 10.

You can find more programming information in the network processor programmer's reference manual (Intel 2004) and the development tools user's guide (Intel 2004).

Configuring the IPV4/V6 Design

You still have some groundwork to do before you unleash your programmers on the IPV4/V6 project. You can develop your design in one of three ways:

- *Designing from scratch.* To design from scratch, you must reinvent everything the Intel IXA Software Framework has been doing for the past several years. See you in six to twelve months...

- *Using the Architecture Tool.* The Architecture Tool produces a skeletal Developer Workbench project, which can be simulated to observe the thread execution and I/O event parallelism. However, this design contains only I/O references and nop instruction fillers; you must insert actual code in place of the nops.

- *Copying and modifying a working design.* In the Architecture Tool, you can import microblocks and copy exactly any design from the applications found on the IXA Framework Applications CD. You can find information about how to obtain this CD on this book's Web site listed in "References." You can then modify the architecture to reflect changes you would like to make. In the Developer Workbench, you can copy an existing project from the example application, give the project a new name, and insert the root source files. All supporting libraries can be found and included. Then you can build the project, run it, change it, build it, and run it. Use this method for the IPV4/V6 project in this book.

Build Settings: Include Libraries

Install all of the applications after you install the Intel IXA SDK. Applications and supporting libraries are installed in the /src directory just under the top IXA_SDK_*n.n* directory. This kit provides many libraries that you can use to put together applications quickly.

Let's browse the Intel IXA SDK 4.0 directory, shown in Figure 6.10. Under /src several important directories appear:

- *Applications.* Example applications for the Intel® IXP2400 Network Processor and the Intel IXP2800 Network Processor. There are core router, IPV4 diffserv, IPV4 forwarder, and mpls categories. Under these categories are Ethernet, ATM, and POS applications.

- *Building blocks.* Microblocks that are used in the applications. Microblocks are the major plug-and-play code blocks used to construct applications. Associated with each microblock is management and exception handling code, which is the component that runs on the Intel XScale® core.

- *Framework.* Provides the Intel XScale core component interface (CCI) and resource manager. This infrastructure provides portability of core components across operating systems and processor generations.

- *Library.* Application-independent libraries with two subcategories:

  - The dataplane library consists of low-level macros that provide a hardware abstraction layer (HAL) just above the microengine instruction set.

  - The microblocks library provides the infrastructure for microblock microengine code. This infrastructure consists of dispatch loop macros that are used to access packet metadata. Using this API layer enables the independent design of microblocks and insulation of the application code from metadata assignment to registers or local memory.

Let's browse a little deeper. Expand ipv4_v6_forwarder/ 4gb_ethernet application directories. There are two projects here: one in microcode and the other in C. By combining these—some microengines in microcode, some in C—and changing the processor type from the Intel IXP2400 Network Processor to the Intel IXP2800 Network Processor, you have something close to what you entered in the Architecture Tool. A complete description of the ipv4_v6 application can be found in the software building blocks design guide (Intel 2004).

Figure 6.10 Intel IXA SDK 4.0 Directory Structure

Copy Freely—You'll Get There Faster

Expand the directory structure to reveal the wbench_project subdirectory of the 4-gigabit Ethernet ingress design, as shown in Figure 6.11. Double-click the dwp file—the one with the red Developer Workbench symbol next to it. This is the way "real" software engineers open projects.

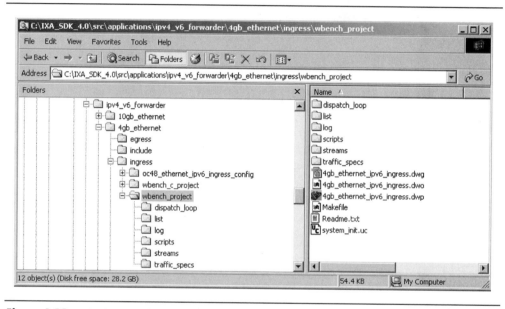

Figure 6.11 Activating the Project

The Developer Workbench key saves project information in the following files:

■ *dwp*—the project configuration file, containing the project's source file names, build settings, and system configuration

■ *dwo*—the project options file, containing display options, such as which default Developer Workbench windows to display, and which information to show or hide

■ *dwg*—a status file, containing settings for the project in the general windows environment

■ *dwt*—a project windows file, containing a list of windows that were active the last time you were in the project

Note   You should not edit these files. The format is subject to change with every re-lease of the SDK. A single character out of place could render one of these files unreadable, and you would have to re-create the project from the beginning.

When moving a project—for example, to a new SDK—only the dwp and dwo files need to be moved. The other project files can be re-created from these files.

Figure 6.12 shows the new project directory structure. Placing your designs under the IXA_SDK_*n.n* directory is a good idea. The project files locations are saved relative to the directory of the project dwp file. The top directory is the IXA_SDK_*n.n* directory. If the application and the libraries it uses are located under this top directory, all file locations can be relative to the project file directory. However, if an application is in another top directory tree, the path to the libraries is fixed; that is, C:\SDK_4.0\… When you get SDK 4.1, your project paths will not point to the new libraries.

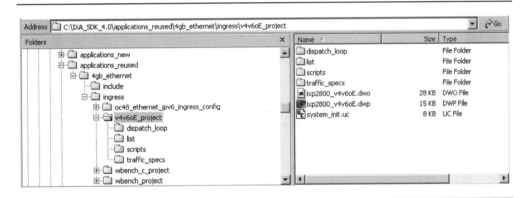

Figure 6.12   The New Project Directory Structure

Adding the Source Files

For this example, the modified project copy is in IXA_SDK_4.0\
!applications_reused. The following steps set up all the necessary project-specific files at the new directory:

1. Copy the complete 4gb_ethernet tree from IXA_SDK_4.0\src\
    applications\ipv4_v6_forwarder   to   IXA_SDK_4.0\!applications
    _reused.

2. In Developer Workbench, create a new project ixp2800_v4v6oE
    under ixp2800_v4v6oE\ingress, as shown in Figure 6.13. This
    creates a directory by the same name. Set the processor family to
    IXP2800 and the version to B0. Save the directory.

3. Copy ixp2800_v4v6oE\ingress\wbench_project sub-directories and system_init.uc to the new project ixp2800_v4v6oE.

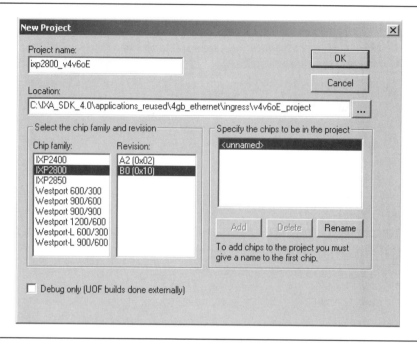

Figure 6.13   Creating the ixp2800_v4v6oE Project

Adding Build Settings

Remember, you are using two source projects to construct the new project. One has build settings for the microcode, and the other has build settings for the C compiler. Figure 6.14 shows the Assembler include directories for the 4gb_ethernet_ipv6_ingress microcode project.

Open the corresponding 4gb_ethernet_ipv6_ingress C project in the directory wbench_c_project. In the Build Settings general dialog, the compiler include directories appear.

The Intel IXA Software Framework uses the preprocessor definition IXP_SIMULATION as a general declaration for all microengines to indicate you are running MEs only in simulation. When IXP_SIMULATION is defined, the microblock initialization routines get table locations and other variables from assemble-time or compile-time constants. When undefined, the Intel XScale core component of the microblock initializes these variables.

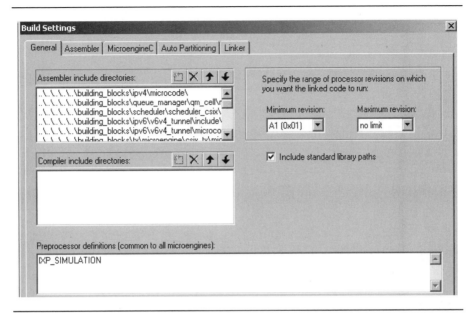

Figure 6.14   Include Settings in the 4-gigabit Microcode Project

The new project has microcode and C code from these two projects. Starting with Intel IXA SDK 4.0, when you use the SDK standard building blocks—microblocks and dataplane libraries—the include paths for these libraries are automatically added when you insert the root files into the new project. Figure 6.15 shows the resulting include directories in the project dwp file.

There is one modification to the two sets of include directories: both source projects have a dispatch_loop subdirectory. In that directory is a dl_system.h that is slightly different for the microcode version and the C version. This difference is to be expected. You merge these into one file later. For now, let the compiler follow the wbench_c_project directory path to find the dispatch_loop include path for the C code. This path is the first COMPILER_INCLUDE directory. Note all paths are relative; that is, your include directories can be followed from the project directory, independent of which version of the SDK you are running.

```
# Developer Workbench Project File
# Format Version 33.05
#********  Do not edit this file ***********

# Begin Project ixp2800_v4v6oE
CHIP_FAMILY = 0x4
CHIP_REVISION_NUMBER = 0x10
DEBUG_ONLY = FALSE
PROJECT_PATH = C:\IXA_SDK_4.0\applications_reused\4gb_ethernet\ingress\v4v6oE_project\
MIN_REVISION_NUM = 0
MAX_REVISION_NUM = -1
INCLUDE_STANDARD_LIBRARIES = FALSE
ASSEMBLER_INCLUDE = .\
ASSEMBLER_INCLUDE = .\dispatch_loop\
ASSEMBLER_INCLUDE = ..\..\..\..\src\include\
ASSEMBLER_INCLUDE = ..\..\..\..\src\library\microblocks_library\microcode\
ASSEMBLER_INCLUDE = ..\..\..\..\src\building_blocks\ipv4\microcode\
ASSEMBLER_INCLUDE = ..\..\..\..\src\building_blocks\queue_manager\qm_cell\microcode\
ASSEMBLER_INCLUDE = ..\..\..\..\src\building_blocks\scheduler\scheduler_csix\
ASSEMBLER_INCLUDE = ..\..\..\..\src\building_blocks\ipv6\v6v4_tunnel\include\
ASSEMBLER_INCLUDE = ..\..\..\..\src\building_blocks\ipv6\v6v4_tunnel\microcode\
ASSEMBLER_INCLUDE = ..\..\..\..\src\building_blocks\tx\microengine\csix_tx\microcode\
ASSEMBLER_INCLUDE = ..\..\..\..\src\building_blocks\rx\microengine\l2_decap\ethernet_decap\microcode\
ASSEMBLER_INCLUDE = ..\..\..\..\src\building_blocks\ipv6\v6_forwarder\include\
ASSEMBLER_INCLUDE = ..\..\..\..\src\building_blocks\ipv6\v6_forwarder\microcode\
ASSEMBLER_INCLUDE = ..\..\..\..\src\building_blocks\ipv4\include\
ASSEMBLER_INCLUDE = ..\..\..\..\src\library\dataplane_library\microcode\
ASSEMBLER_INCLUDE = ..\..\..\..\src\building_blocks\rx\microengine\packet_rx\microcode\
ASSEMBLER_INCLUDE = ..\..\..\..\src\library\microblocks_library\include\
ASSEMBLER_INCLUDE = ..\..\..\..\src\building_blocks\ipv6\natpt\microcode\
ASSEMBLER_INCLUDE = ..\..\..\..\src\building_blocks\ipv6\natpt\include\
ASSEMBLER_INCLUDE = ..\..\..\include\
COMPILER_INCLUDE = ..\.\wbench_c_project\dispatch_loop\
COMPILER_INCLUDE = ..\..\..\..\src\include\
COMPILER_INCLUDE = ..\..\..\..\MicroengineC\include\
COMPILER_INCLUDE = ..\..\..\..\src\library\dataplane_library\microc\
COMPILER_INCLUDE = ..\..\..\..\src\library\microblocks_library\include\
COMPILER_INCLUDE = ..\..\..\..\src\library\microblocks_library\microc\
COMPILER_INCLUDE = ..\..\..\..\src\building_blocks\ipv6\include\
COMPILER_INCLUDE = ..\..\..\..\src\building_blocks\ipv4\include\
COMPILER_INCLUDE = ..\..\..\..\src\building_blocks\ipv4\microc\
COMPILER_INCLUDE = ..\..\..\..\src\building_blocks\rx\microengine\l2_decap\ethernet_decap\microcode\
COMPILER_INCLUDE = ..\..\..\..\src\building_blocks\rx\microengine\l2_decap\ethernet_decap\microc\
COMPILER_INCLUDE = ..\..\..\..\src\building_blocks\ipv6\v6v4_tunnel\include\
COMPILER_INCLUDE = ..\..\..\..\src\building_blocks\ipv6\v6v4_tunnel\microc\
COMPILER_INCLUDE = ..\..\..\..\src\building_blocks\ipv6\v6_forwarder\microc\
COMPILER_INCLUDE = ..\..\..\..\src\building_blocks\ipv6\v6_forwarder\include\
COMPILER_INCLUDE = ..\wbench_c_project\dispatch_loop\
```

Figure 6.15 Include Settings in New dwp

Figure 6.16 shows the general build settings of the new project, with Assembler include directories, Compiler include directories, and the IXP_SIMULATION preprocessor definition.

The next thing to do is insert the source root files into the project. The previous projects were on the Intel IXP2400 Network Processor, which have eight microengines. But four of them run the same code (root = Ethernet_ipv6), so you have to find only five root files. Imagine what you can do with eight spare microengines in the new project. Perhaps you can make it full duplex! The root files to be used from wbench_project\4gb_ethernet_ipv6_ingress are:

■ packet_rx.uc is the rx microblock that receives Ethernet packet segments and re-assembles them in DRAM.

■ qm_cell_code.uc is the queue manager microblock that enqueues and dequeues packets for transmit.

- `scheduler.uc` is the transmit-scheduler microblock that selects packets for transmit.

- `csix_tx.uc` is the transmit microblock that gets packets from DRAM, segments them, and transmits them via the media switch fabric (MSF) interface.

The next few pages describe how to easily insert existing source files from other projects into your new project. If you have SDK 4.0 or later, take a look at the libraries tab on the right side of your Developer Workbench window. If you see the microblocks you need, merely right-click and import them into your project. However, you can benefit from seeing how microblocks are used in other projects.

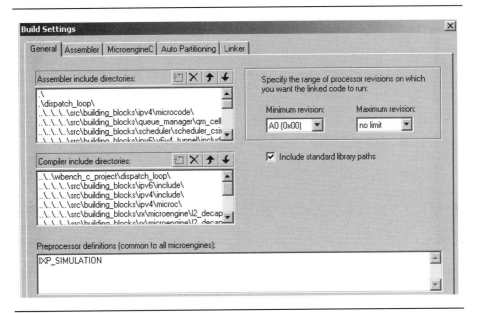

Figure 6.16   Build General Settings in the New ixp2800_v4v6oE Project

In microcode projects, locating the root file is easy. The root file of a microengine is the main file that includes all needed support files. Often the support files are in a building block library that is somewhere in the src/applications directory tree. As shown in Figure 6.17, the project file view lists the files in the project.

The root files have the symbol R next to them. Right-click packet_rx.uc and select Properties **1**. In the Properties dialog highlight the entire file name, right-click, and select Copy **2**. Meanwhile, go back to the new project.

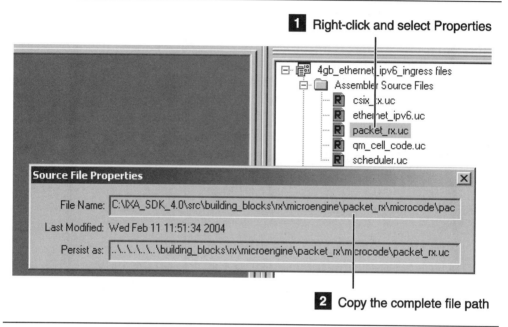

Figure 6.17   Finding the Root File

From the Project menu in the ixp2800_v4v6oE project choose Insert Assembler Source Files. As shown in Figure 6.18, right-click and paste in the File Name box **3**. Select OK. A list of files that are now included in the output window and in the project FileView appears. These files are the Intel IXA libraries used in packet_rx.uc.

3 Paste the complete file path

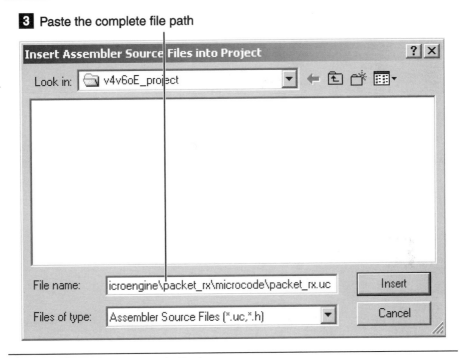

Figure 6.18 Insert Source in Project

You can set the build settings for the source file, just as in the heart-beat example project. In the Build Settings Assembler dialog, create a new list file, packet_rx.list, and then select packet_rx.uc as its root file. Finally, copy the Preprocessor Definitions—also in Build Settings, Assembler dialog—for packet_rx.list from the previous project to this project.

Figure 6.19 shows the resulting project FileView and output windows. Packet_rx.uc is shown as a root file. You are now ready to assemble the project. Right-click the filename (packet_rx.uc) in the FileView and select Assemble. You now have a complete microengine's worth of assembled, ready-to-run code!

Do the same for qm_cell_code.uc, scheduler.uc, and csix_tx.uc, getting the full pathname of the root from the previous project and copying it into the new projects. Assemble the projects. You now have four microengines with ready-to-run code!

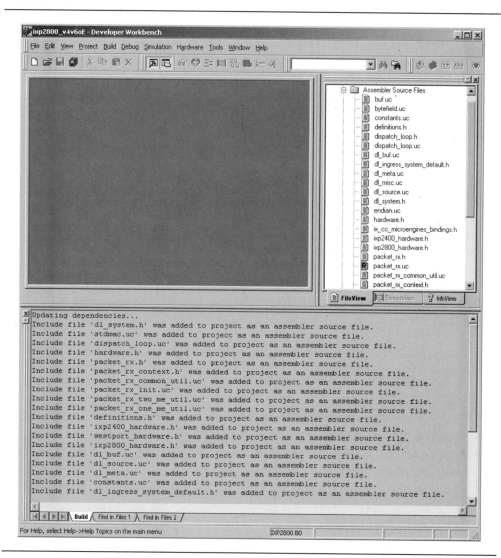

Figure 6.19 Ready to Assemble

You can assemble all of the microengines' code by clicking the build button. What? No build button? If you have not already done so, put the list files in the linker now in the Build Settings, Linker dialog, as you did for the heartbeat project. Now click the build button, shown in Figure 6.20.

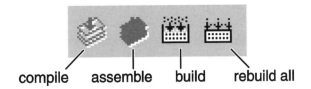

compile   assemble   build   rebuild all

Figure 6.20   The Build Shortcut Buttons of the Developer Workbench Toolbar

All of the microcode is now in the new project. Next, get the C code. The names of the C files are in the Build Settings, Compiler dialog. The C source files to be used from wbench_c_project\4gb_ethernet_ipv6_ingress are:

- *ethernet_ipv6.c* is the application source file for processing packet headers. The application source file is in the FileView of the previous project, residing in the dispatch_loop directory of the wbench_c_project.

- *intrinsic.c* is a compiler library file. From FileView, you determine the file is in IXA_SDK_4.0\MicroengineC\src. This file includes C intrinsics for performing hardware-specific operations.

- *rtl.c* is a compiler library file. From FileView, you determine the file is in IXA_SDK_4.0\MicroengineC\src. This file includes standard C libraries.

Select Insert Compiler Source... from the Project menu. As shown in Figure 6.21, use the windows directory navigation to show the directory wbench_c_project\dispatch_loop. Highlight ethernet_ipv6.c and click Insert. Do the same for intrinsic.c and rtl.c.

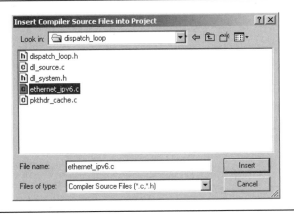

Figure 6.21   Inserting Compiler Source Files in Project

As you did for the microcode files, create a new list file, this time in the build Settings, Compile dialog, as shown in Figure 6.22.

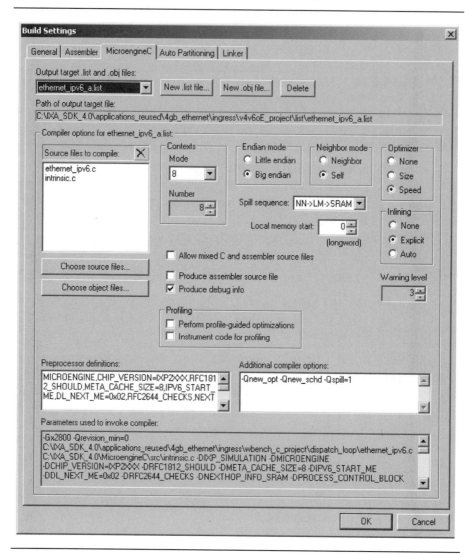

Figure 6.22   Inserting Compiler Source Files in Build Settings

You create a new list file four times, once for each microengine this packet runs on. Call the list files ethernet_ipv6_a.list; ethernet_ipv6_b.list; ethernet_ipv6_c.list; and ethernet_ipv6_d.list. They all have the same three C files.

Copy the preprocessor definitions and additional compiler options from the previous C project to the new project in the Build settings Compiler dialog. Add the list files to the linker. You are ready to rock!

Compile the project, as shown in Figure 6.23. Congratulations!

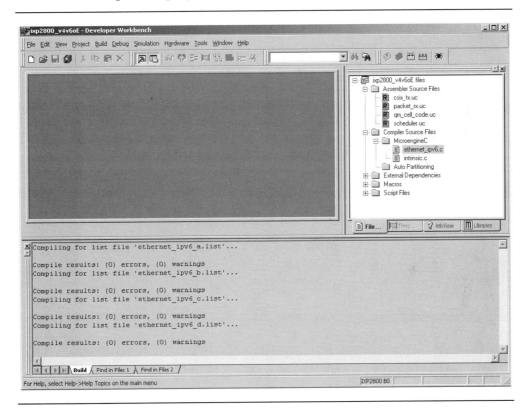

Figure 6.23   The Packet-Processing ME Compiles

Adjusting the System Configuration

Remember, the previous projects were for the Intel IXP2400 Network Processor. This project is for the Intel IXP2800 Network Processor so the system configuration settings are different.

When you select IXP2800 processor family, the workbench provides default clock settings in the system configuration. Choose the Simulation menu and select the System Configuration option. Figure 6.24 shows the default clock settings for all of the chip units in the System Configuration, Clock Frequencies dialog.

Notice the MEs run at 1,400 megahertz and the Intel XScale core runs at 700 megahertz. If this had been an Intel IXP2400 Network Processor, the MEs and the Intel XScale core would be running at 600 megahertz. In addition to getting eight more MEs, the MEs also run 2.3 times faster!

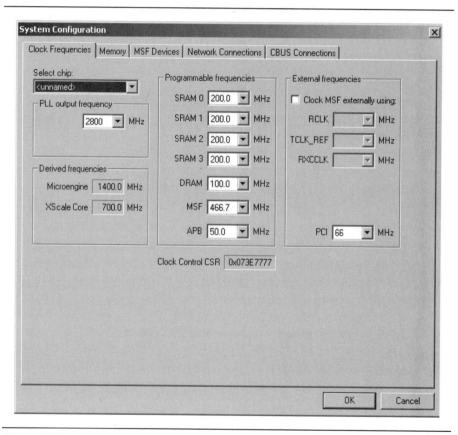

Figure 6.24 System Configuration Clock Settings

However, your application may not run that much faster. Performance is also limited by the speed of SRAM and DRAM, the external memory units. Defaults for SRAM are the same for the Intel IXP2400 Network Processor and the Intel IXP2800 Network Processor. However, DRAM for the Intel IXP2400 Network Processor is DDR, and DRAM for the Intel IXP2800 Network Processor is RDRAM, each with different frequencies and characteristics.

Performance therefore differs when you run your application on the two processors. The application does not scale exactly. For example, the eight threads swapping every 10 cycles and reading SRAM still show the ME as busy on the Intel IXP2400 Network Processor, but show the Intel IXP2800 Network Processor's ME as stalled, waiting on memory completion. But, of course, the Architecture Tool would have told you that!

Figure 6.25 shows the Memory settings tab of the System Configuration Memory dialog.

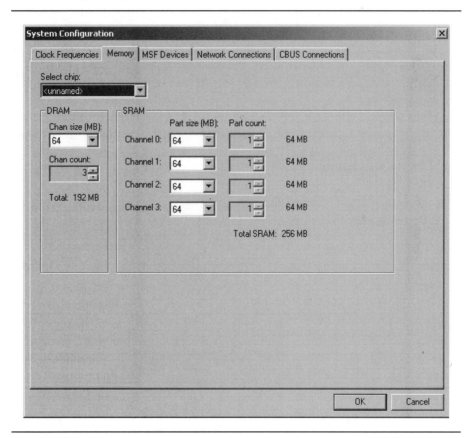

Figure 6.25   System Configuration Memory Settings

Notice there are four channels of SRAM and three channels of DRAM. For Intel IXP2400 Network Processors, you would have two channels of

SRAM and one channel of DRAM. The defaults are 64 megabytes for all channels in both types of processor. You should adjust the sizes to match those you entered in the Architecture Tool.

Figure 6.26 shows the MSF Device configuration in the System Configuration, MSF Devices dialog. Because the previous project uses SPHY and CSIX devices and both processors support these device types, you are in luck. You can merely copy the Device ID and port entries to the new project. However, if the Intel IXP2400 Network Processor project uses a Utopia device, there are differences.

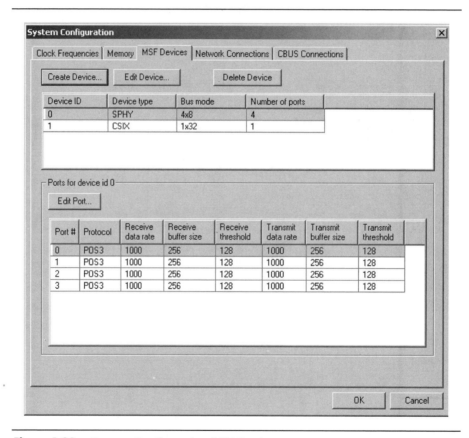

Figure 6.26 System Configuration MSF Devices

Figure 6.27 shows the System Configuration Network Connections dialog. This dialog specifies which of the devices to connect to receive and transmit sides of the processor.

You can connect two network processors using the System Configuration, CBUS Connections dialog. The CBUS is a low-bandwidth bus that can be used for synchronization messages between the processors that are in the same platform or system. For further information on the MSF interfaces, supported devices, and network devices of these two processors, refer to the appropriate hardware reference manual (Intel 2002–3) that covers the type of processor for which you are designing.

Save your project frequently. At any time you can choose Save All from the File menu to capture all project settings and windows options.

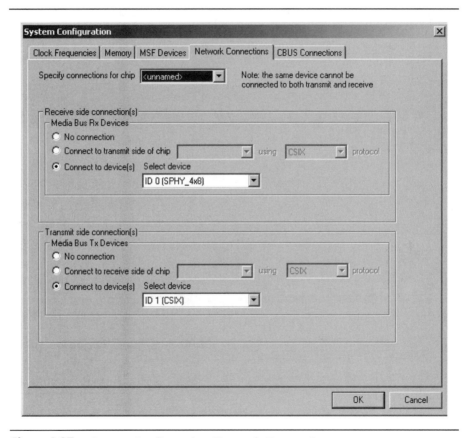

Figure 6.27   System Configuration Network Connections

Summary

In this chapter you have learned two important procedures:

- The fastest way to try out small code snippets.

- How to quickly put together a complete packet-forwarding application, reusing code from existing projects.

As you learned in the Architecture Tool, you can also drag and drop microblocks into a high-level design drawing, analyze the drawing, and generate the Developer Workbench project and the code for a wide variety of designs based on the Intel IXA Software Framework. The more you practice, the faster you will become.

Part III
The Microcode Programmer

Chapter 7

The Assembler

The trouble with programmers is that you can never tell what a programmer is doing until it's too late.

—Seymour Cray

This chapter covers the basics of writing microcode, the assembly language of the microengine. You learn how the Assembler works and what it does for you. You also learn the syntax of the microcode file, including preprocessor directives, register naming, and some coding guidelines to keep you out of trouble. From reading this chapter, you'll know how to write macros and instructions that move data around the IXP2XXX network processors. You'll also know the instruction set categories and syntax with a neat two-page summary of the instruction set. Because your job is to write a driver for receiving packets, you use the task diagram generated by your architect to write key code segments that touch the hardware, writing CSRs, allocating a buffer, transferring packet data from the MSF (media switch fabric) to DRAM, and sending messages to the IP stack through a scratch ring. You configure the Assembler build parameters and run the Assembler in the Developer Workbench. You also run the Assembler standalone from the command line. This chapter contains tips for writing more efficient and maintainable code. For additional information, refer to the programmer's reference manual (Intel 2004) and the user's guide for the development tools (Intel 2004). You can find other good examples of application development in the programming guide (Johnson and Kunze 2003).

If you are an old-timer, you probably define microcode as the specification of the fields of a processor's instruction word, just as the execution data path sees them. However, microcode for IXP2XX network processors is defined differently. For them, microcode is a format that represents the microengine's instruction word in a much more readable syntax. In fact, microcode is more accurately described as *symbolic assembly language*. The syntax consists of opcode, result operand, source operands, required qualifiers, and optional qualifiers. The operands are named by you and thus have meaningful names, such as ip_dest_address—unless you really like calling them foo and bzz.

Here is the basic form of microcode:

```
opcode[parameter1, parameter2, …], option1, option2, …
```

The opcode identifies the type of instruction, much like any assembly language. Parameters of the instruction are enclosed in square brackets. They are operands, operation to be performed, or constants. Options are just that: optional qualifiers that further specify the actions the instruction takes. Here are some examples:

```
// Decrement a GPR by 1:
alu[time_to_live, time_to_live, -, 1]

// Increment a statistics counter:
scratch[incr, --, port_packet_counts, port_id]
```

What the Assembler Does

When you select New Source File from the Developer Workbench File menu, you get the editing window. You then enter the source, consisting of comments, preprocessor commands, and microcode. When you save this information, the default file extension is uc. As you learned in the Workbench heartbeat project, just insert the file in the project, and you are ready to assemble it. Figure 7.1 illustrates the assembly process. This section describes each step of the process.

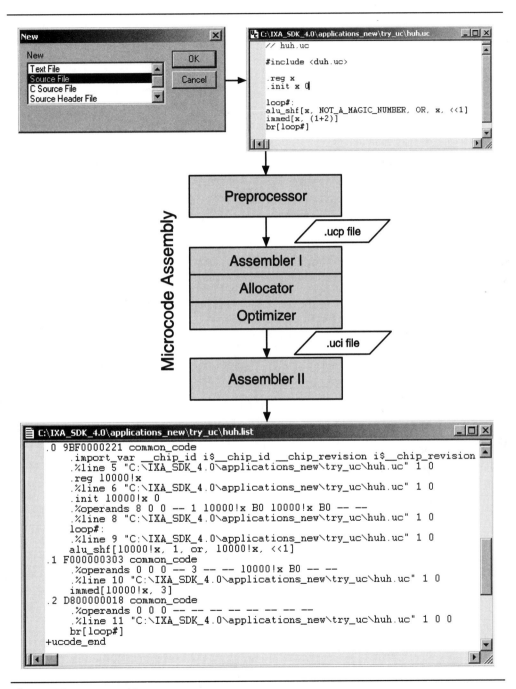

Figure 7.1   Assembly Process

Preprocessor

The preprocessor reads and parses the .uc file as well as any included files named by #include statements. The preprocessor then does the following, as needed:

- Evaluates constants and expressions as specified by #define and #define_eval
- Performs token expansion
- Performs expression tests such as isnum, !isnum, strstr, and streq
- Conditionally executes preprocessor commands and inserts code lines as specified by #if and #ifdef, #while, #for
- Performs macro expansion, capturing #macro definitions and substituting code lines in place of macro invocations

The intermediate output file produced by the preprocessor is the .ucp file.

Assembler I

The main Assembler reads the .ucp file from the preprocessor and does the following:

- Parses the ucp text and creates microword objects
- Performs sanity check on each microword
- Resolves labels for targets of branches
- Checks transfer registers for correctness
- Performs microcode restriction checks based on the chip type

Allocator

The Allocator does the following:

- Computes a flow-graph of code paths for the entire microengine
- Splits registers and signals symbolic variables that are logically independent
- Computes intersections and live-ranges for symbolic variables
- Assigns physical registers and signals to variables
- Scattered throughout these steps, performs various checks to detect coding problems

Optimizer

The Optimizer does the following:

■ Following the flow-graph, moves instructions to fill defer shadows

■ Removes and replaces nop instructions

■ Prints the microword list to the .uci file

Assembler II

The final Assembler reads the .uci file written by the Assembler and does the following:

■ Converts ASCII microword text to hexadecimal-formatted microwords

■ Prints the list file with assignments, live ranges, linker directives, microwords, and debug information

Chapter 6 discusses how to set up the linker and run a complete build from the Developer Workbench. The same linker dialog applies to all .list outputs, whether they are from the Assembler or the Compiler.

What is in a Microcode Source File?

The microcode source file has a .uc extension. When using the workbench editor, key words such as preprocessor commands and microinstruction opcodes are colored blue. Comments are colored green. The source file consists of:

■ Comments

■ Preprocessor commands

■ Executable code

Comments

There are three forms for comments:

```
/* Spanning multiple lines.
   This is a C-style comment.
   */
// To end of a line. This is a C-style comment.
; To end of a line. Shows up in debugger list view.
```

C-style comments can be used for copyright statements, macro low-level design descriptions, assumptions, and other design information. Semi-colon-delimited comments are passed on to the debugger, whereas C-style comments are not. The semicolon comment form is useful for providing debug information, such as what a particular piece of code is really doing. What the piece of code is doing may be obvious. On the other hand, you could come back to that piece in three months and be totally lost without the comment.

Preprocessor Commands

The include statement is used to insert other microcode files. Typically, a microengine has a single root .uc file that includes a hierarchy of definition and library files. The two forms of the include statement are:

- `#include <>` search using the tool include paths
- `#include ""` begin the search relative to the including file, then continue the search using the tool include paths

Definition files (.h suffix) can be shared by many tools: assembler, micro-engine C compiler, the C compiler for the Intel XScale® core, Architecture Tool, and simulator. Using definition files is a powerful way to define common application parameters. However, you do need to be aware of the subset that is common to all of the tools that read the definition file. The following preprocessor keywords are common to all of the Developer Workbench tools:

- `#include`. Inserts another file.
- `#define`. Defines a token.
- `#undef`. Undefines a token previously defined by `#define`.
- `#ifdef` *const*. Includes following lines up to `#else` or `#endif`, if the token *const* is currently defined.
- `#else`. Includes following lines up to `#endif` if preceding conditional was not true.
- `#endif`. Ends the lines included by `#ifdef` or `#else`.

Note that `#if` is not present in this list and is not supported by the simulator command line. Because the simulator command line is a C-interpreter, conditional expressions are written in C syntax.

Don't make the mistake of using the preprocessor directive `#define_eval` in a common definition file and trying to read it with the assembler and C compiler. `#define_eval` is supported only by the assembler. `#ifdef IXP_MICROCODE` around the `#define_eval`, when used in a common file. `#define_eval` evaluates the line at the declaration, as opposed to `#define`, which evaluates at the instances of use.

The `#define` code segment should always be followed by `#undef` at the end of the scope of the constant definition to clean up the name space. Otherwise, you might be causing unwanted substitutions in some other programmer's code.

The following examples give you the basics of writing microcode Assembler preprocessor commands.

Defining and Using Constants

This example uses `#define`, `#if`, `#ifdef` and `#define_eval` constructs. Because preprocessor commands can perform extensive calculations or evaluations, using `#warning` statements to print intermediate results to the Assembler output is often useful.

Constants Example

```
1    #define abc 2
2    #define_eval abc (abc + 1)
3
4    #define def (a c) clueless !@#$
5
6    #define_eval xyz abc/**/abc
7
8
9    #if (DEBUG_VERBOSE == 1)
10        #warning "abc is" abc
11        #warning "def is" def
12
13        #if ((isnum (xyz)) && (xyz > 32))
14            #warning "xyz is" xyz
15        #else
16            #error "you can't use xyz:" xyz
17        #endif
18   #endif
19
20   #define OPTIMISTIC
21
22   #ifdef OPTIMISTIC
23        #warning "you have learned something"
24        #undef OPTIMISTIC
25   #endif
26
27   #ifndef OPTIMISTIC
```

```
28          #warning "you have much to learn, grasshopper"
29    #endif
```

Lines 1–2

> The token `abc` is first defined as 2, then is redefined. In the redefinition, 2 is substituted for `abc` and incremented by 1, establishing the new value of `abc`. With `define_eval`, the token is expanded or evaluated at the time of the `define_eval`. With `define`, the token is expanded or evaluated at the time of use.

Line 4

> The token `def` is defined as a line of arbitrary characters. This definition is fraught with danger and can result in errors if the token is used in actual code. The `#warning` in the output should tell you this is a useless and probably incorrect token. Instead of a `#warning`, you could place a `#error` test on this token.

Line 6

> The token `xyz` is defined as a concatenation of `abc` and redefined `abc`. The expansion and concatenation of the tokens should result in the number 33.

Lines 9–18

> A conditional is used to determine whether to issue warnings, based on the settings of `DEBUG_VERBOSE`. If `xyz` is a number and it is greater than 32, issue a warning. Otherwise, issue an error.

Lines 20–29

> The token `OPTIMISTIC` is defined, a warning is issued, and then it is undefined. Then if `OPTIMISTIC` is undefined, another warning is issued. You are thus forewarned, warned, and double-warned.

Building It

You may or may not want the intermediate token values the preprocessor produces. The Assembler build settings can be used to turn DEBUG_VERBOSE on or off. To display the Build Settings dialog in the Developer Workbench, click Settings from the Build menu, as shown in Figure 7.2. Enter DEBUG_VERBOSE in the Preprocessor definitions box.

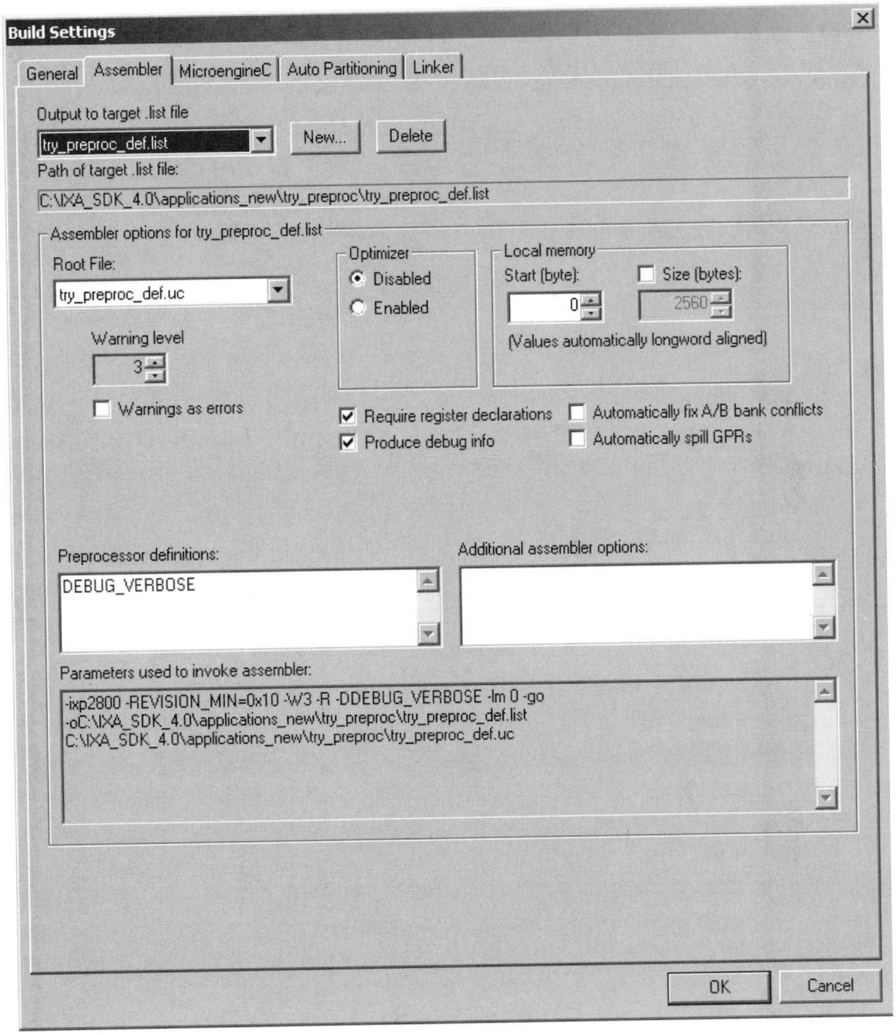

Figure 7.2 Build Settings for DEBUG_VERBOSE

For trying simple examples, you don't have to configure the Linker settings. Clicking Assemble in the top Build menu assembles the current source window. Figure 7.3 shows the resulting warnings in the Assembler output when DEBUG_VERBOSE is defined.

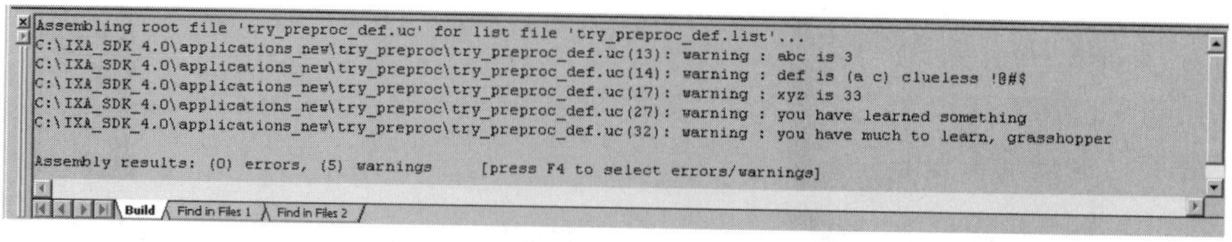

```
Assembling root file 'try_preproc_def.uc' for list file 'try_preproc_def.list'...
C:\IXA_SDK_4.0\applications_new\try_preproc\try_preproc_def.uc(13): warning : abc is 3
C:\IXA_SDK_4.0\applications_new\try_preproc\try_preproc_def.uc(14): warning : def is (a c) clueless !@#$
C:\IXA_SDK_4.0\applications_new\try_preproc\try_preproc_def.uc(17): warning : xyz is 33
C:\IXA_SDK_4.0\applications_new\try_preproc\try_preproc_def.uc(27): warning : you have learned something
C:\IXA_SDK_4.0\applications_new\try_preproc\try_preproc_def.uc(32): warning : you have much to learn, grasshopper

Assembly results: (0) errors, (5) warnings      [press F4 to select errors/warnings]
```

Build   Find in Files 1   Find in Files 2

Figure 7.3   Assembler Output, Preprocessor `#define` and `#define_eval`

Define with Arguments

You can use the `#define` code segment with arguments, in the same way as in C. For include files that are common to both the Assembler and the C Compiler, this definition is preferable to `#define_eval`. In this example, the `#define macro` sum is used in the operand of an instruction and is evaluated when the instruction is instantiated. The result is loaded with the value 3.

```
#define sum(x,y) (x+y)

.reg result
immed[result, sum(1,2)]
```

Constant Expression as an Argument

If all you want to do is add constants to produce an argument, the preceding example may be coded using a constant expression:

```
#define BASE 1
#define OFFSET 2

.reg result
immed[result, (BASE + OFFSET)]
```

Macro in a Preprocessor Loop

Macros are defined using a `#macro` ... `#endm` construct. Assembler macros are used for multiple line substitution; that is, all of the lines between `#macro` and `#endm` are expanded. If a macro has arguments, the argument tokens are substituted when the macro is used. Later in this chapter, you'll see how to define macros with arguments. In this example, you create a macro that defines and undefines the token OPTIMISTIC, then evaluates inside a loop. Figure 7.4 shows the source code window and Assembler output.

1 Define the Macro

```
C:\IXA_SDK_4.0\applications_new\try_preproc\try_preproc_while.uc

// try_preproc_while.uc

#macro whatssup
    #ifndef OPTIMISTIC
            #warning "you are useless"
            #define OPTIMISTIC
    #else
            #warning "you have no code"
            #undef OPTIMISTIC
    #endif
#endm


#define _LOOP_COUNT 4

#while (_LOOP_COUNT > 0)
    whatssup
    #define_eval _LOOP_COUNT (_LOOP_COUNT -1)
#endloop
```

2 Expand the Macro

```
Assembling root file 'try_preproc_while.uc' for list file 'try_preproc_while.list' using stand-alone settings...
C:\IXA_SDK_4.0\applications_new\try_preproc\try_preproc_while.uc(5): warning : you are useless
C:\IXA_SDK_4.0\applications_new\try_preproc\try_preproc_while.uc(17): warning : The previous warning occurred while expanding macro.
C:\IXA_SDK_4.0\applications_new\try_preproc\try_preproc_while.uc(8): warning : you have no code
C:\IXA_SDK_4.0\applications_new\try_preproc\try_preproc_while.uc(17): warning : The previous warning occurred while expanding macro.
C:\IXA_SDK_4.0\applications_new\try_preproc\try_preproc_while.uc(5): warning : you are useless
C:\IXA_SDK_4.0\applications_new\try_preproc\try_preproc_while.uc(17): warning : The previous warning occurred while expanding macro.
C:\IXA_SDK_4.0\applications_new\try_preproc\try_preproc_while.uc(8): warning : you have no code
C:\IXA_SDK_4.0\applications_new\try_preproc\try_preproc_while.uc(17): warning : The previous warning occurred while expanding macro.

Assembly results: (0) errors, (8) warnings    [press F4 to select errors/warnings]

Build  Find in Files 1  Find in Files 2
```

Figure 7.4   Assembler Output, Preprocessor #macro and #while

Preprocessor Strings

This example illustrates the use of Assembler preprocessor strings to initialize values for a variable number of arguments. Macros take a fixed number of arguments. In this case, the argument list is treated like a long string, strstr is used to find the space that delimits each argument, strleft is used to get the next argument, and strright is used to remove the argument just parsed from the string. Finally, the argument name is used in an immed instruction.

Preprocessor Strings Example

```
6     // set initial values of a variable number of arguments
7     // to 0, 1, 2,...
8     //
9     #macro _set_vars_ascending[args]
10    #define SET_COUNTER 0
11
12    #define_eval __tmp 'args'
13    #while (!streq('__tmp', ''))
14        #define_eval __index (strstr('__tmp'," "))
15        #warning "__index is" __index
16        #if (__index == 0)
17            #define_eval __name '__tmp'
18            #define_eval __tmp ""
19        #else
20            #define_eval __name (strleft('__tmp',__index-1))
21            #define_eval __tmp (strright('__tmp',-__index))
22        #endif
23
24        immed[__name,SET_COUNTER]
25        #define_eval SET_COUNTER (SET_COUNTER+1)
26    #endloop
27
28    #undef SET_COUNTER
29    #endm
30
31    .reg global ab bc cd de ef
32    _set_vars_ascending[ab bc cd de ef]
```

Lines 8–28

Define the macro.

Lines 15–21

Determine __name and __tmp for each iteration. The first iteration initializes them all.

Line 31

Use the macro.

Try inserting some #warning statements to show the evaluations of __tmp and __name for each iteration of the loop.

Microcode

You should challenge yourself to write microcode that is easy to read. Declarations, naming conventions, and code structure all play important roles in the maintainability of your ever-increasing code-base.

Register Naming

When writing microcode, you can give symbolic names to the various register types in the microengine listed in Table 7.1. The variable name is a string of alphanumeric characters, including "_". However, in some cases, you need to specify the register type in the name.

Table 7.1   Register Name Designations

Type of Register	Variable Name
GPR, local to thread	No special notation
GPR, global to all threads of ME	@*name*
SRAM transfer register	$*name*
DRAM transfer register	$$*name*
Next Neighbor register	n$*name*

Declarations

Declare all register variables before use with a *.reg* statement. The assembler then detects problems such as misspellings or unused register variables.

```
.reg table_addr
immed[table_addr, NOT_A_MAGIC_NUMBER]
```

Declare transfer register variables to be used in I/O instructions with the *.reg* statement. When grouping more than one transfer register, declare the order of the registers with a .xfer_order statement. Declare signals to be used with the *.sig* statement. Use meaningful names.

```
.reg $qos $output_port
.xfer_order $qos $output_port
.sig tb_sig
sram[read, $qos[0],  table_addr, 0, 2], sig_done[tb_sig]
```

Keywords can be used in some register declarations to indicate special use, as follows:

.reg *keyword variable_name*

Keyword meanings:

- *volatile*. This register remains allocated at all times in the micro-engine. Use this keyword for registers that can change value unexpectedly, such as another thread writing over it. This keyword can never be de-allocated.

- *global*. Force the scope of this register to be at microengine level. Otherwise, the name scope is that of the code block or module.

- *visible*. Make a transfer register visible to another microengine. Use this keyword for neighbor write or cap reflect operations, where one microengine writes to another's transfer registers. The producing microengine will declare the same register as *remote*.

- *read, write*. Declare a transfer register's direction. If not specified, both read and write transfer registers are allocated.

- *remote*. The named transfer register is declared *visible* in another microengine and is presumably the target of a neighbor write or cap reflect.

Code Structure Guidelines

The following guidelines for microcode structure should keep you out of trouble:

- *Don't use magic numbers*. Simply sticking an address, a threshold value, or a configuration decode in an immed instruction, and using it is easy, but someone else reading your code will find these terms nearly impossible to decipher. Instead, define the numbers with meaningful names and place the names in a separate include file.

- *Declare register variables near their use*. You might start out declaring registers at the top of the file, but as the file grows, you will begin to see natural partitions for the code. Having the declaration in the partition greatly increases the robustness of the code. For example, you could move a code block to another file easily if the register declarations are with the code block.

- *Scope code blocks*. Within the delimiters .begin and .end, all register declarations are scoped. Scoping can be used to avoid naming conflicts with variable names such as *temp*.

■ *Use macros.* You can shape code blocks into macros and reuse them as if they were functions. Beware: a macro performs code substitution. Using a 200-line macro twice is 400 lines of code. In this case, branch to a .subr code block so that return uses fewer instructions. However, the overhead of branch and return is several instructions, plus possible copies for arguments and return values. Substituting small macros without subroutines is better. Also, if you are writing a driver or a context pipe stage, you most likely have a small code size for the microengine and can use macros without subroutines for best performance.

■ *Hide the spaghetti.* As much as possible, keep intricate branch choices inside a macro or within a code block that is visible all at one time in the editor. Branches within the macro should generally be low-level conditionals or branches within a fully-implemented algorithm. Use structured programming constructs .if, .else, and .while wherever possible.

■ *Maintain clean interfaces.* A macro that accesses a register variable that is not passed in as an argument or declared in the macro is hiding important information from a reader and most likely results in nonportable, unmaintainable code. The only exception is a system access interface to shared data. In the Intel® Internet Exchange Architecture (Intel® IXA) software framework, the only access to shared variables within the microengine is through the interface macros dl_meta_set* and dl_meta_get*. This type of interface abstraction eliminates the problem of your code breaking another programmer's code due to dangling or mismatched register declarations.

■ *Achieve the right level of partitioning.* Achieving the right level may take several iterations on your code. Major decisions in the program flow should be explicit outside the macro. Thread parallelism, such as interaction with other threads and units, should not be hidden. The Architecture Tool helps you formulate the task partitioning. You can also use the Architecture Tool to look at the task partitioning of existing microblocks.

■ *Use consistent macro naming and format conventions.* For example, macro definition could have the convention

partition_sub-partition_verb(outs, ins, constants, labels)

with a comments template above the macro definition describing the parameters.

■ *Clean up after yourself.* If you set a register and don't use it or use a register without initializing it, the assembler produces warnings. Warnings can accumulate quickly if you don't periodically clean them up. Other programmers looking at your code will not be able to tell a real problem from a nonproblem. If you define constants for your own use and don't undefine them, you may cause some strange substitutions in the next programmer's code.

Libraries

Microcode libraries can be used to speed your code development. These building blocks have been used in a wide variety of applications and are well tested. They have been hand-tuned to achieve best performance. Best of all, they are free!

Macros

The template for all microcode libraries is the macro. The Assembler preprocessor syntax for macros is

```
#macro name[optional_param1, optional_param2, …]
    //lines_of_code
#endm
```

You should use macros to:

■ Support code re-use and ease of programming

■ Hide complexity, particularly hardware dependencies

■ Improve code readability and maintainability

For example, the following macro satisfies all three reasons. It is easier to write move(a, b), then to write the full alu format for passing the B operand through to the result and taking no action on the A operand.

```
// copy the value of parameter2 to parameter1

#macro move[parameter1, parameter2]

    // lines of code, such as
    alu[parameter1, --, B, parameter2]

#endm

// use it
move(b, c)
move(a, b)
```

In its simplest form, the macro provides substitution of lines of code. However, the most common use of macros is to define a block of code with input and output parameters, much like a function. In this form, the parameter names in the definition get substituted with the actual names at the macro instantiation.

Note

> You can choose one of three ways to go to the macro definitions:
>
> ■ In the project workspace, view any of the projects in the applications provided on this book's Web site (for URL see "References"). Select FileView and then navigate the hierarchy to Macros/ By Name. Then click the macro name to go to the source definition.
>
> ■ Use Find in Files at the Developer Workbench toolbar. Enter the macro name in the Find What box. Enter *.uc in the In files box. Normally *uc is the default, so you don't have to do this. Enter the directory where the search should start; for example, C:\IXA_SDK_4.0. Check Look in subfolders. You not only find the macro definition, but all uses of it. Click any line to go to the microcode file.
>
> ■ When you see the use of a macro in source code—it looks like an instruction, but the name is not blue, right-click the macro and select Go To Macro Definition.

Dataplane Library

Now look at the move macro in the dataplane library:

```
#macro move(out_result, in_src)
    #if (isnum(in_src))
        immed32[out_result, in_src]
    #else ;  ! isnum(in_src)
        alu[out_result, --, b, in_src]
    #endif     ; (isnum(in_src)
#endm
```

The #if tests whether the in_src parameter is a number. If so, it invokes another macro, immed32, to load a number into the result. Look up the definition of the immed32 macro in the dataplane library. You can see that immed32 tests the size of the number and whether the bits in the number can fit in a 16-bit field. It then instantiates one or two immed instructions. By now you have guessed that the immed instruction can load a 16-bit constant. If your constant is 32 bits, you need two immed instructions to load the two halves.

With the dataplane library move macro you can:

```
#define NOT_A_MAGIC_NUMBER 0x42424242
move(b, NOT_A_MAGIC_NUMBER)
move(a, b)
```

Many of the macros in the dataplane library test whether macro parameters are numbers and instantiate instructions accordingly. For example, if you want to shift a variable left and mask it, you could have several combinations of constants and variables. If the constants don't fit in an instruction, one or two immeds are needed. If the shift amount is a variable, the variable must be passed through the A operand of the instruction preceding the shift. The complexity is enough to make you want to program in C. The C statement `a = (b<<c)&&0xffff);` looks like this in microcode:

```
immed[tmp, 0xffff]
alu[--, c, OR, 0]
alu[a, tmp, AND, b, <<indirect]
```

Or you can use the macro `alu_shf_left`:

```
// shift b left by c then mask it with 0xffff
alu_shf_left(a, 0xffff, AND, b, c)
```

The macro `alu_shf_left` handles the various constant and variable combinations, instantiating the optimum code.

Microblocks Library

The microblock library has both C and microcode versions. Microblocks in microcode are large macros. Typically, they are much larger than dataplane macros and have hand-tuned code sequences for best performance. In addition, microblocks are the major building blocks of applications. As you learned in Chapter 6, plunking down a few microblocks is the fastest way to achieve a working packet-forwarding application. Before you start writing code, take a look in the building blocks library to see if there are microblocks you can use.

In the Ethernet_ipv6.uc root file in the 4gb_Ethernet_ipv6_ingress project is the microblock v6v4_tunnel_decap. The purpose of this microblock is to remove a layer 3 tunnel header to get to the real layer 3 header. The microblock has an init macro, a run-time macro:

```
v6v4_tunnel_decap_init()
v6v4_tunnel_decap()
```

The init macro is called at start-up time, and the run-time macro is called inside the dispatch loop—the repeating loop that the thread executes. Depending on the packet, the 4gb_Ethernet_ipv6_ingress may execute the following microblocks while in the dispatch loop:

- *dl_source()* —get the next packet
- *ether_decap_classify()* —classify layer-2 and remove the Ethernet header
- *v6v4_natpt_translate()* —perform NAT if needed
- *ipv4_fwder()* —classify layer-3 if ipv4
- *v6v4_tunnel_decap()* —remove tunnel layer-3
- *ipv6_forwarder()* —classify layer-3 if ipv6
- *v6v4_tunnel_encap()* —add tunnel layer-3
- *dl_qm_sink()* —enqueue the packet

In the dispatch loop, the microblock dynamically specifies which microblock must follow by setting the dispatch loop parameter `dl_next_block`. Plug and play!

Controlling the Hardware Features

Your driver has the distinguished job of actually interfacing with the hardware. The driver uses global system parameters, formats and sets the contents of control status registers (CSRs), and moves data to and from external bus interfaces.

Definitions and Initialization

Static system configuration definitions are typically held in definition files, as described previously in the section *Include Files*. Arranging these definitions into generic and chip-specific sections or files is recommended. The generic definitions specify sizes, number of ports, number of microengines used for certain tasks in a way that is independent of the type of processor. The processor-specific definitions control the formatting of CSR fields or indirect instruction words. The goal is to achieve portability with no changes to the code. For example, when chip type is defined in the assembler build settings, the correct CSR formats are used due to judicious use of #if statements. This setting gives you forward compatibility. Or, perhaps you will want to run the same code on different performance versions of your product, one on an Intel® IXP425 Network Processor, another on an Intel® IXP2400 Network Processor, yet another on an Intel® IXP2800 Network Processor.

Dynamic definitions can be made using *import_var*. The *import_var* declaration states that a program running on the Intel XScale core does the initialization. For microblocks, the dynamic definition is done by the core component of the microblock and is useful for memory regions that can vary in size from application to application. For example, in some networks, your route table may only need to support 50,000 routes. In others, it may need to support 1 million routes. The base addresses for tables can be dynamically adjusted at system startup to accommodate the sizes needed.

```
// during initialization
#ifdef USE_IMPORT_VAR
    .import_var TRIE_TABLE_SRAM_BASE
#else
    #define TRIE_TABLE_SRAM_BASE 0x400
#endif


// later when it is needed
immed32(route_table_base, TRIE_TABLE_SRAM_BASE)
```

All IXP2XXX network processors have CSRs that must be initialized. You will most likely initialize from the Intel XScale core. The CSRs are mapped to addresses in I/O space. The SDK library provides a HAL interface for writing and reading CSRs. However, in early simulations, initializing certain CSRs from microcode might be easier. The code can be conditionally compiled using the IXP_SIMULATION definition in build settings. To write a CSR from microcode, use the CAP (CSR addressing proxy) write command:

```
cap[write, $xfer_register, CSR_NAME]
```

CAP is a unit that intercepts CSR reads and writes and forwards them to the appropriate hardware unit.

Runtime

In a network processor, runtime means real time. You cannot afford to waste cycles. Packet data continues to arrive; if you do not handle the data, the port receive device will overflow. Therefore, certain CSRs must be read and written by microcode at runtime. For example, your rx driver needs to inform the MSF that a thread can receive an autopush—notification and status for packet data that has just arrived. The rx driver informs the MSF by writing to the MSF thread freelist. MSF CSRs are addressed mapped. They are written with msf fast write or write commands:

```
// add thread to freelist
msf[fast_wr, --, MY_THREAD_NUMBER, RX_THREAD_FREELIST_0]

// write two transmit control words (TCW) to MSF
// and send ME thread a signal when it is done
msf[write, $tcw0, tcw_addr, 0, 2], sig_done[tcw_sig]
```

A fast write command carries write data embedded in the command and can be used in both cap and msf commands. This command is faster because no data needs to be pulled from transfer registers. Up to 14 bits of immediate data, or the keyword ALU, can be specified in the instruction itself. The ALU keyword indicates the data is 32 bits and comes from the ALU result of the preceding instruction.

Moving Data Between Units

Thanks to transfer registers, moving large amounts of data to and from memory is extremely easy in the IXP2XXX network processors. A single instruction performs inter-unit moves. The syntax is:

```
target[operation, transfer, address1, address2, size]
```

The target is one of the units; for example, SRAM, DRAM, MSF, scratch, PCI. The operation is most often a read or a write. The transfer argument specifies the first transfer register in a sequence. The address arguments are added to from a memory address. The size determines the number of transfer registers to use.

Optional arguments specify the event signal to use for completion and other actions to be taken. The token sig_done[*signal_name*] allows the ME thread to perform asynchronous I/O to continue executing while the memory operation is being performed. A ctx_arb[*signal_name*] later in the code causes the thread to swap out and be eligible to swap back in when the signal is received.

```
// transfer data from SRAM to ME
sram[read, $data, a0, a1, size32], sig_done[s]

// lines of code to cover latency

ctx_arb[s]
```

The token `ctx_swap[signal_name]` causes the thread to swap out following this instruction and be eligible to swap back in when the signal is received.

```
// transfer data from SRAM to ME
sram[read, $data, a0, a1, size32], ctx_swap[s]
```

Optimally, the thread should be a good ME citizen and swap out frequently to let other threads on the same ME have a chance to run. But you can take advantage of asynchronous I/O to overlap the memory operations:

```
sram[read, $data0, a0, a1, 2], sig_done[s0]
// lines of code
sram[read, $data2, a2, a3, 2], sig_done[s1]
// lines of code
ctx_arb[s0, s1]
```

An SRAM read on the Intel IXP2800 Network Processor takes about 120 cycles. With eight threads swapping, if each executed an average 15 lines of code between reads, the microengine would be 100 percent busy.

Depending on the target unit, a target unit can support many possible operations. For example, the scratch unit supports the operations listed in Table 7.2:

Table 7.2　Scratch Unit Operations

Operation	Definition
read	Reads scratch memory starting at the specified address into the specified transfer registers.
write	Writes scratch memory starting at the specified address from the specified transfer registers.
swap	Swaps the contents of a transfer register with the data at the address.
set	Sets the bit or bits at the specified address according to a bit mask provided in the transfer register.
clr	Clears the bit or bits at the specified address according to a bit mask provided in the transfer register.

Table 7.2   Scratch Unit Operations *(continued)*

Operation	Definition
incr	Increments the value of the data at the specified address by one.
decr	Decrements the value of the data at the specified address by one.
add	Adds the value of the transfer register to the data at the specified address.
sub	Subtracts the value of the transfer register from the data at the specified address
test_and_set	Same as the set operation. Reads the premodified value to the read transfer register.
test_and_clr	Same as the clr operation. Reads the premodified value to the read transfer register.
test_and_incr	Same as the incr operation. Reads the premodified value to the transfer register.
test_and_decr	Same as the decr operation. Reads the premodified value to the transfer register.
test_and_add	Same as the add operation. Reads the premodified value to the read transfer register.
test_and_sub	Same as the sub operation. Reads the premodified value to the read transfer register.
get	Gets data from the ring specified in the address and return it to the specified transfer registers.
put	Puts data from the specified transfer registers to the ring specified in the address.

The SRAM unit supports a similar set of operations, plus a set of queueing operations, like enqueue and dequeue.

Figure 7.5 shows possible paths for packet-related data. The ME controls the movement of data between the units using the I/O instructions for MSF, DRAM, SRAM, scratch, PCI, or crypto units.

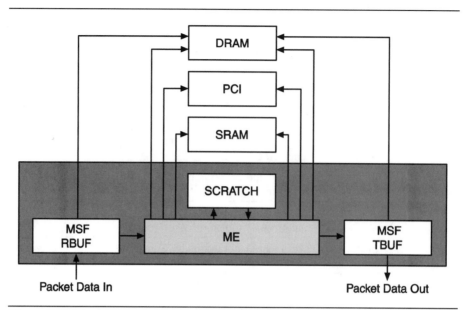

Figure 7.5   Datapaths Between Units

Using MSF instructions, the ME can move data from the receive buffer (RBUF) to the ME transfer registers, or from ME transfer registers to the transmit buffer (TBUF). Using dram instructions, the ME can move data from RBUF to DRAM, or from DRAM to TBUF. Up to 64 bytes can be moved at a time.

```
// transfer data from RBUF to ME
msf[read, $data, a0, a1, size32], sig_done[s]

// transfer data from RBUF to ME
msf[read64, $data, a0, a1, size64], sig_done[s]

// transfer data from RBUF to DRAM
alu[--, …]; alu result contains RBUF address in 18:5
dram[rbuf_rd, --, a0, a1, size64], sig_done[s], indirect_ref

// transfer data from ME to TBUF
msf[write, $data, a0, a1, size32], sig_done[s]

// transfer data from ME to TBUF
msf[write64, $data, a0, a1, size64], sig_done[s]

// transfer data from DRAM to TBUF
dram[tbuf_wr, --, a0, a1, size64], sig_done[s], indirect_ref
```

The size parameter takes on the characteristic of the target unit. For example, the size of dram transfers is always in multiples of 64-bit words—8 bytes. The size of sram and scratch transfers is always in multiples of 32-bit words—4 bytes. The transfers between ME and MSF can be either 4 byte (read, write) or 8 byte (read64, write64).

You will most likely store packet data in DRAM. The devices on the MSF receive network interface generally are unforgiving, so you must move the data into a DRAM buffer at full line rate. You have no excuses for not keeping up—such as you were looking into the packet and wandering through a lot of exception code. DRAM is large, slow, and cheap, relatively speaking. DRAM requires two completion signals to cover the event that the data width spans multiple controllers. The Assembler inserts the second signal in the instruction word using an even/odd pair.

```
// transfer data from DRAM to ME
dram[read, $data, a0, a1, size64], sig_done[s0]

// transfer data from ME to DRAM
dram[write, $data, a0, a1, size64], sig_done[s0]
```

SRAM, on the other hand, is smaller, faster, and more expensive. If you need fast access and your data structure does not fit in scratch memory, put the data structure in SRAM. Use SRAM for lookups, classification, and connection information, especially if your code has little work to do while waiting for the memory operation to complete.

```
// transfer data from SRAM to ME
sram[read, $data, a0, a1, size32], sig_done[s]

// transfer data from ME to SRAM
sram[write, $data, a0, a1, size32], sig_done[s]
```

Next Neighbor

Adjacent microengines can send messages to the next neighbor (NN) microengine—next larger microengine number. The NN communication can be direct between the same thread contexts—for example 0 to 0, 1 to 1—or through the NN ring. Direct NN variables prepend n$ to the variable name:

```
move(my_reg, $nprev_me_reg);   get from previous ME
move(n$next_me_reg, my_reg);   put to next ME
```

When sending through the NN ring, the producer ME must check ring fullness. The pointer syntax *n$index++, refers to the NN ring in-pointer.

```
nn_full#:
br_inp_state[NN_FULL, nn_full#]
move(*n$index++, my_reg)
```

The consumer checks ring empty. The CTX_ENABLES CSR is used to set the empty threshold. This way, if the message consists of more than one word, the ring looks empty if the entire message has not yet been written.

```
nn_empty#:
br_inp_state[NN_EMPTY, nn_empty#]
move(my_reg, *n$index++)
```

Inside the ME

You've seen the *alu* instruction. In one cycle, an operation can be performed on two source registers and the result written to a destination register. Alu instructions also set condition codes. The alu operations are +, +16, +8, +carry, -carry, -, B-A, B, ~B, AND, ~AND, AND~, OR, XOR. Check them out in the programmer's reference manual (Intel 2004).

Figure 7.6 shows the microengine register groups you will be working with. For the syntax groups for the microengine version 2 instruction set, refer to Appendix A.

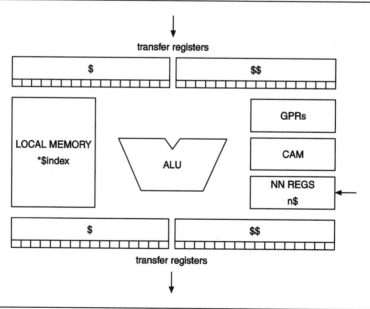

Figure 7.6   Microengine Registers

Using Transfer Registers

As you have seen, you can read and write data between transfer registers and units outside the ME. The transfer registers are holding registers that let you continue executing instructions while an I/O operation is being performed. You can have more than one I/O operation in progress at the same time by using different subsets of the transfer registers.

The $ transfer registers are typically used for SRAM and $$ transfer registers for DRAM. There are read (from external unit) and write (to external unit) sets, bringing the total to four sets of 64 bytes. The notation is historical, stemming from the original Intel® IXP1200 Network Processor. In the IXP2XXX network processors, you can actually read from any memory into $ or $$ transfer register sets. Future processor generations may further blur the distinction between read and write sets—meaning you will be able to read and write any memory with all four sets, plus the ME will be able to read and write all four sets.

Transfer registers can be treated like arrays. The .xfer_order declaration groups a series of transfer registers in ascending index order, which is the order all data is loaded or stored for I/O instructions. Data is loaded to a read transfer register and stored from a write transfer register using I/O instructions. The following declaration and instruction reads three 8-byte quadwords from DRAM into $$pkt_a[0] through $$pkt_a[5]. Later, you can read more of the packet header{$$pkt_b) and append it to the previous array ($$pkt_a). Notice that transfer register array element size is 4 bytes, whereas the DRAM reference count size unit is 8 bytes.

```
// $pkt_a is 24 bytes, $pkt_b is 40 bytes
.reg $$pkt_a[6] $$pkt_b[10]
.xfr_order $$pkt_a $$pkt_b

dram[read, $$pkt_a[0], pkt_addr, 0, 3], sig_done{s0]
// some code
...

// wait for dram read to complete
ctx_arb[s0]

// parse and classify the header
...
// decide you need more header
dram[read, $$pkt_b[0], pkt_addr, 24, 5], sig_done{s0]
```

Conditionals

In microcode, branch and jump instructions are used to continue execution at instructions other than program counter (PC) +1. To identify a branch target you must insert a label before an instruction. An unconditional branch goes to the label specified. A conditional branch goes to the label if the condition code specified is true. In actual execution, additional cycles are needed to calculate the new program counter value and begin execution at the branch target label. These additional cycles are called the branch shadow. Figure 7.7 illustrates the effect of the branch shadow on actual execution.

The alu instruction sets condition code flags to indicate whether the result was zero, overflow, carry-out, or negative. The conditional branch tests selected flags to determine whether to branch. During actual execution, if a conditional branch is taken, a three-cycle penalty of aborted instructions occurs, until the branch target instruction begins to execute. If the branch is not taken, there is no penalty. When you are writing source code to fit within a cycle budget, you must take this penalty into consideration. Choose the proper branch opcode—for example, branch if equal versus branch if not equal—to achieve no penalty in the normal cases, while taking the penalty in the exception cases.

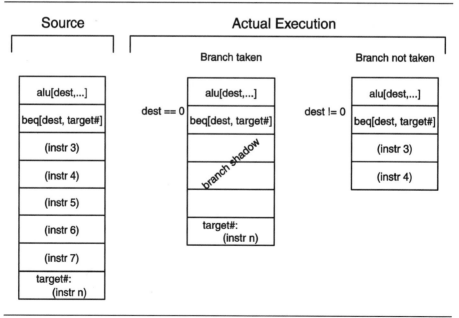

Figure 7.7   Branch Taken or Not Taken Execution

In some cases you know there is a 50-50 chance that the branch will be taken. To avoid the branch penalty, you can cause instructions to be executed in the shadow by using the defer[n] optional token on the branch instruction. For example,

```
beq[dest, target#], defer[2]
```

causes the next two instructions following the branch always to be executed.

If optimization is turned on, the Assembler tries to move instructions to fill the defer slots, inserting defer[n] for you. Figure 7.8 shows one of the optimizations the Assembler does.

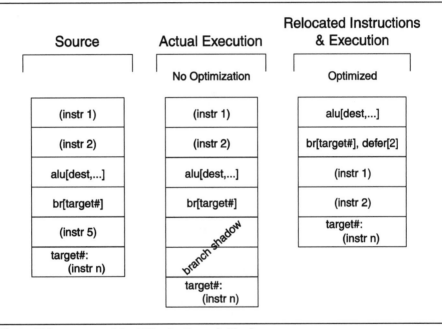

Figure 7.8   Assembler Fills the Branch Shadow

In this example, the unconditional branch goes to a target and would normally have a branch shadow of two cycles. The Assembler moves instructions into the shadow, and inserts `defer[2]`. The Assembler flags the moved instructions in the output list file.

As you can imagine, if-then-else code sequences can get quite convoluted, with multiple branches and defer shadows. The assembler preprocessor provides a structured assembly syntax, using `.if`, `.elif`, `.else`, and `.endif` to construct simple if-then-else decisions. Both `.if` and `.elif` can perform a comparison of a register variable to a constant, or a register variable to another register variable. This form is much more readable than a sequence of branch instructions.

Conditional Code Example

```
1    // in ppp.h, the RFC standard type decode for IPV4 in PPP
2    #define PPP_IPV4 0x21
3
4    // in dl_system.h, unique microblock ids are assigned
5    #define BID_IPV4 0x22
6
7    // in a ppp_classify microblock source file
8    #include <dl_system.h>
9    #include <ppp.h>
10
11   #macro ppp_classify(in_header, IN_HEADER_OFFSET)
12   .begin
13   .reg type
14
15    ppp_get_pkt_type(type, in_header, IN_HEADER_OFFSET)
16
17    .if (type == PPP_IPV4)
18        dl_meta_set_header_type(PPP_IPV4_TYPE)
19        move(dl_next_block, BID_IPV4)
20    .elif (type == PPP_IPV6)
21        // Others supported in microengine
22    .else
23        // Send the packet to core
24        dl_meta_set_header_type(UNKNOWN_TYPE)
25        dl_set_exception(BID_POS, 1)
26        move(dl_next_block, BID_EXCEPTION)
27    .endif
28
29      .end
30   #endm
```

Lines 17–27

This if-then-else construct is used to conditionally execute based on packet header type.

Loops

Structured assembly also includes a while loop construct, which inserts a label and branch instruction. Microengine threads typically perform initialization then go into an endless loop:

```
// init code
.while (expression)
//code inside loop
.endw
```

Subroutines

Use a `.subr` / `.endsub` delimiters to identify a subroutine. Before branching to the subroutine, use the `load_addr` instruction to capture the return PC. After the subroutine, return to the return PC with an `rtn` instruction.

Interthread Communication

You know that 128 threads can be running at the same time. Just how do they communicate? For example, some communication is a simple handshake, possibly involving a signal or a flag in shared memory. Other communication is in the form of a message, with type and data passed from one thread to the next. Messages may be synchronous, as in mailboxes, or asynchronous, as in rings. Communication may be within the microengine, between adjacent microengines, or global. Messages have single or multiple producers and consumers. With the IXP2XXX network processors, you can do all of these. Microengine Assembly language is simple. C is simple. Interthread communication is the key to it all playing together. Here is a short list of the methods:

- *Pipe.* With the autopartitioning (AP) C compiler, you can see how simple gets and puts are used to hand-off state from one packet-processing stage to another. The compiler takes care of the synchronization between producer and consumer.

- *Msgq.* The dataplane library has a msgq interface, which is an abstraction of scratch and SRAM rings for sending asynchronous messages.

■ *Next neighbor.* A microengine may write directly to the adjacent microengine's next-neighbor registers. One thread can write to a corresponding thread in the next microengine or to a ring accessible by all threads of the next microengine.

■ *Signal.* One thread may signal any other thread. Signals are used for synchronization purposes to prevent race conditions, such as a downstream thread read of data that is not yet valid.

■ *Reflect.* One thread may write to transfer registers of another thread.

■ *Ring.* Scratch and SRAM rings are used as FIFOs to hold messages from any producer, including the Intel XScale core, to be read by any consumer.

■ *Queue.* Enqueue and dequeue is primarily used to enqueue and dequeue packet descriptors.

■ *Linked List.* SRAM linked lists are used for freelists of buffer pointers.

■ *Absolute Register.* Absolute registers are global to the threads of a microengine. Threads on the same microengine can communicate with one another through dedicated registers.

■ *Local Memory.* Local memory (LM) is global to the threads of a microengine. Threads on the same microengine can communicate with one another through dedicated LM locations.

You can find many examples for microcode operations in the applications on this book's Web site, listed in "References."

Putting Together Rx_Packet

According to your architect, when packets arrive in the processor, your microengine is the first to notice they are there. Your microengine runs the rx_packet microblock. Let's take a look at the rx_packet1 task flow diagram from the Architecture Tool, shown in Figure 7.9. Note that the OC192 rx_packet1 and rx_packet2 tasks that run on two microengines are combined to form the one microengine rx_packet task for 4-gigabit Ethernet on the Intel IXP2800 or IXP2850 Network Processor.

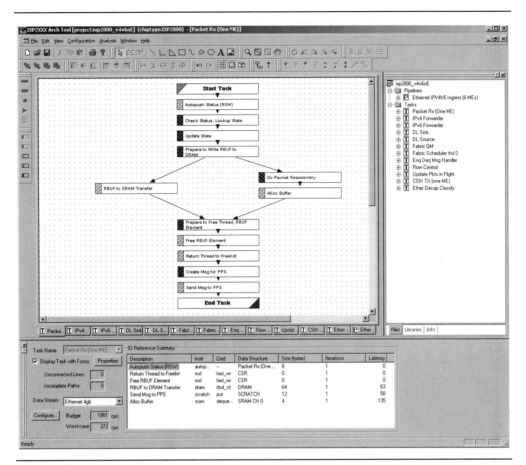

Figure 7.9   Rx_Packet1 Task Flow

At the end of initialization, the `rx_packet` thread puts itself on the MSF thread freelist to request an autopush:

```
msf[fast_wr, --, rx_freelist, freelist_reg]
```

Also, before packet data is transferred to DRAM, a buffer must be allocated. The buffer is obtained from a buffer freelist:

```
sram[dequeue, buf_handle, sram_qa_addr, 0],
    sig_done[req_sig]
```

Following existing `rx_packet` code is easy from the source editor in the Developer Workbench. As shown in Figure 7.10, starting from the top-level loop in rx_packet.uc, right-click the macro to go to source code ■. Note that the Find in files feature also is useful for looking for code examples.

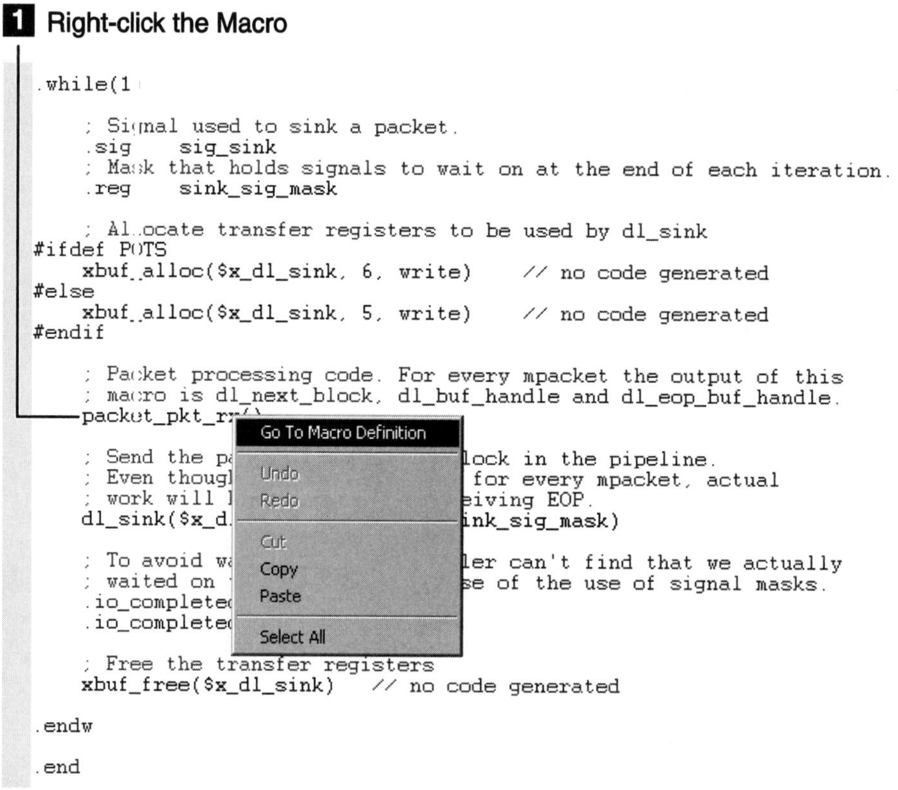

---

1 **Right-click the Macro**

```
.while(1

    ; Signal used to sink a packet.
    .sig    sig_sink
    ; Mask that holds signals to wait on at the end of each iteration.
    .reg    sink_sig_mask

    ; Allocate transfer registers to be used by dl_sink
#ifdef POTS
    xbuf_alloc($x_dl_sink, 6, write)      // no code generated
#else
    xbuf_alloc($x_dl_sink, 5, write)      // no code generated
#endif

    ; Packet processing code. For every mpacket the output of this
    ; macro is dl_next_block, dl_buf_handle and dl_eop_buf_handle.
    packet_pkt_rx()
                    Go To Macro Definition
    ; Send the p                        lock in the pipeline.
    ; Even thoug    Undo                for every mpacket, actual
    ; work will     Redo                eiving EOP.
    dl_sink($x_d                        ink_sig_mask)
                    Cut
    ; To avoid w    Copy                ler can't find that we actually
    ; waited on     Paste               se of the use of signal masks.
    .io_complete
    .io_complete    Select All

    ; Free the transfer registers
    xbuf_free($x_dl_sink)   // no code generated

.endw

.end
```

Figure 7.10   Going to a Macro Definition

When packet data is received, the MSF writes—autopushes—the thread's transfer registers with receive status word (RSW) and signals the thread. Note that Intel IXP2400 Network Processor and Intel IXP2800 Network Processor have slightly different receive status word formats. The thread then extracts information from the receive status word, such as port number:

```
#if IS_IXPTYPE(__IXP28XX)
      alu[port_num, rsw1, AND, 0xFF]; [7:0] is port
#else
      alu[port_num, rsw1, AND, 0xF] ; [3:0] is port
#endif
```

For Ethernet, packets are reassembled to buffer space in DRAM. The buffer location and current offset in the buffer is kept in local memory (LM), indexed by port. Using the port number, a jump instruction goes to the port-specific code segment that reads and updates LM state.

```
alu[*l$index0[RXC_LM_REF_CNT_OFFSET],
    *l$index0[RXC_LM_REF_CNT_OFFSET], -, 1]
```

The RBUF element for the data is in the RSW. There is now enough information to perform the reassembly of packet data in DRAM. The transfer from RBUF to DRAM is done with a dram instruction. The RBUF address is specified in the alu result of the instruction just previous to the dram instruction.

```
dram[rbuf_rd, --, dram_addr, 0, max_16],
    indirect_ref, sig_done[req_sig]
```

The thread assigns the packet-for-packet processing by the next microengine using the next neighbor ring:

```
alu[*n$index++, --, b, in_curr_buf_handle]
// plus other metadata
```

or using the scratch ring:

```
scratch[put, $sink[0], 0, rx_mcast_out_ring, 3],
    sig_done[scratch_write_signal]
```

The rx_packet thread now loops back to repeat the operation for other packet data segments.

Choosing Assembler Build Settings

The Assembler can do much more than your usual Assembler. It can move instructions into branch shadows, which is the dead time while a new program counter is being calculated and loaded, resolve register bank conflicts, spill register usage into LM. Figure 7.11 shows the Build Settings dialog for the 4-gigabit Ethernet IPV4/IPV6 project.

1 Enable Warnings **2** Fill Defer Shadows **3** Fix Conflicts, Spill to LM

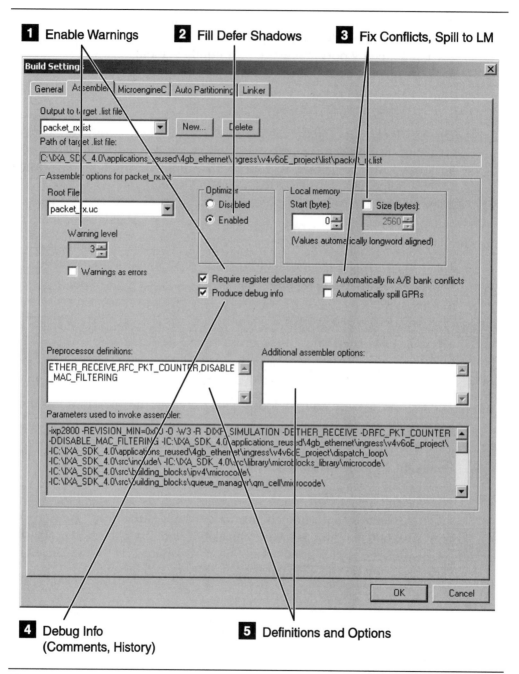

4 Debug Info
(Comments, History)

5 Definitions and Options

Figure 7.11 Assembler Build Settings

Running from the Command Line

You can run the assembler from a Windows† command line or UNIX command line. The input is a .uc root file, and the output is the .list file.

To perform a full build from command line, run the assembler and the linker—uca and ucld. The assembler must be run once for each microengine to produce a list file containing binary, code, comments, debug information, and linker directives. The linker creates a uof file from the assembled list files. Here is the command line syntax for assembling microcode:

```
uca [options] microcode_file.uc
```

Table 7.3 lists the most frequently used assembler options.

Table 7.3   Frequently Used Assembler Options

Option	Description
-h	List the options (print usage). Help!
-o *list_file*	Use list_file as the generated output file. Because of assemble-time definitions, you may produce more than one list file from the same source.
-ixp2xxx	Produce microengine version 2 code.
-O	Enable optimization. Always try this. You will be surprised at how good the Assembler is at hiding instructions inside defer branch shadows.
-Of	Automatically fix register A/B bank conflcts. This rarely occurs, so only turn this on when it does (you should know about it first).
-g	Add debugging info to the output list file. This information includes comments and support for simulation history features.
-I*directory*	Add this directory to the end of the list of include file directories.
-D*name*	Define a preprocessor token.
-D*name=value*	Define a preprocessor token with value.

The linker is then run to produce the object file format (uof). The linker can take list files generated by the Assembler or the Compiler. Here is the command line syntax for linking microengine code:

```
ucld [options] input_file.list
```

Table 7.4 lists the most frequently used linker options.

Table 7.4   Frequently Used Linker Options

Option	Description
-h	List the options (print usage). Help!
-o *outfile*	Name the output uof file.
-g	Include debug information.

For the example heartbeat.uc test file of Chapter 6, the command lines for uca and ucld are:

```
uca -ixp2xxx -o heartbeat.list -O -g heartbeat.uc
ucld -o heartbeat.uof -g heartbeat.list
```

For a more detailed list of assembler and linker command line options, refer to the development tools user's guide (Intel 2004).

Summary

In this chapter you have studied the microengine Assembly language and the Assembler. You have learned the assembly process, from source code, through assembler, to linker output. You have experimented with preprocessor definition, loops, macros and strings. You have learned instruction and variable naming syntax and semantics, and have written simple instructions and dataplane macros. You have learned how to move data around the units in the processor, including caching the packet in local memory. You have tweaked the build settings to produce optimized results. You have studied code snippets from the rx_packet microblock. Finally, you have learned to run the assembler and linker from the command line. You are now dangerous!

Part IV
The C Programmer

## Chapter 8

The Microengine Compiler Landscape

One of the main causes of the fall of the Roman Empire was that, lacking zero, they had no way to indicate successful termination of their C programs.

—Robert Firth

When your program has finished initialization, each of your 128 little threads go into an endless loop. Each thread continues to iterate its tasks on new sets of data. The sum total of all this parallelism is that packets are processed in parallel at maximum data rate. Precisely the goal!

This section discusses the high-level language tools. Your architect has partitioned the packet-forwarding design into high-level language stages and assembly-level language stages. If you are a C programmer, you are in the right chapter. Here you learn about the two modes of the C Compiler: autopartitioning and explicit partitioning. You can decide which mode you want to use for your design. Based on your decision, you can become expert in one or both modes by reading the following three chapters.

Your Task Assignment

As a C programmer, you probably want to write everything in C. In reality, you cannot afford to lose any cycles in some pieces of code, such as the MSF (media switch fabric) receive and transmit interface. Let the driver programmers tweak that code. You can do the packet processing and classification. Typically, microengines are assigned to perform packet processing tasks, and usually there is plenty of headroom. Thus, you can make the tradeoff: elegant, beautiful, maintainable, portable C for a small percentage of performance loss in the packet-processing stages.

The top portion of Figure 8.1 shows the program flow for a typical data-forwarding application, similar to the one your architect set up in the Architecture Tool. Assuming the control plane software—meaning the configuration and setup of network connection and associated state—is done in the Intel XScale® core or in a host, your dataplane application stores and forwards packets at the highest possible rate. The high-level view of this application is a run-to-completion process, in which a packet is received, reassembled, validated, classified, modified, queued, scheduled, and transmitted. If you had only one kind of packet coming through, this code would be straight-line without any branches, except for a loopback to the beginning to start on a new packet. Given packet variations and exceptions, the actual code is much like a tree. However, it can still be partitioned into processing stages—the days of monolithic code are long gone, my friend. In fact, this partitioning is desirable for many reasons:

- Top-level execution flow is readily understood.

- Code blocks are more maintainable. Bug fixes can be contained within the block.

- Code development can proceed in parallel, because interfaces between stages are clearly defined.

The bottom portion of Figure 8.1 shows the IXP2XXX network processors. One thing is true about current and future processors: the number of MEs varies. The basic partitioning problem is to map the code stages to MEs.

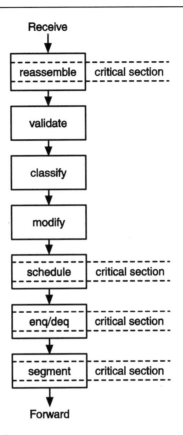

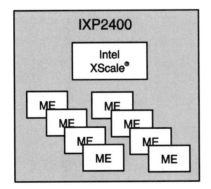

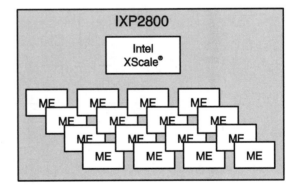

Figure 8.1   The Partitioning Problem

Your forwarding performance dictates how many threads are needed for each stage. The number of threads needed is arrived at by the equation:

$$throughput = stage\ cycle\ latency\ /\ number\ of\ threads\ allocated$$

Each stage can run as many threads as needed. Each thread works on a different packet. Threads can run in two major ways:

- *Pipelined.* Stages are very short—instruction latency and throughput is very high. Threads may read/modify/write shared data. Shared data may have to be read and updated in order.

- *Parallel.* Stages can be variable in length. Order and sharing are not issues, although you may need a reordering ring at the end of these to feed into ordered pipeline stages that follow.

Figure 8.2 shows the allocation of some of the stages for your design.

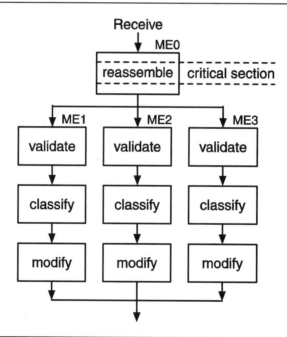

Figure 8.2   Parallel Versus Pipeline, ME Assignment

If the stage has a critical section—that is, code that reads and writes variables common among packets—you must do something to ensure the atomicity of the read/modify/write. This something usually involves signaling or other synchronization. If the threads run in order, the next thread is known; therefore, the synchronization signal can be readily sent to it. Rather than read and write from external memory, threads in the ME can utilize the CAM and read/write from local memory if there is a CAM hit on a shared address. This process is often called a context pipeline stage. In this example, ME0 is a context pipeline stage.

If the stage does not have read/modify/write of shared variables, and the code can be executed out of order, threads can be allocated to run in parallel. Packet header validation, lookups, classification and header modification can all be done in this way. ME1, ME2 and ME3—or many MEs in the case of the IXP2XXX network processors—can be assigned for parallel execution.

Figure 8.3 shows the thread execution.

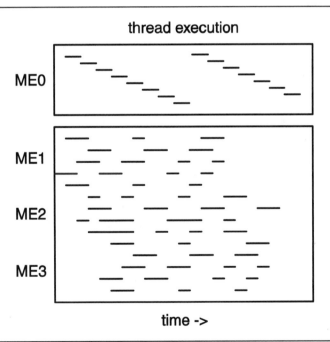

Figure 8.3   Parallel versus Pipeline, Thread Execution

The context stage threads are running in order, and the packet validation/classification/modification threads are running in parallel.

If you have done multithreaded programming, you understand the complexity of synchronizing threads around critical sections or working on packets in order. Consider the portability of your code. Performance requirements alter the partitioning in the following ways:

■ A pipeline stage runs differing numbers of threads. The identification of thread to signal for synchronization changes. Thread sequence may go 0 to 3 then wrap, 0 to 7 then wrap, or may go across MEs and wrap.

■ Communication between MEs is often done via next neighbor (NN) registers and signals. Again, communication requires hard-coded ME and signal designations.

The ME and signal numbering in the code can make it difficult to change the number of threads or microengines allocated to a stage. With some clever #defines, you may achieve some degree of portability. Achieving portability becomes increasingly difficult as you attempt to run the same code on different processors at varying performance levels. You must determine how many threads are needed to achieve maximum parallelism and then implement the necessary synchronization between threads. On the other hand, you can let the autopartitioning compiler do it for you.

Choosing the Compiler Mode

The two compiler modes—explicit-partitioning and autopartitioning—are like two different compilers. Throughout this book, they are called the EP compiler and the AP compiler. Much of the code inside the compilers, such as optimizations, is the same, but there are two executables. Table 8.1 shows a comparison of the two compiler modes.

Table 8.1   Compiler Mode Comparison

Feature	Explicit-Partitioning	Autopartitioning
Signals	Specified by programmer	Inserted by compiler
Intrinsics for hardware access	Yes, with signals for I/O	Yes, without signals
_asm Assembly language sections	Allowed	Not allowed
Microengine assignment	Specified by programmer	Assigned by compiler
Thread-specific code	Allowed	Not allowed
Code organization	In main() per microengine	In PPSs

You can see the main differences are that you can specify signals in the EP compiler, but not in the AP compiler. I/O intrinsics—hardware-abstraction functions—while similar, have signals for the EP compiler and not for the AP compiler. Also, assembly language statements are allowed in the EP compiler. Due to the wide variety of target implementations, assembly language is not allowed in the AP compiler. The AP compiler performs ME assignment to a set of available microengines—you make the MEs available in the Development Workbench Linker dialog. Using the EP compiler, you can control which threads of a ME execute a block of code. In contrast, the AP compiler controls thread allocation. And finally, the top level program for the EP compiler is in a main(), per ME. The top-level program for the AP compiler is encapsulated in a set of packet processing stages (PPSs).

Performance Considerations

The performance of the Compilers varies, depending on the type of code. The Compiler performance has historically improved with each new release as new optimization cases are covered. Figure 8.4 shows the improvement of the EP compiler over several releases. With the current release, the compiler actually does better than a comparable hand-crafted microcode design in some cases.

At the printing of this book, it is too early to provide performance numbers for the AP compiler. However, the expectation is that the AP compiler will achieve at least the same level of performance as the EP compiler on the same source code. You make the tradeoff. You can design application functions in pure C that run on both compilers; for example, keep the critical section code in separate functions.

Both compiler modes allow you to annotate code with critical path information, giving the compiler key information about which code segments to optimize for performance. The EP compiler annotation specifies that one path is more critical than alternate paths; for example, in a conditional if-than-else construct. The AP compiler annotation specifies a performance throughput requirement for the path.

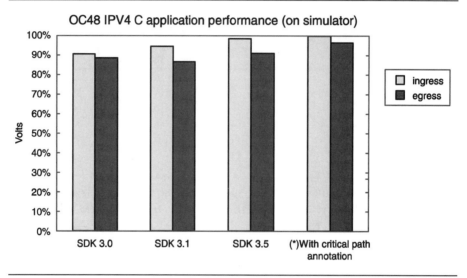

Figure 8.4   Compiler Performance Comparison with Handcrafted Microcode

Summary

In this chapter, you have been introduced to the two C compiler modes: explicit partitioning and autopartitioning. Each has characteristics that you want:

◼ Near-complete control—almost as much as straight microcode—of the result.

◼ Software portability to different processors and performance levels.

You have also seen the issues regarding two types of partitioning of code stages to threads and MEs:

◼ Pipelined threads

◼ Parallel threads

Chapter **9**

Microengine C Compiler

C is often described, with a mixture of fondness and disdain varying according to the speaker, as "a language that combines all the elegance and power of assembly language with all the readability and maintainability of assembly language."

—MIT Jargon Dictionary

Congratulations! You have chosen a very portable way to write your code, with more control of the resulting compilation and additional options for shooting yourself in the foot using the Microengine C Compiler. The Microengine C Compiler and associated language extensions have also been referred to as the explicit-partitioning (EP) mode of the C compiler. As a shorthand notation in this book, it is referred to as the EP compiler, meaning this tool compiles for one microengine (ME).

Well, are we using C or aren't we? What we're using is C±. Our version of C is missing certain features that are of little use to a network processor, such as floating-point arithmetic and recursion. However, our version has additional features for controlling where data is stored in the network processor and for accessing hardware features such as CRC, CAM, next neighbor (NN), rings, queues, and the hash unit. You can write most of your code in pure C with no network processor specific language extensions and intrinsics. Occasionally, you will need greater control. Sometimes CSRs simply do not behave correctly unless you are very explicit with them. Keep this hardware-specific code partitioned away from the pure C, lest the pure C become contaminated. This means: think about what you're doing if you want to port your code to the next generation of IXP2XXX network processors.

What the Compiler Does

Because a microengine's program space is limited—8,000 instructions for the Intel® IXP28XX Network Processor; 4,000 instructions for the Intel® IXP24XX Network Processor—the C compiler always compiles the entire program for an ME using interprocedural optimization techniques that eliminate unnecessary instructions. In this model, the compiler writes the intermediate result to an object file. Common code used in multiple MEs is best compiled to an object file to reduce overall compile time. The full build can include the object file and specific source files for the ME.

When linking all source and object files, the compiler performs a global analysis and calls the code generator for each function in the complete program. At this point, the entire call graph and global usage of all variables is known, allowing for much better code generation than would be possible compiling one function or even one source module at a time. Figure 9.1 illustrates the C compilation process.

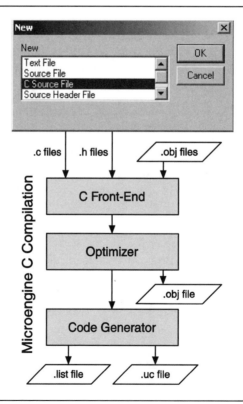

Figure 9.1   C Compilation Process

What's in the Source Files

As already mentioned, the C source file contains standard C±. The additional features enable you to control thread and I/O parallelism. The missing features are not needed in real-time packet-forwarding applications.

Datatypes

As you can see in Table 9.1, most C data types, excluding floating-point, are supported. If the microengine had a floating-point unit, it would be much larger, resulting in fewer MEs. You wouldn't want that would you? For packet processing, simple approximations are accurate enough, and are also much faster.

Although the C compiler supports chars and shorts, their use is not recommended, because insertion and extraction of these types take additional cycles. Because the microengine contains so many GPRs, using variables in 32-bit form is most efficient. When multiple states are stored, it is useful to place them in packed structs. For example, route table entries and packet header formats can be declared as structs. The one-time insert or extract is a good tradeoff versus increasing the size of expensive SRAM to accommodate sparsely populated table data.

Table 9.1   Data Type Summary

Datatype	Size	Supported	Signed	Unsigned
char	8 bit	x	x	x
short	16 bit	x	x	x
int/long	32 bit	x	x	x
long long	64 bit	x	x	x
enum	32 bit	x	x	N/A
pointers	32 bit	x	(only for ptr arithmetic)	x
float/double	N/A	N/A	N/A	N/A
struct	variable	x	N/A	N/A
union	variable	x	N/A	N/A
array	variable	x	N/A	N/A

Although signed types are supported, don't use them unless you absolutely must. Packet data and table lookup structures are not signed. Extracting a signed char from a struct takes two instructions. Extracting an unsigned char compiles to one instruction.

Variables can be declared for location in a specific memory type. The variable can be local to threads, shared by threads in an ME, or shared by threads of multiple MEs such as export, import, remote, and visible. With explicit partitioning, you specify where variables go and how they are shared using the __declspec modifier on the variable declaration. Table 9.2 is a summary of the data attributes that are allowed.

Table 9.2 Allowed Data Attribute Summary

	Thread local	Shared	Export/Import	Remote/Visible
GPR	x	x		
Xfer reg	x			x
Signal reg	x			x
Next Neighbor	x			x
Local Memory	x	x		
SRAM	x	x	x	
DRAM	x	x	x	
Scratch	x	x	x	
RBUF	(pointer only)			
TBUF	(pointer only)			

Take a Walk Through C Coding Techniques

This section is your basic Hello World in Microengine C. In this section, you walk through enough code examples to feel comfortable with the nuances of explicit microengine C programming. Do not skip this part!

In addition to your main source file, you must link in the support libraries. If you don't use them, the code is not compiled in. You may be unaware of even calling a support function, but you will use the libraries frequently; their use happens indirectly. You must link to the following three libraries:

- *libc.c*—Standard library, string, and memory functions

- *intrinsic.c*—hardware register access functions and nonstandard library, asynchronous I/O functions specific for the IXP2XXX network processors

- *rtl.c*—Arithmetic, multiply, divide, unaligned access support functions

Create a C source file and add it to a test project. Use Project > Insert Compiler Source Files…, to insert new files into the project. Library files can be found by browsing to:

```
ixa_sdk_4.0\MicroengineC\src\
```

In build settings, name the new list file and specify the source file plus supporting libraries, as shown in Figure 9.2.

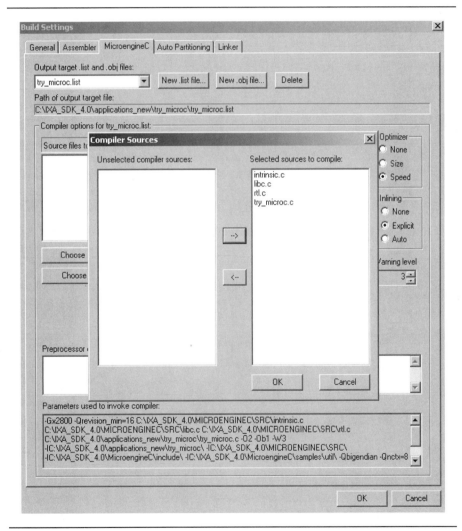

Figure 9.2   Including Support Libraries in Build Settings

Start with something simple, so you can readily compare source code with the resulting compiled microcode. To bring in all of the declarations for datatypes and supporting libraries, always include ixp.h at the top of the file.

```
#include <ixp.h>

main()
{

__declspec(shared sram) int *data1 = (int *)4;
__declspec(shared sram) int *data2 = (int *)8;

*data2 = 42;

*data1 = *data2;

}
```

The IXP2XXX Product Line has several memory types, each with its own characteristics. With the Microengine C Compiler, you can specify exactly where data should be stored using the __declspec type modifier.

- *Local memory.* Local memory (LM) is in the ME. Minimum LM access is four cycles. An address pointer is set with one instruction; after three intervening cycles have passed, the location can be used. In the intervening cycles, other instructions can execute.

- *Scratch.* Scratch memory is on-chip and is global to all of the MEs and to the Intel XScale® core. Typical access times are less than 80 cycles for an IXP28XX network processor.

- *SRAM.* SRAM memory is off-chip. Typical access time is under 130 cycles for an IXP28XX network processor. SRAM is also referred to as narrow RAM because the size of access is smaller than DRAM.

- *DRAM.* DRAM memory is off-chip. Typical access time is less than 300 cycles for an IXP28XX network processor. Most efficient use of DRAM requires an access of larger size, such as 32 bytes.

Note | Access times vary, depending on the type of processor and frequency setting for the memory channel.

If you do not declare a memory type, the compiler assigns variables to GPRs. When all of the GPRs are taken, the compiler spills the variable assignments to LM. If LM is full, it spills them to SRAM. You can change the spill sequence in the Developer Workbench build settings dialog or through –Qspill build switch at the command line.

If you add the shared sram qualifier to the type declaration, the compiler assumes the data is shared by all MEs, and places it in SRAM. As you can see in this example, pointer access is normal C syntax.

Note

> Taking an address of a variable means the variable is either declared as a pointer (*var) or its address is used (&var).
>
> If a variable is declared as shared—no memory qualifier—and its address is taken, the compiler also assigns it to SRAM.
>
> If a variable is declared as shared and its address is not taken, the compiler might allocate the variable to shared storage within the ME, such as an absolute GPR.

In the Build Settings Linker dialog that displays when you select that option on the Build menu, assign the list file to an ME. You are now ready to simulate. Start debugging by clicking the "bug". Run 300 cycles. Display Thread History by clicking the Thread History button. To expand the thread line of ME 0:0, right-click and select Expand Threads for Microengine 0:0. Right-click again on a thread line and you can select Display Memory References. What do you see? All of the threads are writing and reading SRAM. Your code has been loaded to ME 0:0, and all eight threads are executing it in parallel! Right-click again on one of the thread lines and select Go To Instruction. Both the Thread History View and the Thread List appear, as shown in Figure 9.3.

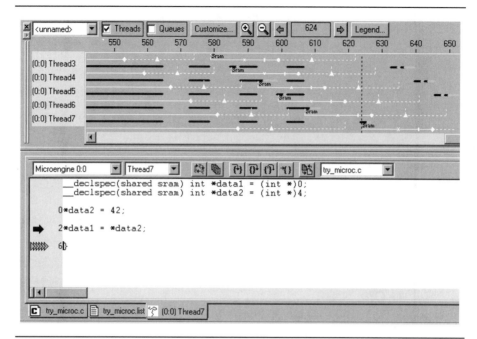

Figure 9.3   Thread List, Source View

The code looks just like your source code, doesn't it? The left border shows the currently executing line of code. To see the corresponding microcode instructions, click the Toggle View button. The four lines of C source are implemented with six lines of microcode, as shown in Figure 9.4. The compiler assigns different names to the registers, but you can see your source code in comments /*****/ just above the instruction. If you know your sram instructions, you can recognize b0, b1, and a1 as addresses, and $0 as read and write transfer registers. The reference count in the sram instructions is 1, indicating one 32-bit word is read or written.

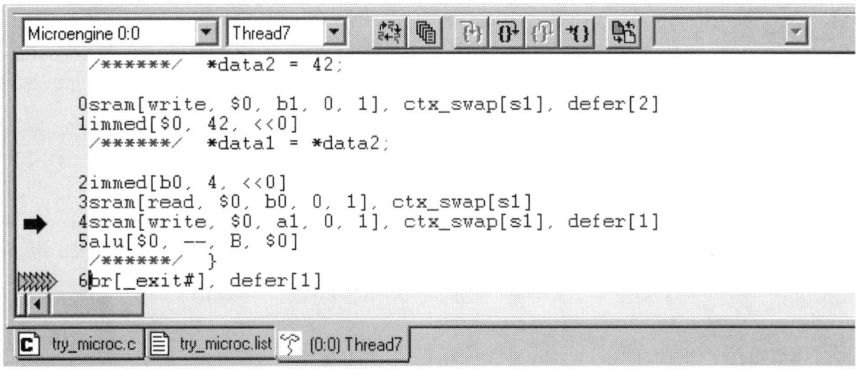

Figure 9.4 Thread List, Toggled to Instruction View

Wait a minute! The initial addresses of the pointers data1 and data2 were assigned in the source file, yet no instructions exist to do this. The compiler has provided a directive to the debugger to initialize two GPRs with these addresses. When you run in simulation, initialization is done by the loader DLL when the microcode is loaded. When you run on real network processor hardware, initialization is done by the microcode loader from the Intel XScale core. The try_microc.list file confirms initialization as follows:

```
.%init_reg A1 0x4
.%init_reg B1 0x8
```

When the first sram write executes, the compiler places a ctx_swap and defer[2] qualifiers on the instruction. The defer[2] qualifier causes the following two immed instructions to be executed in the dead cycles that occur while the thread is swapping out. The dead cycles are known as defer shadows. They occur during the branches and context swaps. The Assembler and Compiler attempt to fill defer shadows by moving instructions out of their normal order into the defer cycles. The first immed instruction after the write loads the transfer register for the write.

Know what your compiler does for you by toggling between source code and microcode in the List View. You can hover with your cursor over the variable names to see the values at any selected simulation cycle.

Structs

In the previous example, you accessed SRAM by declaring the type—shared sram—and using pointers in assignment statements. These were single word accesses—the minimum read/write size. Declaring struct variables and using their pointers in assignments cause single memory accesses with multiple-word reference counts. Figure 9.5 and Figure 9.6 illustrate a memory copy from SRAM into the ME, then from the ME to memory.

```
Microengine 0:0  ▼  Thread7  ▼  [icons]  try_struct.c  ▼
      #include <ixp.h>

      main()
      {

      typedef struct my_data{
          unsigned int a;
          unsigned int b;
      } my_data_t;

      __declspec(shared sram) my_data_t *table_entry1;
      __declspec(shared sram) my_data_t *table_entry2;

      table_entry1 = (__declspec(shared sram) my_data_t *)0x10;
      table_entry2 = (__declspec(shared sram) my_data_t *)0x8;
    2 table_entry1->a = 0;
{*} table_entry1->b = 0;
    6 table_entry2->a = 42;
 {*} table_entry2->b = 43;

    8 *table_entry1 = *table_entry2;

   14 }
```

Figure 9.5   Thread List, Struct Example Toggled Source View

In the source code view, the PC location is approximate. The actual PCs and corresponding source code can be seen in the instruction view. Each member of each struct is initialized on a separate source line. However, the compiler recognizes the proximity of the members and combines the memory access into single two-word write (PCs 1, 5). The transfer registers are loaded in the defer shadow of the sram instructions. The copy is then performed with a two-word sram read (PC 9) and a two-word sram write (PC 11).

```
┌─────────────────────────────────────────────────────────────────┐
│ Microengine 0:0    ▼  │ Thread7 ▼ │  ⬚ ⬚ ⬚ ⬚ ⬚ ⬚  ⬚           │
├─────────────────────────────────────────────────────────────────┤
│         /******/  table_entry1->b = 0;                          │
│                                                                 │
│ ▶▶▶▶  0immed[a0, 16, <<0]                                       │
│       1sram[write, $0, a0, 0, 2], ctx_swap[s1], defer[2]        │
│         /******/  table_entry1->a = 0;                          │
│                                                                 │
│       2immed[$0, 0, <<0]                                        │
│         /******/  table_entry1->b = 0;                          │
│                                                                 │
│       3immed[$1, 0, <<0]                                        │
│         /******/  table_entry2->b = 43;                         │
│                                                                 │
│       4immed[a0, 8, <<0]                                        │
│       5sram[write, $0, a0, 0, 2], ctx_swap[s1], defer[2]        │
│         /******/  table_entry2->a = 42;                         │
│                                                                 │
│       6immed[$0, 42, <<0]                                       │
│         /******/  table_entry2->b = 43;                         │
│                                                                 │
│       7immed[$1, 43, <<0]                                       │
│         /******/  *table_entry1 = *table_entry2;                │
│                                                                 │
│       8immed[b0, 8, <<0]                                        │
│       9sram[read, $0, b0, 0, 2], ctx_swap[s1], defer[1]         │
│      10immed[a0, 16, <<0]                                       │
│      11sram[write, $0, a0, 0, 2], ctx_swap[s1], defer[2]        │
│      12alu[$0, --, B, $0]                                       │
│      13alu[$1, --, B, $1]                                       │
└─────────────────────────────────────────────────────────────────┘
```

Figure 9.6   Thread List, Struct Example Toggled to Instruction View

For structs declared for specific memory types, the compiler typically aligns the struct to the boundary required by the type. Declaring aligned(4) ensures that the compiler aligns this structure to a 4-byte boundary—use aligned(4) for SRAM, aligned(8) for DRAM. Future chips could have wider SRAM options requiring aligned(8) so try to align your data structures to 8 byte boundaries.

```
__declspec(shared sram aligned(8)) my_data_t *table_entry;
```

Structs can also be used to pack data in GPRs and memory. Without any pack qualifiers, the members align according to their size:

- char aligns to a 1-byte boundary
- short aligns to a 2-byte boundary
- int aligns to a 4-byte boundary

Instead of using one GPR per variable, the following struct packs four variables into two GPRs—two 32-bit words:

```
typedef struct my_data{
    unsigned int a;
    unsigned short b;
    unsigned char c;
    unsigned char d;
} my_data_t;
```

If the longest members are not first, alignments may occur. The following struct has gaps caused by the alignment. The struct occupies three 32-bit words:

```
typedef struct my_data{
    unsigned char a;        // 1 pad byte to align b
    unsigned short b;
    unsigned char c;        // 3 pad bytes to align d
    unsigned int d;
} my_data_t;
```

The packed qualifier is used to eliminate the gaps. The following struct occupies only two 32-bit words:

```
typedef __declspec(packed) struct my_data{
    unsigned char a;
    unsigned short b;
    unsigned char c;
    unsigned int d;
} my_data_t;
```

Bitfields are useful for defining odd-size fields or for packing as many fields as possible into a struct. However, alignments can occur to prevent a bitfield from crossing a 32-bit boundary. For example, the following struct occupies three 32-bit words and has 32 wasted bits:

```
typedef struct my_data{
    unsigned int a:20;      // pad 12 bits to align b
    unsigned int b:20;      // pad 12 bits to align c
    unsigned int c:24;
} my_data_t;
```

To pack bitfields across the int boundary, use the packed_bits qualifier. The following struct occupies two 32-bit words:

```
typedef __declspec(packed_bits) struct my_data{
    unsigned int a:20;
    unsigned int b:20;
    unsigned int c:24;
} my_data_t;
```

For packet headers, you don't have the luxury of placing larger members first or using standard C sizes. Bitfields enable you to use structs to define your network headers, whatever the sizes or order of the members may be. This one doesn't require the `packed_bits` qualifier:

```
typedef struct ipv4_hdr{
    unsigned int version:4;
    unsigned int hdr_len:4;
    unsigned int tos:8;
    unsigned int total_len:16;
    unsigned int id:16;
    unsigned int flags:3;
    unsigned int frag:13;
    unsigned int ttl:8;
    unsigned int protocol:8;
    unsigned int cksum:16;
    unsigned int sa:32;
    unsigned int da:32;
} ipv4_hdr_t;
```

Unions

Often when working on small struct members in the microengine, you may want to move portions of the struct to memory in blocks. Use a union to define one structure for data manipulation and another for member sizes that match memory access reference sizes:

```
typedef __declspec(packed align) struct{
    union{
        struct{
            unsigned int    p1    :16,
                            p2    :16,
                            p3    :16,
                            p4    :16;
        }paramsform;
        struct{
            unsigned int    a;
            unsigned int    b;
        }copyform;
    };
}data_t;
```

Assigning paramsform members to memory results in expensive and slow read/modify/write operations. Assigning copyform members as follows produces a single memory write:

```
my_data_t pkd;
__declspec(shared sram) int answer[2] = {0,0};

pkd.paramsform.p1 = 1;
pkd.paramsform.p2 = 2;
pkd.paramsform.p3 = 3;
pkd.paramsform.p4 = 4;

answer[0] = pkd.copyform.a;
answer[1] = pkd.copyform.b;
```

Optimizations

Don't be alarmed if the compiler optimizes away much of your code. If results aren't used, the instruction code that computed the result disappears! The compiler also optimizes away constant expressions. In the following example, the sum of four struct members is reduced to a single immed instruction:

```
#include <ixp.h>

main()
{
typedef struct my_data{
    unsigned int a:8;
    unsigned int b:8;
    unsigned int c:8;
    unsigned int d:8;
} my_data_t;

my_data_t pkd;
__declspec(shared sram) int *answer = 0;

pkd.a = 1;
pkd.b = 2;
pkd.c = 3;
pkd.c = 4;

*answer = pkd.a + pkd.b + pkd.c + pkd.c;
}
```

The compiled result, shown in Thread List instruction view, is just two instructions:

```
/******/  *answer = pkd.a + pkd.b + pkd.c + pkd.c;
sram[write, $0, b0, 0, 1], ctx_swap[s1], defer[1]
immed[$0, 11, <<0]
```

Asynchronous I/O in C

As mentioned previously, DRAM access times are much longer than SRAM access times. If you read DRAM by using it on the right side of an assignment, your thread swaps out and is not eligible to run again for 300 cycles. A look at Thread History view while simulation is running shows that the microengine is idle for most of this time. As Carlson mentions (Carlson 2003), you now are memory-bound—wasting time waiting for memory. You want to strike a balance between being memory-bound and being compute-bound.

To fill in those idle cycles, asynchronous I/O intrinsics can be used. With these intrinsics, you can make one or more memory accesses run while the thread continues to execute. The basic I/O intrinsic form is:

```
mem_op(&data, &address, count, sync_type, signal);
```

The following example performs two sram operations in parallel with a dram operation.

Asynchronous I/O Code Example

```
1    #include <ixp.h>
2
3    main()
4    {
5
6    SIGNAL      sram_signal;
7    __declspec(sram) unsigned int *sram_addr;
8    __declspec(sram_write_reg) unsigned int swrite = 41;
9    __declspec(sram_read_reg) unsigned int sread;
10
11   SIGNAL_PAIR dram_signal;
12   __declspec(dram) unsigned int *dram_addr;
13   // Dram reads 8-byte words
14   __declspec(dram_write_reg) unsigned int dwrite[2] = {42,
     43};
15   __declspec(dram_read_reg) unsigned int dread[2];
16
17   sram_addr = (__declspec(sram) unsigned int *) 0x20;
18   dram_addr = 0;
```

```
19
20    dram_write(dwrite, dram_addr, 1, sig_done,&dram_signal);
21
22    sram_write(&swrite, sram_addr, 1, ctx_swap,&sram_signal);
23
24    sram_read(&sread, sram_addr, 1, sig_done,&sram_signal);
25
26
27    // do something else, then
28    wait_for_all(&dram_signal, &sram_signal);
29
30    __free_write_buffer(&dram_write_reg)
31    __free_write_buffer(&sram_write_reg)
32    }
```

Lines 6–9

> Declare a variable in SRAM, plus the transfer registers and signal to be used for the asynchronous SRAM write and read.

Lines 11–15

> Declare a variable in DRAM, plus the transfer registers and signal pair to be used for the asynchronous DRAM write.

Lines 17–18

> Set addresses.

Lines 20–24

> DRAM and SRAM intrinsic functions perform the writes and reads.

Line 28

> Wait for the signals that indicate the completion of the I/O.

Lines 30–31

> Give a hint to the compiler that the write transfer registers are now free to be re-allocated.

The code that we have just analyzed beats on memory pretty hard since the MEs are doing little else but issuing memory references. To run this code on only one thread, kill off all but thread 0:

```
if (__ctx() != 0) ctx_wait(kill);
```

The resulting Thread History View of Figure 9.7 shows the parallel memory operations.

Figure 9.7   Thread History, Asynchronous I/O

Interthread Signaling

A key difference between explicit-partitioning (EP) and autopartitioning (AP) C is the handling of signals. In AP C, signals are not allowed. The AP C compilation handles the signals for you. In EP C, you perform thread synchronization using signal intrinsics. The Microengine C Compiler supports six types of interthread signaling:

- `signal_same_ME()`. Signal another thread context in the same ME.

- `signal_same_ME_next_ctx()`. When running the threads of a microengine round robin in order, signal the next (current +1, with wrap to 0) thread context.

- `signal_prev_ME()`. Send a signal to a specific thread context of the previous neighbor ME.

- `signal_prev_ME_this_ctx()`. Send a signal of the same thread context as sender of the previous neighbor ME.

- `signal_next_ME()`. Send a signal to a specific thread context of the next neighbor (NN) ME.

- `signal_next_ME_this_ctx()`. Send a signal the same thread context as sender of the NN ME.

Next Neighbor

Adjacent MEs can send messages to the next neighbor (NN) ME—next larger ME number. The NN communication can be direct between same thread contexts—for example 0 to 0, 1 to 1—or through the NN ring. When NN communication is context to context, NN variables are declared using `__declspec(nn_remote_reg)`.

When using the NN ring for inter-ME communication, the producer checks whether the ring is full. If the ring is not full, the producer writes the message to the ring:

```
if !(inp_state_test(inp_state_nn_full)
    nn_ring_enqueue_incr(message);
```

The consumer checks whether the ring is empty. If the ring is not empty, the consumer reads the message from the ring:

```
if !(inp_state_test(inp_state_nn_empty)
    message = nn_ring_dequeue_incr();
```

Inline Assembly Language in Microengine C

Assembly language—also called microcode—can be inserted to take advantage of the network processor's functionality that is difficult to represent in C. To use microcode, declare non-memory variables as the operands, then encapsulate the assembly language statements in __asm{}.

```
#include <ixp.h>

main()
{

__declspec(shared sram) int y[2] = {42, 1};
__declspec(shared sram) int *z;
int arg1, arg2, result;

z=0;
arg1 = y[0];
arg2 = y[1];

__asm{ alu[result, arg1, +, arg2] }

*z = result;

}
```

For example, in the add with carry (alu +carry) operation, the carry argument is a hidden variable supplied by the hardware from the previous alu result. This operation is used in the IPV4 checksum calculation. The C unsigned int variables x0 through x5 are the aligned 20-byte IPV4 header:

```
sum = x0;
__asm
{
    alu[temp_zero, --, B, 0]

    alu[sum, sum, +, x1]
    alu[sum, sum, +carry, x2]
    alu[sum, sum, +carry, x3]
    alu[sum, sum, +carry, x4]
    alu[sum, sum, +carry, 0]
    ld_field_w_clr[x1, 1100b, sum]

    alu_shf[shfted_sum, --, B, sum, <<16]
    alu[sum, x1, +, shfted_sum]

    alu[save_carry, 1, +carry, temp_zero]
    alu_shf[shfted_x1, --, B, x1, <<16]
    alu[x1, save_carry, +, shfted_x1]

    alu_shf[shfted_x1, --, B, x1, <<16]
    alu[sum, sum, +, shfted_x1]
}
```

Path Annotation

You can provide hints to the compiler to prioritize optimization of one path over others. In the case of if-then-else constructs, the compiler has no way of knowing which is the most-used path. Place the critical path intrinsic in the preferred path:

```
__critical_path(n);
```

For applications with multiple paths, you can specify a priority level from 0 to 100 as follows:

```
if (expr)
{
    __critical_path(20);

    //not most, not least critical path code
}
else if (expr)
{
    __critical_path(100);

    // most critical path code
}
else
{
    // least critical path code
}
```

Back to Your Task: Packet Processing

You can work the packet in network or big-endian order, as specified in the RFCs. Here is the RFC 791 header specification for IPV4:

```
0                   1                   2                   3
0 1 2 3 4 5 6 7 8 9 0 1 2 3 4 5 6 7 8 9 0 1 2 3 4 5 6 7 8 9 0 1
+-+-+-+-+-+-+-+-+-+-+-+-+-+-+-+-+-+-+-+-+-+-+-+-+-+-+-+-+-+-+-+-+
|Version|  IHL  |Type of Service|         Total Length          |
+-+-+-+-+-+-+-+-+-+-+-+-+-+-+-+-+-+-+-+-+-+-+-+-+-+-+-+-+-+-+-+-+
|         Identification        |Flags|     Fragment Offset     |
+-+-+-+-+-+-+-+-+-+-+-+-+-+-+-+-+-+-+-+-+-+-+-+-+-+-+-+-+-+-+-+-+
|  Time to Live |    Protocol   |        Header Checksum         |
+-+-+-+-+-+-+-+-+-+-+-+-+-+-+-+-+-+-+-+-+-+-+-+-+-+-+-+-+-+-+-+-+
|                       Source Address                          |
+-+-+-+-+-+-+-+-+-+-+-+-+-+-+-+-+-+-+-+-+-+-+-+-+-+-+-+-+-+-+-+-+
|                    Destination Address                        |
+-+-+-+-+-+-+-+-+-+-+-+-+-+-+-+-+-+-+-+-+-+-+-+-+-+-+-+-+-+-+-+-+
|                       Options                 |    Padding     |
+-+-+-+-+-+-+-+-+-+-+-+-+-+-+-+-+-+-+-+-+-+-+-+-+-+-+-+-+-+-+-+-+
```

When you read the packet into the ME, the headers load into the transfer registers in network order. Figure 9.8 and Figure 9.9 show the contents of the transfer registers for IPV4 over Ethernet 802.3 and 802.3, respectively.

$pkt[0]	Ethernet Source Address Bytes 0-31		
$pkt[1]	Ether Source Address 32-47	Ether Dest Address 0-15	
$pkt[2]	Ethernet Dest Address Bytes 16-47		
$pkt[3]	Length or Protocol(16)	Vers(4) IHL(4)	TOS(8)
$pkt[4]	Total length(16)	Identification(16)	
$pkt[5]	Flags (3) Frag Offset(13)	Time to Live(8)	Protocol(8)
$pkt[6]	Header Checksum(16)	IP Source Address 0-15	
$pkt[7]	IP Source Address 16-31	IP Dest Address 0-15	
$pkt[8]	IP Dest Address 16-31		
$pkt[9]			

Figure 9.8   IPV4 over Ethernet 802.3 in Transfer Registers

$pkt[0]	Ethernet Source Address 0-31		
$pkt[1]	Ether Source Address 32-47	Ether Dest Address 0-15	
$pkt[2]	Ethernet Dest Address 16-47		
$pkt[3]	Length or Protocol(16)	DSAP(8)	SSAP(8)
$pkt[4]	Control(8)	Vers(4) IHL(4) TOS(8)	Total len 0-7
$pkt[5]	Total len 8-15	Identification(16)	Flags (3) Frag 0-4
$pkt[6]	Frag 5-12	Time to Live(8) Protocol(8)	Cksum 0-7
$pkt[7]	Cksum 8-15	IP Source Address 0-23	
$pkt[8]	IP Src 24-31	IP Dest Address 0-23	
$pkt[9]	IP Dest 24-31		

Figure 9.9   IPV4 over Ethernet 802.2 in Transfer Registers

Note that the IP headers for these start at byte offset 17 for 802.2 and 14 for 802.3. If you receive IP over Ethernet SNAP, the layer-3 offset is 22. Other data-link layer protocols can effectively cause the start of the IPV4 header to be at any byte offset.

Typically, your code assumes a specific header alignment, such as the header always starts at byte 0, so that all field extractions are aligned relative to the alu path 32-bit word size. You don't really want to have separate sets of code, one for each byte alignment. If IP header verification and classification takes 200 instructions, a separate set for each byte alignment would take 4 x 200 instructions. The byte_align_block_be intrinsic can solve this problem for you. The following code reads 32 bytes of header from DRAM, then aligns and writes 20 bytes of IP header to local memory:

```
// declare dram packet buffer
typedef struct{
    union
    {
        struct{
            unsigned int pkt_hdr_in_mem[8]
            unsigned int pkt_rest_in_mem[504]
        }pkt_struct;
        pkt_array[512]
    }
} pkt_in_mem_t:
    __declspec (dram) pkt_in_mem_t pkt_buf;

// declare 48 bytes to hold packet header from DRAM
__declspec (dram_read_reg) unsigned int pkt[8];

// local memory packet address
#define LM_CACHE_ADDR 0

int offset = 14;          // if Ethernet 802.3
int i;
// initialize pkt buffer
for {i=0; i<8; i++} {
    pkt_buf.pkt_array[i] = 0;
}
// read pkt buffer and align header
pkt = pkt_buf.pkt_struct.pkt_hdr_in_mem;
byte_align_block_be(5,
        (unsigned int *) LM_CACHE_ADDR,
        (unsigned int *) pkt, offset);
```

Figure 9.10 shows the resulting IPV4 header in local memory. Now that's much better!

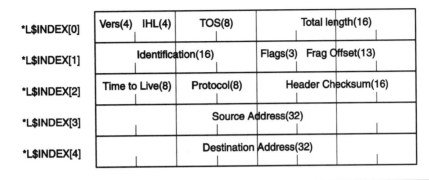

	Vers(4) IHL(4)	TOS(8)	Total length(16)	
*L$INDEX[0]				
*L$INDEX[1]	Identification(16)		Flags(3) Frag Offset(13)	
*L$INDEX[2]	Time to Live(8)	Protocol(8)	Header Checksum(16)	
*L$INDEX[3]	Source Address(32)			
*L$INDEX[4]	Destination Address(32)			

Figure 9.10 IPV4 Header in Local Memory

Explicit-Partitioning C in the Developer Workbench

You can use the Developer Workbench Compiler Build Settings dialog, shown in Figure 9.11, to fine-tune your compiler output. This dialog provides the following options:

■ *Number of contexts.* **1** An ME can be configured to run in either eight or four thread contexts mode. Choose four if you need twice as many GPRs and the ME is doing very little I/O—also, if you don't need eight threads running. The default is eight. Within the mode selection, you can indicate the exact number of contexts to run. The compiler automatically kills the unused contexts.

■ *Big-endian or little-endian.* **2** This option determines the mapping of bytes in memory. Standard network order is big-endian (byte 0 to 3, left to right).

■ *Neighbor mode.* **3** If this ME does not interface to another ME via NN registers, choosing self mode gives you more registers.

■ *Optimizations.* **4** Optimize for size or speed. Be careful if selecting no optimization; your resulting microcode instructions may not fit. Spill sequence determines where spills go if variables do not fit in GPRs. If spilling to local memory, specify the starting address the compiler can use. Inlining is good for real-time applications.

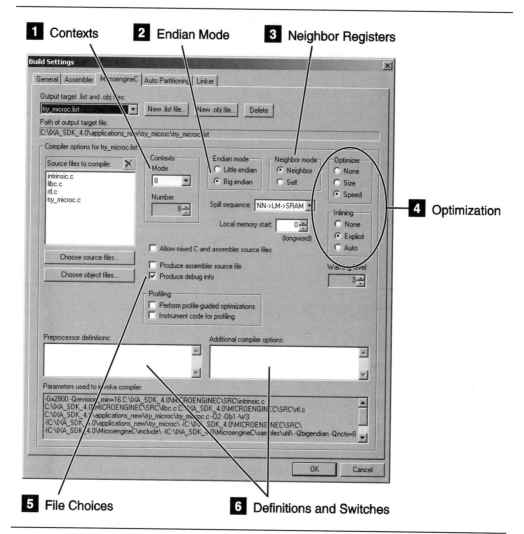

Figure 9.11 Build Settings

- *Files.* **5** In general, use __asm statements instead of mixing C and assembler source files. Produce assembler source file if you want to see just microcode; however, it is always better to write your own microcode because you control the variable names. Producing debug info is essential for debugging in simulation.

- *Definitions and switches.* **6** Specify #defines and other infrequently used compile switches, as needed.

Running the Compiler from the Command Line

You can run the compiler from a Windows[†] command line or UNIX command line. Two kinds of compilation are supported, as shown in Table 9.3:

Table 9.3   Two Kinds of Compilation

Inputs	Outputs
.c, .i source or intermediate files	Separate .obj files
Any combination of .c, .i or .obj files	One .list file

Use the –c command line switch to compile to separate object files. If code blocks are reused on multiple MEs, you get a faster overall compilation run by producing separate object files in a first pass and a final list in a second pass of the compiler.

To perform a full build from command line, run the assembler and the linker—uccl and ucld. You must run the ME C Compiler once for each ME to produce a list file containing binary, code, comments, debug information, and linker directives. The linker creates a uof file from the .list files. Here is the command line syntax for compilation:

```
uccl [options] file.c
```

Table 9.4 lists the most frequently used compiler options.

Table 9.4   Frequently Used Compiler Options

Option	Description
-? or -help	List the options (print usage). Help!
-D*name[=value]*	Specifies a #define symbol. The value is 1 if omitted.
-I*path[;path2...]*	Paths to include files, prepended before environment variable UCC_INCLUDE.
-c	Produce separate object files.
-F*ename*	Specifies the name of the list file. Default is the first source file.
-Ob*n*	Inlining control: n=0, none; n=1, explicit(inline functions declared with __inline or __forceinline(default); n=2, any (inline functions based on compiler heuristics, and those declared with __inline or __forceinline).

Table 9.4   Frequently Used Compiler Options *(continued)*

Option	Description
-On	Optimize for: n=1, size(default); n=2, speed; n=d, debug (turns off optimizations and blows your code into very huge size).
-Qspill=*n*	Selects alternative storage areas chosen when variables spill out of GPRs. Most-preferred to least-preferred.
	n=0: LM > NN > SRAM
	n=1: NN > LM > SRAM
	n=2: NN only. Halt if not enough NN
	n=7: no spill. Halt if any spilling required.
-Qnn_mode=*n*	n=0: neighbor(default)
	n=1: self. Use this if you spill to next neighbor regs.
-Zi	Produce debug information.

Run the Linker to produce the object file format (uof). The Linker can take list files generated by the Assembler or Compiler. Here is the command line syntax for linking microengine code:

```
ucld [options] input_file.list
```

Table 9.5 lists the most frequently used Linker options.

Table 9.5   Frequently Used Linker Options

Option	Description
-h	List the options (print usage). Help!
-o *outfile*	Name the output uof file.
-g	Include debug information.

For the example, `try_microc.c` cases of this chapter, the command lines for compiling and linking are:

```
uccl try_microc.c
ucld -o try_microc.uof -g try_microc.list
```

For a more detailed list of compiler command line options, refer to the development tools user's guide (Intel 2004) and the reference manual for the Microengine C language (Intel 2004).

The C Programmer: Job Summary

By now you have discovered that if you want to write C that runs fast, you need to know what to expect from the Compiler. The Microengine C Compiler produces code that typically performs very close to hand-crafted microcode. However, if you use too many intrinsics, your code could begin to look like microcode in C syntax. Try to use structs and pointer assignments instead of memory intrinsics where possible to make your code more portable.

In this chapter you have learned the basics of C programming for microengines. For more information about programming, refer to the complete microengine coding guide (Johnson and Kunze 2003). For the complete set of functionality, see the reference manual for Microengine C Language (Intel 2004). You can also find examples on this book's Intel Press Web site, listed in "References."

Chapter 10

C Compiler: Autopartitioning Mode

I have stopped reading Stephen King novels. Now I just read C code instead.

—Richard O'Keefe

Congratulations! You have chosen the most portable way to write your code. This compiler partitions high-level C source to multiple MEs and takes care of parallel I/O references, signals, and partitioning for you. If you want to write Assembly code, you are in the wrong chapter. If you want to partition your C code to individual MEs, you are in the wrong chapter. If you want to signal one thread from another, or wait on parallel I/O completion signals, you are in the wrong chapter. However, you are in the right chapter if you want to learn:

- What the autopartitioning (AP) compiler does
- Syntax of AP C for IXP2XXX network processors
- How to compile from the Developer Workbench
- How to compile from the command line

The code examples in this chapter are from the latest Intel® Internet Exchange Architecture (Intel® IXA) Software Framework, under development at the time of the printing of this book. The actual code in the Intel IXA Software Framework CD may vary slightly from this version.

Design Refresh

Just to refresh your mind once again, your project is an IPV4/IPV6 router. The big picture drawing from the Architecture Tool is shown in Figure 10.1.

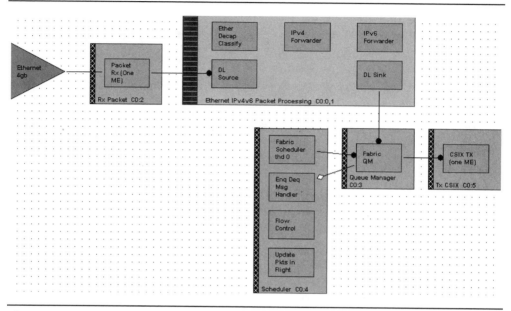

Figure 10.1   The Architecture Specification

All you really want to do is get a packet—packet rx—classify it for protocol, verify it, look up the destination, and enqueue it for transmit. At least the first two pipeline partitions in this view seem to be candidates for writing in C. Clearly, you can write simple procedural code up to the point where the packet is enqueued. Don't worry about other threads, just write code for what is done on one packet at a time.

Most of your code is in the second functional partition, Ethernet IPV4/V6 packet processing. As you saw in the Architecture Tool analysis, to get to the desired line rate, you need more than one ME. The autopartitioning compiler maps your C onto multiple MEs, as many as are needed to meet the specified path rate.

What the Compiler Does

Figure 10.2 shows the compilation process. Source files are typical C source and header files as well as optional intermediate files from the output of the compiler's first optimization phase. Source files are organized as a top-level program that is a run-to-completion sequence of packet-processing stage (PPS) functions and lower-level supporting functions. The compiler does the following for the compilation phases:

- Front-end, the source C language parser, is the same parser used by other Intel compilers.

- Intermediate form and optimizations are typical compiler conversions, including translation to atomic statements and instruction formation for IXP2XXX network processors. Common optimizations include:
    - Function inlining and single-copy function inlining
    - Algebraic simplification
    - Migration of data from memory to virtual registers
    - Propagation of constants and partial constants
    - Value numbering
    - Dead code elimination
    - Suppression of partial redundancies
    - Invariant reassociation and hoisting
    - Strength reduction
    - Induction variable replacement
    - Compression of switch statements
    - IXP2XXX network processor-specific optimizations

- Autopartitioning is the phase in which the code is distributed across multiple MEs and multiple threads. The compiler performs the following transformations:
    - Partition to context and functional pipeline stages
    - Allocate to MEs (multiprocessing) and threads (multithreading)
    - Migrate variables under CAM management and local memory
    - Insert signaling for I/O operations and interthread communication
    - Insert inter-PPS message communication
    - Instruction-level optimizations

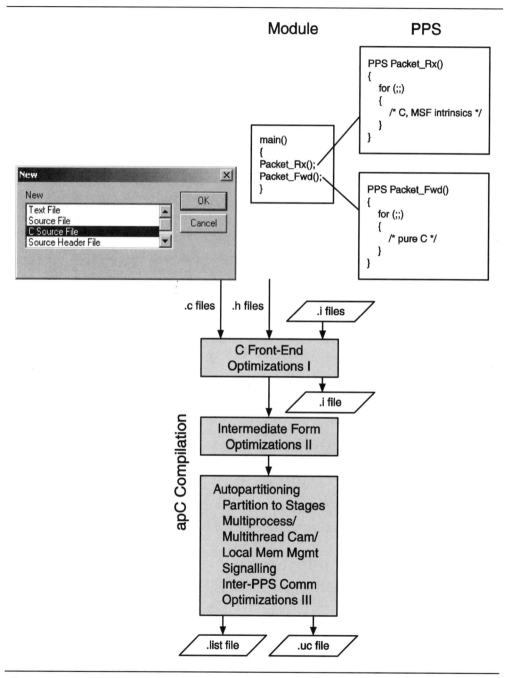

Figure 10.2 Autopartitioning Compiler Process

The output of the compiler is a set of uc or list files, depending on the build switches. The uc files are microcode-only files. The list files include microcode, instruction words, and debug information. The list files may then be run through the linker to produce the final loadable binary image.

Syntax

The compiler generally conforms to the ANSI/ISO/C99 C standard. However, it does present a subset of the language, plus IXP2XXX network processor-specific extensions for C±.

The compiler does not support the following functions because network processor applications can be readily implemented without them and they may be detrimental to the performance of a real-time system.

- *Floating-point.* Calculations for metering and WRED do not have to be as precise as required by standard floating-point.

- *Function pointers.* If these are implemented, extract instructions are needed to copy arguments and results.

- *Recursion.* Additional copies of arguments are required. Loops are much more efficient.

The compiler also enforces a lower maximum—lower than C99—for the number of cases in a switch statement. Remember, this is for real-time fast-path packet processing.

IXP2XXX network processor-specific language extensions include:

- *Support for the PPS construct.* This support is the top-level partitioning of the application. Instantiation of the PPS by the compiler automatically results in synchronization between software pipeline stages.

- *Pipe interface between PPSs.* The compiler supports basic put and get ring functions for communication between PPSs.

- *Critical path annotation.* Budgets may be placed on selected code paths to guide the compiler performance optimizations. Your Architecture Tool project's data stream rate specification is used here.

- *Storage class declaration.* Variables can be qualified by memory type and channel. You can use the results from the Architecture Tool analysis to ensure balanced bandwidth across memory channels.

- *Intrinsics.* The intrinsics provide a hardware-abstraction layer for accessing network processor functionality.

- *Loop counts.* The loop count directive provides a hint to the compiler regarding the typical number of iterations that occur for loops.

- *Load-time memory allocation.* Some variables, such as the addresses of tables and other memory structures, can be specified as import variables. The compiler places the .import_var linker directive in the list file. The directive is then passed to the loadable binary (uof) and made available to the Intel XScale® core applications at runtime. The microengine driver in the Intel XScale core supports an API for the insertion of the value into the instruction.

Designing with PPSs

If you want good results from a compiler, you must provide some direction although with the autopartitioning compiler, the need for direction is kept to a minimum. The top design must be structured as a series of PPSs. The PPS is a function with no arguments; that is, essentially an unending for (;;) loop. As shown in Figure 10.3, one PPS hands off to the next through a pipe API.

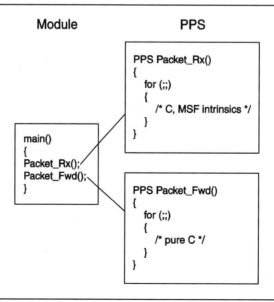

Figure 10.3   PPSs in a Compilation Module

In this example, the PPS function `Packet_Rx()` performs packet re-assembly. As you learned in the Architecture Tool, several media switch fabric (MSF)-related operations must be performed, such as asking for new packet data from the network—an abstraction for putting a thread on the freelist; freeing an RBUF element; getting a buffer from a buffer freelist; and transferring the data to DRAM.

The `sram_dequeue` intrinsic is used to get the buffer as follows:

```
#define BUF_CHAN        0      /* Q SRAM channel */
#define BUF_FREELIST    16     /* Q Array entry  */
uint32_t meta_ptr;

meta_ptr = sram_dequeue(BUF_CHAN, BUF_FREELIST);
```

The AP compiler intrinsics are simpler than the comparable ones for the EP compiler. For the AP compiler, there is no signal synchronization type or signal. If needed, the AP compiler makes this operation asynchronous to meet the path budget.

The autopush status word is defined as a hardware-specific struct in ixplib.h, where one of the members is the rbuf element number. The `msf_recv()` intrinsic is used to ask for the autopush status:

```
msf_rsw_t rsw;
rsw = msf_recv(0);
```

The `dram_rbuf_read()` intrinsic is used to transfer RBUF data to DRAM. The addresses for each must be calculated, as well as the number of quadwords. Note that 64-bit words are the unit size for DRAM transfers. The following code is from the AP compiler PackerRx() microblock, with the path:

IXA_SDK_4.0\
src\building_blocks\rx\microengine\packet_rx\c\packet_rx.c

```
rbufAddress = RBUF_TBUF_BASE + (rsw.rbuf_elem <<
RBUF_ELEMENT_SHF);
:
dataPtr = Dl_BufGetData(curBufHandle);
dramAddress = &dataPtr->data[(packetRxSopBufferOffset >> 3)];
nquadWords = rsw.byte_count >> 3;
if (rsw.byte_count & 0x7)
{
    nquadWords++;
}
dram_rbuf_read(dramAddress, rbufAddress, nquadWords);
```

Following the transfer of data from RBUF to DRAM, the `msf_rbuf_free` instrinsic is used to free the rbuf element:

```
msf_rbuf_free(rsw.rbuf_elem);
```

The `pipe_put()` and `pipe_get()` functions do communication between PPSs. Inside the `Packet_Rx()` PPS, you assemble the message to send to `Packet_Fwd()` PPS and place the put:

The code for the entire PPS PacketRx_Pps() is shown below. The file name is:

IXA_SDK_4.0\src\applications\ipv4_diffserv\
oc192_pos\ingress\wbench_c_project\dispatch_loop\packet_rx_pps.c

Packet Reassembly Example

```
69    PPS PacketRx_Pps(void)
70    {
71
72        /* Stores return value of call to PacketRx() */
73        int32_t packetRxResult;
74
75        /* Arguments passed to PacketRx() */
76        dl_buf_handle_t dlBufHandle, dlBufHandleEop;
77        packet_rx_msg_data_t packetRxMsgData;
78
79        /* Stores outgoing Packet Rx message */
80        packet_rx_msg_t packetRxMsg;
81
82        /* Initialize the buffer freelist */
83        Dl_BufInit();
84
85        /* Set the system init done flag to 1 */
86        systemInitDoneFlag = 1;
87
88        /* Do MSF Rx and Packet Rx initialization */
89        MsfRxInit();
90        PacketRx_Init();
91
92        /* Paranio: wait for system init done flag to be set*/
93        while (systemInitDoneFlag != 1);
94
95
96        for(;;)
97        {
98
99            PATH(PPS_CRITICAL_PATH);
100
```

```
101            packetRxResult = PacketRx(&dlBufHandle,
      &dlBufHandleEop, &packetRxMsgData);
102
103            /* Check if packet is fully reassembled */
104            if (packetRxResult != PACKET_RX_EOP)
105                continue;
106
107            /* Check if packet fits in one buffer */
108            if (dlBufHandle.eop)
109            {
110                /* Packet fits in one buffer */
111
112                PATH(PPS_CRITICAL_PATH);
113                packetRxMsg.minpkt.sopBufHandle =
      dlBufHandle;
114                packetRxMsg.minpkt.inputPort =
      packetRxMsgData.inputPort;
115                packetRxMsg.minpkt.freeListId =
      BUF_FREELIST_0;
116                packetRxMsg.minpkt.rxStat = 0;
117                packetRxMsg.minpkt.headerType = 0;
118                packetRxMsg.minpkt.bufferSize =
      packetRxMsgData.packetSize;
119                packetRxMsg.minpkt.bufferOffset =
      packetRxMsgData.sopBufferOffset;
120            }
121            else
122            {
123                /* Packet fits in multiple buffers */
124
125                packetRxMsg.largepkt.sopBufHandle =
      dlBufHandle;
126                packetRxMsg.largepkt.eopBufHandle =
      dlBufHandleEop;
127                packetRxMsg.largepkt.packetSize =
      packetRxMsgData.packetSize;
128                packetRxMsg.largepkt.bufferOffset =
      packetRxMsgData.sopBufferOffset;
129            }
130
131            /* Send outgoing Packet Rx message */
132            while COUNT(1) (1)
133            {
134                if
      (!pipe_full_scratch(&packetRxToDiffservPipe))
135                {
136                    PATH(PPS_CRITICAL_PATH);
137                    pipe_put_scratch(&packetRxToDiffservPipe,
      (uint32_t *)&packetRxMsg, sizeof(packetRxMsg) >> 2);
138                    break;
```

```
139                    }
140              }
141
142        } /* for(;;) */
143
144   } /* PacketRx_Pps() */
```

Lines 72–80

> Declare data structures.

Lines 82–93

> Perform initializations before the for (;;) loop begins.

Line 99

> Identify a critical path.

Line 101

> Execute the `packet_rx` driver microblock. Get a buffer, get the auto-push, reassemble, free the RBUF element.

Lines 113–129

> Assemble the pipe message.

Lines 132–138

> Send the pipe message. Use the COUNT(1) directive to specify loop count. The compiler assumes this directive typically does not have to retry.

How about that? You've just used up an ME for `Packet_Rx()`. Except for the few intrinsics, `Packet_Rx()` and `Packet_Fwd()` are written in pure C. No worries. Get the packet, validate it, perform lookups, modify it, bend it, fold it, and mutilate it.

Critical Path Annotation

A critical path inside a PPS can be designated with the PATH(*n*) directive:

```
#define MIN_PKT 1
PPS Packet_Rx()
{
    for (;;)
    {
    PATH(MIN_PKT);
    /* packet proccesing code */
}
```

The argument *n* identifies a path. You can have many paths, each with a different budget. However, at a minimum you want your min-size packet critical path to be specified. Compiler build switches set the budget for each path, allowing the budgets to be specified differently when the code runs on different network processors while leaving the source code intact. The command line switch –QT specifies budget in terms of rate per second. For example, the following switch specifies a budget of 5 million packets per second for your MIN_PKT path:

```
-QT1=5000000
```

Storage Class Declarations

An autopartitioning mode program can qualify variables with storage types. Key distinctions can thus be made to keep data on-chip, or to choose fast or slow access:

- SCRATCH—fast on-chip
- SRAM—fast off-chip
- DRAM—slow off-chip

In addition, channel designations can be made to enforce a balanced distribution of memory bandwidth.

The segment ixplib.h provides the definitions for the preferred storage class declarations. Place the storage class before the type in the variable declaration:

```
#define NUM_ROUTES 200000
    typedef struct my_data{
        uint32_t a;
        uint32_t b;
    } my_data_t;

    SRAM_1 my_data_t table_entry[NUM_ROUTES];
```

You just used 1.6 megabytes of SRAM. The storage class qualifiers are:

- DRAM
- SRAM—let the compiler choose which SRAM channel—defaults to 0
- SRAM_0—place the variable in SRAM channel 0
- SRAM_1—place the variable in SRAM channel 1
- SRAM_2—place the variable in SRAM channel 2
- SRAM_3—place the variable in SRAM channel 3
- SCRATCH

The number of channels you have depends on the type of IXP2XXX network processor. For complete portability, you could provide another layer of indirection with preprocessor macros to apply the appropriate storage class based on the type of processor.

Comparison of Compiler Mode Syntaxes

Table 10.1 shows the key differences between EP and AP compiler syntaxes. Key differences are that the EP compiler uses `__declspec(tag)` to declare storage classes and other qualifiers. The AP compiler uses well-known symbols, such as SRAM and DRAM, without the `__declspec` operator. For variables shared between threads, the default for the AP compiler is shared. The default for the EP compiler is nonshared. The `__declspec` shared qualifier must be used in the EP compiler for shared variables. Regarding critical-section variables, for the AP compiler, the `pps_unique()` operator is used to declare variables that are not critical-section variables. For example, packet header modifications are unique for a given loop iteration of the PPS. When declaring storage classes, the AP compiler has a specific qualifier for each storage type and memory channel—SRAM, SRAM_0, DRAM, and so on. The EP compiler uses the `__declspec(sram)`, etc., operator. In addition, the AP compiler uses `__packed` and `__packedbits` qualifiers, also #defined as PACKED and PACKED_BITS. The EP compiler uses `__declspec(packed)` and `__declspec(packed_bits)`. And finally for signals, the AP compiler does not have any event synchronization arguments in its intrinsics. The last two arguments of EP compiler I/O reference intrinsics are synchronization type and signal variable.

Table 10.1   Compiler Mode Syntax Comparison

AP compiler	EP compiler
/* Default is shared across loop iterations */ uint32_t var;	/* Default is unique to thread */ /* Declare if shared across threads*/ __declspec(shared) uint32_t var;
/* Default is shared across loop iterations */ /*Declare if unique to each iteration */ uint32_t p = __pps_unique(expr);	/* Default is unique to thread */ uint32_t p = (expr);
SRAM uint32_t **var;** /* implied channel 0 */ SRAM_0 uint32_t **var;** /* channel 0 */ SRAM_1 uint32_t *var; SRAM_2 uint32_t *var; SRAM_3 uint32_t *var;	/* specify channel via upper address bits */ __declspec(sram) uint32_t *var;

Table 10.1   Compiler Mode Syntax Comparison *(continued)*

AP compiler	EP compiler
DRAM uint64_t *var;	__declspec(dram) uint64_t var;
SCRATCH uint32_t *var;	__declspec(scratch) uint32_t *var;
PACKED struct S {...};	__declspec(packed) struct S{...};
PACKED_BITS struct S {...};	__declspec(packed_bits) struct S{...};

scratch_add(uint32_t data,
    SCRATCH uint32_t *address);
	scratch_add(__declspec(sram_write_reg)
	void *data,
	    volatile void __declspec(scratch)
	*address,
	    sync_t sync,
	    SIGNAL *sig_ptr);

scratch_get_ring(uint32_t *data,
    SCRATCH uint32_t *address,
    uint32_t nwords);
	scratch_get_ring(
	    __declspec(sram_read_reg) void *data,
	    volatile void __declspec(scratch)
	*address,
	    uint32_t nwords,
	    scratch_ring_ind_t ind,
	    sync_t sync,
	    SIGNAL *sig_ptr);

Register classes managed by the compiler	Register classes specified by user: sram_read_reg, sram_write_reg, dram_read_reg, dram_write_reg, nn_local, nn_remote, etc.

Writing High-Level C in the Developer Workbench

Source editing is the same for either mode of the AP C compiler. The Developer Workbench provides the following:

- *Standard library support*. Include paths are set to AP compiler standard libraries.

- *Path Budgets*. AP build settings include path budget settings.

- *Resources*. A build settings dialog defines the processor resources available for use by the compiler.

- *Linker settings*. In the linker, you specify which MEs are available for use by the AP compiler. Other MEs can be used by the EP compiler or Assembler.

Figure 10.4 shows the build settings dialog for the autopartitioning C compiler. The key differences with the microengine C Compiler build dialog are the presence of Resources and Critical Paths Budgets.

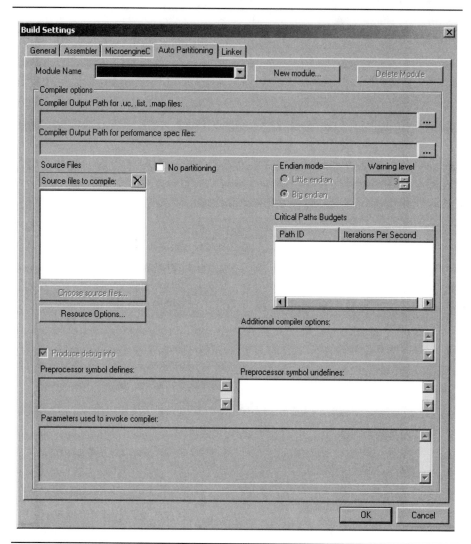

Figure 10.4   Autopartitioning Compiler Build Settings

Resources

The compiler must know which processor resources are available for use. Resources include:

■ Memory sizes

■ Memory bus frequency

■ Scratch rings

To determine what resources are available, in the AP compiler build settings, click Resources to view the default resources, as shown in Figure 10.5. The default resources are obtained from the chip configuration.

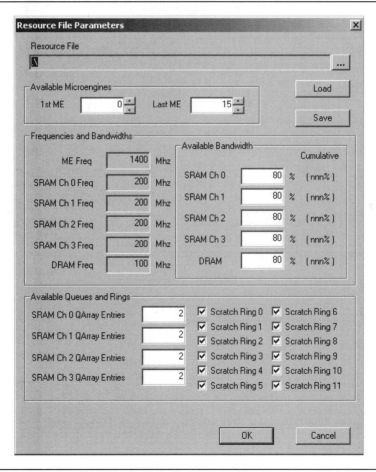

Figure 10.5 Autopartitioning Compiler Resources

The resource specification window allows you to dedicate a portion of the processor resources for the AP compiler by filling in the available bandwidth, scratch rings, and queue array entries information.

Which Microengines Get the Autopartitioned Result?

You can allocate the compilation module to a group of MEs using the Linker tab in the Build Settings dialog, shown in Figure 10.6.

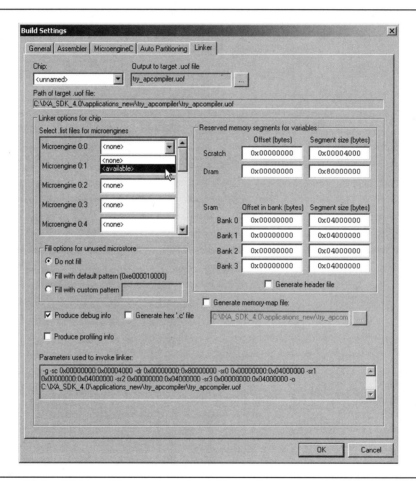

Figure 10.6 Making Microengines Available: Linker Settings

▬ **Running from the Command Line**

You can run the AP compiler from a Windows or UNIX command line. Table 10.2 lists the most frequently used command-line switches.

Table 10.2   Frequently Used Command-line Switches

Option	Description
-help	List the options (print usage). Help!
-Qap	Always do this to invoke the autopartitioning compiler.
-D*name[=value]*	Specifies a #define symbol. The value is 1 if omitted.
-U*name*	Undefines a #define symbol.
-I*path[;path2…]*	Paths to include files.
-E	Preprocess input files and stop.
-O1	Compile without full autopartitioning.
-O1	Compile with full autopartitioning. This action should be done in conjunction with a PATH budget, to enable the compiler to partition PPSs to meet budget.
-o*filename*	Write compiler output to filename.
-Qbigendian	Compile in big-endian byte order. Default.
-Qlittleendian	Compile in little-endian byte order.
-QMresource_spec= *[filename]*	Specify resources such as memory size and frequency via the resource specification file.
-QT=*[path budget]*	Specify budget for one or more critical paths. Specified as the number of times per second this path is executed.
-S	Generate microcode assembly language and stop.
-W*[0-4]*	Warning level. W0 suppresses all warnings.
-Zi	Produce debug information.

You can then run the linker to produce the object file format (uof). The linker can take list files generated by Assembler or Compiler. The following is the command line syntax for linking microengine code:

```
ucld [options] input_file.list
```

Table 10.3 lists the most frequently used linker options.

Table 10.3 Frequently Used Linker Options

Option	Description
-h	List the options (print usage). Help!
-o *outfile*	Name the output uof file.
-g	Include debug information.

Summary

In this chapter you looked at the new autopartitioning C compiler. You have learned:

- What the compiler does
- Supported and unsupported standard C syntax
- Language extensions, including:
  - PPS
  - Inter-PPS communication
  - Path annotation
  - Storage class declarations
  - Intrinsics
  - Loop counts
  - Load-time import variables
- Designing a real PPS for the packet receive partition
- A comparison of syntactical differences between the two compiler modes

This information should provide the basics for getting you started with the compiler. For more information, refer to the user's guides for the development tools (Intel 2004) and the C Compiler Autopartitioning mode (Intel 2004).

Part V
The Test Engineer

Chapter 11

Packet Generation

Once a day a cheap, gaudy packet arrived upward from St. Louis, and another downward from Keokuk. Before these events, the day was glorious with expectancy...

—Mark Twain, *Life on the Mississippi*

Now your design builds without errors. If you could only throw a packet at it and see what happens. This chapter is for the test engineer. However, programmers may also want to run a few packets through just to make sure the design is not totally broken. In this chapter, you learn how to configure and generate packets for your simulation. You select protocols, build protocol-specific packet flows, choose distribution algorithm and rates for aggregates of flows, and attach flow aggregates to ports on the IXP2XXX network processors. In the next chapter, you run the simulation with your packets and your IPV4 router.

The Network Traffic Simulator

The Developer Workbench has a PacketSim module that feeds bytes through MAC Device Simulators to the simulator. A network traffic simulator (NTS) is a dynamic-link library that generates packets and sends them byte-by-byte to the PacketSim interface or receives packets from the PacketSim interface and validates them. There are many ways to generate packets for simulation:

■ *From a file.* The NTS can read a file defining the packets. The file can be a standard sniffer or other file format. To achieve a continual stream of packets, the NTS can repeat the set of packets. Danger: don't try this with packets that have sequence numbers. Early packet generators for IXP2XXX network processors generated packets from a format called datastreams. You may still see some .strm files in the application examples.

■ *Generated on the fly.* From a script interface, stream specifications can identify the layering of protocols for each stream and set values for the fields of protocol headers. The packet generator can then create packets that fit the specifications. The streams are then added to a port configuration; rate and distribution algorithms are then assigned. Earlier application toolkit releases used the NetSim NTS to provide this capability.

■ *Generated on the fly, hierarchical.* Independent definition of protocol, flow or stream, and algorithm, with hierarchical assembly of the packet header at runtime. Following NetSim, Intel developed PacketGen. PacketGen provides a completely flexible method of assembling packets, allowing you to layer protocol headers in any order, control rates and distributions, and reuse definitions in more than one design.

Figure 11.1 shows the objects used by PacketGen: protocols, flows, aggregates, and ports.

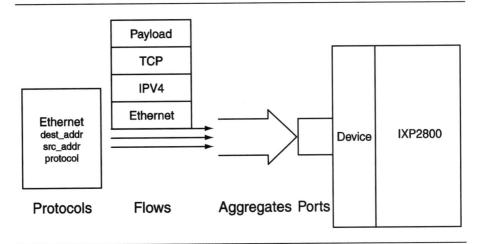

Figure 11.1 PacketGen Objects

Protocols

Protocols add information to a packet that facilitates moving the packet around the network. The protocol consists of a header at the front and, optionally, a trailer at the back added to the packet data. Because standards writers are prolific, encapsulating header after header for packets, protocols are layered 1 through 7. Often a packet has more than seven layers, but the seventh layer is considered to be one big layer with lots of user-application wrappers. The lowest software layer, not counting the physical layer, is layer 2, called the data-link layer. Ethernet, ATM, and PPP are data-link layer protocols. IPV4 and IPV6 are layer 3, called the Network Layer. The layer names are standard.

PacketGen defines protocols through protocol metadata (pmd) files, which define all fields of a protocol, the size of each field, names to be used when referring to the field in scripts, and default settings. The software toolkit contains one large pmd file for all protocols it supports. You can define your own custom protocols through separate pmd files and add them in through the PacketGen initialization dialog.

Having separate objects for protocol definitions separates the objects from how they are used. For example, the PacketGen GUI reads the pmd definitions and presents the protocols in a graphical way for the construction of packet groups, called flows.

Flows

Flows represent groups of packets that share a common characteristic, such as a key field with the same value. For example, IP packets are frequently grouped in five-tuples, which identify a connection by source address, destination address, source port, destination port, and protocol. The flow can be further characterized by rate or other traffic parameter that specifies quality of service (QoS). You arbitrarily define flows to set up test cases for your design. If your design is a router, you may want to create flows with different destination IP addresses that are also in the route table. You create the route table with an initialization routine in script and send packets with IP destination addresses that are looked up using longest-prefix-match. You then read the route table to get the next hop data-link header and the output port. When you run your design, verify that the packet was forwarded on the correct output port. If you are doing layer 4 forwarding—for example, TCP over IP over Ethernet—your design might use a hash-lookup to get QoS, next hop, and output port.

Aggregates

A more recent trend in packet forwarding is the aggregation or tunneling of multiple flows in a single flow. The flexible nature of the stack definition using PacketGen is illustrated in Figure 11.2.

When individual five-tuple-based flows enter or exit the molten core of the World Wide Web, they may be sent over physical connections that have a fixed rate. For example, digital subscriber link (DSL) modems limit all data passing through to the modem rate. Therefore, any flows can be aggregated and sent through a single flow at any point in the network. When building a PacketGen stack, the aggregation looks like flows within a flow. The aggregation protocol layer—for example, the layer-2 tunneling protocol L2TP—may or may not be there. With PacketGen, you can arbitrarily group the flows into aggregates and set distribution and rate characteristics for the aggregate. In PacketGen, the flow aggregate and its attributes are known as the *traffic configuration*.

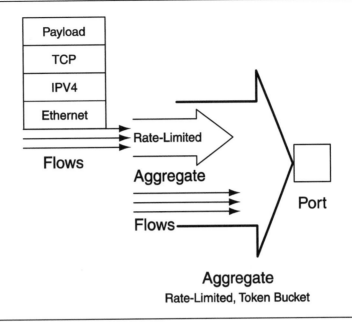

Figure 11.2   Flow Aggregates

Ports

The most common aggregation point for flows is the port. In PacketGen, the port represents an interface on the MAC device connected to the processor. In simulation, both the MAC device and the processor are simulated. To be used, a flow aggregate is assigned to a port. You can define a set of flow aggregates for testing purposes and use that set on separate processors.

In PacketGen, the direction of flows and ports is from the perspective of the processor; that is, making a flow or port a receive port means the processor receives packets from the flow on the given port. The designated port is where generated packets go. Conversely, making a flow or port a transmit port means the processor transmits packets to the flow from the given port where packets go for validation or logging.

Packet Simulation Options

Now you must define the packet simulation using PacketGen GUI. But first, you must choose PacketGen.

Figure 11.3 shows the simulation menu on the Developer Workbench top toolbar. Before you forget, make sure Enable Packet Simulation is checked **1** on the menu. When enabled, the workbench creates the correct simulation startup script and uses it when you actually run the simulation.

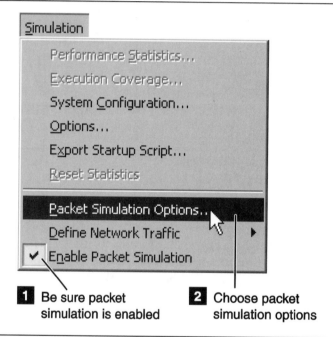

Figure 11.3   Simulation Top Menu

For packet simulation, you use the Simulation menu to:
1. Select the packet generator using Packet Simulation Options.
2. Define flows using Define Network Traffic.
3. Configure flow aggregates using Define Network Traffic.
4. Set simulation startup, stop, and history options using Options.

Now **2** select Packet Simulation Options from the Simulation menu. The Packet Simulation Options dialog appears, as shown in Figure 11.4.

1 Select PacketGen   **2** Click Initialize

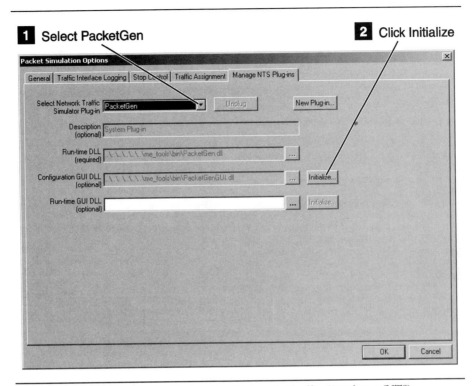

Figure 11.4   Selecting the PacketGen Network Traffic Simulator (NTS)

In the box labeled Select Network Traffic Simulator Plug-in, select PacketGen **1**. The path pointers to the PacketGen DLLs are then shown in the run-time DLL and configuration GUI DLL, respectively. The SDK-supplied tools, DLLs, and protocol are always in the same directory: ixa_sdk_*.*/me_tools/bin. Click Initialize **2** to load and initialize the Packet-gen GUI DLL.

The run-time DLL has an interface to PacketSim, which simulates a network wire. PacketSim requests a byte at a time from NTS DLL, based on port wire rate, as the simulation progresses. PacketSim requests a byte at a time from the packet generator at the port wire rate as soon as the function `ps_start_packet_receive()` is called from the script interface. You generally call this function after the MEs have run through any initialization routines to avoid device overflow when just getting started.

If you have your own generator, enter the generator's name in the top box and the path to your DLL in the Run-time DLL box. The GUI DLL is optional. The GUI DLL is used only for configuring protocol-specific flows and aggregates; it is not needed to run simulation. In fact, you can configure flows completely through the command-line script interface.

PacketGen GUI automatically loads the default protocol metadata file PacketGenProtocols.pmd, which defines all of the protocols supported by PacketGen, including:

- Layer 4—UDP, TCP

- Layer 3—IPV4, IPV6

- Layer 2—Ethernet, PPP, MPLS, HDLC, ATM, CSIX

Protocol Metadata File Format

The pmd format is a standard Extensible Markup Language (XML) file. This section discusses the PacketGen syntax and the definition of Ethernet and IPV4 protocols.

The following metadata file defines a custom protocol for use in PacketGen. With custom protocols, you can specify arbitrary field sizes and values to build up the protocol, including header, trailer, CRC, or checksum calculation algorithms and length calculations.

Custom Protocol pmd Example

```
1    <?xml version="1.0" encoding="utf-8" ?>
2    <!-- Metadata Definition File -->
3    <!-- Format Version='1.01' -->
4
5    <Metadata>
6
7      <Protocol name ="swFabric">
8        <Header>
9          <Field name="switchId" width='16' value='0xFFFF'/>
10       </Header>
11       <Trailer></Trailer>
12     </Protocol>
13
14     <! Copy schedule and payload portion from default pmd>
15
16   </Metadata>
```

Line 1

Identify the XML version.

Lines 5, 16

Identify the packet metadata region.

Lines 7–12

Specify the protocol.

Lines 8–10

The header has one 16-bit field, named switchId, with default value 0xFFFF.

IPV4 No Options pmd Example

```
7    <! Inserted inside Metadata region>
8
9    <Protocol name="IPv4" alias="ipv4">
10     <Header>
11       <Field name="Version" alias="ver"
12         width='4' value='4'/>
13       <Field name="Internet Header Length" alias="hlen"
14         width='4' valueType="LENGTH" value='5'>
15         <Length unitSize='32'>
16         <Range begin='START_OF_HEADER'
17           end='END_OF_HEADER'/>
18         </Length>
19       </Field>
20       <Field name="Type Of Service" width='8' value='0'/>
21       <Field name="Total Length" width='16'
22         valueType='LENGTH'>
23         <Length unitSize='8'>
24         <Range begin='START_OF_PACKET'
25           end='END_OF_PACKET' />
26         </Length>
27       </Field>
28       <Field name="Identification" width='16' value='0' />
29       <Field name="Flags" width='3' value='0' />
30       <Field name="Fragment offset" width='13' value='0'/>
31       <Field name="Time to live" alias="ttl"
32         width='8' value='255' />
33       <Field name="Protocol" alias="protocol"
34         width='8' value='0' />
35       <Field name='Header Checksum' width='16'
36         valueType='CHECKSUM'>
37         <Checksum>
38         <Range begin='START_OF_HEADER'
39           end='END_OF_HEADER' />
40         </Checksum>
```

```
41          </Field>
42          <Field name="Source Address" alias="src_addr"
43            width='32' value='0' displayFormat="IPV4ADDR" />
44          <Field name="Destination Address" alias="dest_addr"
45            width='32' value='0' displayFormat="IPV4ADDR" />
46        </Header>
47        <Payload maxSize="65535"/>
48        <Trailer></Trailer>
49      </Protocol>
```

Lines 11–12

The IPV4 version field is 4 bits wide, with a default value of four. The alias is the name used when using this field in simulation command-line function or procedure. The name "Version" identifies the field in the GUI. You may want the GUI to have a pretty name with spaces and the command line to have a shorthand name using underscores. If both are the same, just use the name attribute.

Lines 13–19

The IPV4 Internet header length field is 4 bits wide, with a default value of five. The value of this field is a length type, calculated as the number of 32-bit units from start-of-header to end-of-header, which, coincidentally is always five if there are no options. And because we did not define an options field, there can be no options.

Lines 21–27

The IPV4 total length field is a 16-bit field. The value of this field is a length type, calculated as the number of 8-bit units from start-of-packet to end-of-packet.

Lines 35–41

The IPV4 checksum field is a 16-bit field. The value of this field is an IP CHECKSUM type, calculated from start-of-header to end-of-header.

Lines 42–45

The IPV4 source and destination address fields are 32-bit fields that have the IPV4ADDR display format. In the resulting GUI, you can edit the standard IPV4 address dot syntax (nnn.nnn.nnn.nnn).

Lines 42–45

There is no trailer for the IPV4 protocol layer. However, the trailer metadata delimiters—with nothing in them—are provided for clarity.

Ethernet pmd Example

```
50    <! Inserted inside Metadata region>
51
52    <Protocol name="Ethernet" alias="ethernet">
53      <Header>
54        <Field name="Destination Address" alias="dest_addr"
55          width='48' value='0' />
56        <Field name="Source Address" alias="src_addr"
57          width='48' value='0' />
58        <Field name="Protocol Type" alias="protocol_type"
59          width='16' value='0x0600' />
60      </Header>
61      <Payload minSize = "46" maxSize = "1500"/>
62      <Trailer>
63        <Field name="FCS" width='32' valueType='CRC'>
64          <Crc width='32' polynomial='0x4C11DB7'
65            initialValue='0xFFFFFFFF'
66            finalXorValue='0xFFFFFFFF' reflected='true'
67            finalResultProcessing='BYTESWAP'>
68            <Range begin='START_OF_HEADER'
69              end='END_OF_PAYLOAD' />
70          </Crc>
71        </Field>
72      </Trailer>
73    </Protocol>
```

Lines 54–57

The display format default for the 48-bit destination and source address fields is hexadecimal.

Lines 62–72

The trailer has a frame check sequence (FCS) 32-bit field. The value type of the FCS is CRC, calculated from start-of-header to end-of-payload—everything but the FCS field. The PacketGen CRC performs a 32-bit CRC calculation using the given polynomial, given the initial and final values.

You can place the custom protocol in a separate pmd file and load this file as part of the PacketGen GUI initialization.

Based on the pmd definitions, the GUI automatically configures dialog windows for creating protocol stacks for your packets. You see the protocol selection later when you are configuring flows. More are added with each release of the Intel® Internet Exchange Architecture (Intel® IXA) SDK tools.

Finally, choose open to use the pmd file and click OK back in the Packet Simulation Options dialog. PacketGen is ready to use!

Defining Network Traffic

For the IPV4 router initial tests, you now define a few flows with the desired network stack and IP destination addresses. Follow the steps shown in Figure 11.5.

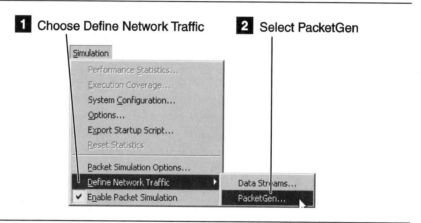

Figure 11.5   Enter Menu For Flows and Aggregates

The Define Network Traffic dialog displays. Select the Flows Specification tab to display the Flows Specification dialog, as shown in Figure 11.6.

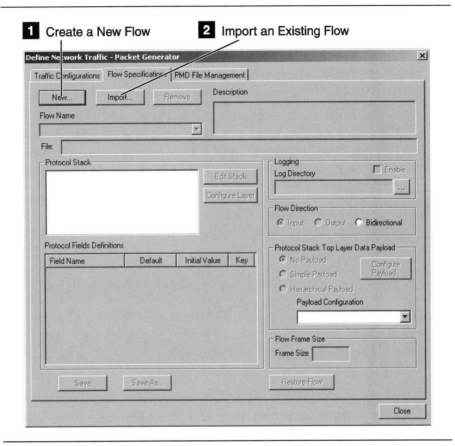

Figure 11.6   Flow Definition Dialog

Using the Flows Specification dialog, you can specify new flows **1**, save them, or import existing flows **2**. Think about your test plan. What flows would you like to set up? For example, you might want to create these test cases:

■ *A fat pipe*—a single flow at full line rate
■ *Test all queues*—flows that stream packets to all fabric queues
■ *Mix of packet rates*—flows with rate distribution
■ *Min-size packets*
■ *Max-size packets*

- *Variable size packets*

- *Test QoS*—high, low, and medium priority flows to test whether high priority flows are chosen over low priority

- *RFC1812 exception addresses*—packets with illegal addresses that should be dropped

- *Header errors. Invalid IP headers*—incorrect version, time-to-live, bad checksum, incorrect total length packets

- *WRED*—oversubscribe the test system by sending in packets at a higher rate than can be transmitted. Check that low priority packets are dropped.

- *Round robin*—run the sets of flows in round-robin fashion

- *Token bucket*—run the sets of flows using a token-bucket distribution

Furthermore, the test suite should be useful for more than one design; for example, applications with different performance ranges. The separation of flows and flow aggregates become useful when you need to use the same packet content on different designs. Flows can specify the packet content, whereas the flow aggregates can separately specify rate parameters and distribution.

You have no flows to import, so create a few. Click New in the Flows Specification dialog. Because the new flow is eventually saved to a file, you create the name and specify the location now, as shown in Figure 11.7.

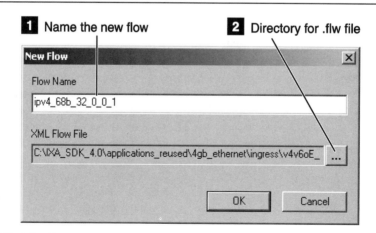

Figure 11.7 Naming and Locating a New Flow

You can make derived flows from existing flows, so after the first few, the process is amazingly fast. Think about the names early in the development of test flows, so that you can sort through them later for reuse. For example, the flow name ipv4_68B_32_0_0_1 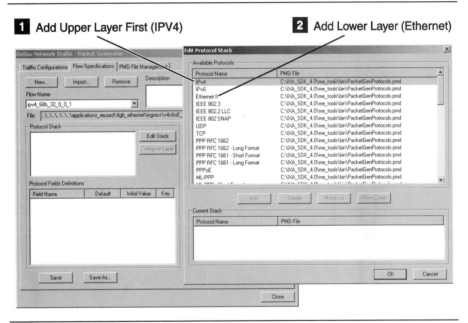 might signify an IPV4 packet, frame size 68 bytes, IP destination address 32.0.0.1. The destination address is also used in an `add_route()` call in the application initialization routine in order to load the route table. The flow is written to a file with a .flw suffix. Create a common directory for test flows used in multiple projects. To find the new directory, browse the directory structure using the ... button ❷.

Back in the Flows Specification dialog, click Edit Stack. The Edit Protocol Stack window appears, as shown in Figure 11.8.

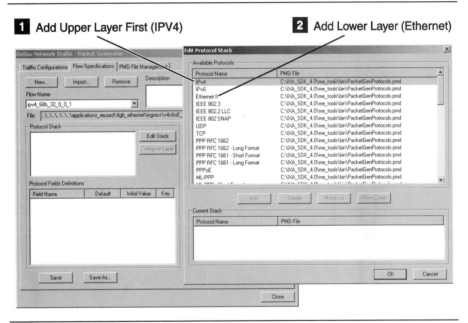

Figure 11.8   Building the Protocol Stack for a Flow

The available protocols, previously loaded from the protocol metadata files, are shown at the top of the Edit Protocol Stack dialog. The protocol stack for your flow is at the bottom. Highlight the desired flows in the available protocols list and click Add to move them to the current stack.

The current stack is shown as a standard network stack. The Data Link layer—for example, Ethernet ❷—should be on the bottom and upper layers—for example IPV4 ❶—should be above. This is the lowest encapsulating layer that represents the packet interface between the MAC device and the IXP2XXX network processor. If the protocols moved to the current stack are in the wrong order, highlight the ones you want to move and use the Move Up or Move Down buttons to place them in the correct order in the stack. If you add top through bottom, in that order, you do not need to move them (now he tells me). Click OK.

Select any layer of your protocol stack **1**; a list of Protocol Field Definitions appears. Double-click any Field Name entry **2** to bring up the editing window for the field, as shown in Figure 11.9. The default settings for this dialog are defined in the pmd file. Depending on its field specification, the protocol might have a fixed or computed width, a fixed or computed value, default value, or display format **3**.

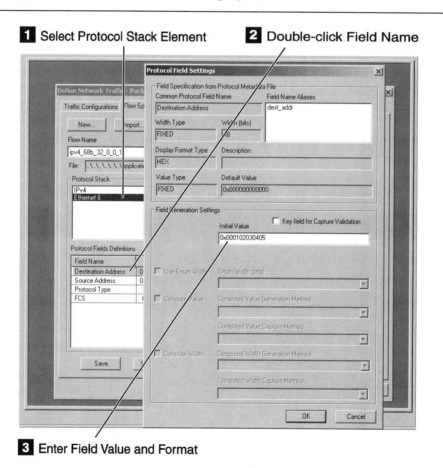

Figure 11.9   Editing a Protocol Field

Table 11.1 compares the pmd format name with the GUI dialog name for each protocol field parameter. PacketGen supplies a C-API that enables you to design C functions in a DLL that computes width or values for selected fields. The pmd specifies the format. The GUI provides the option to specify the default value or the function to compute the value. For internally computed values, such as padding, crc, checksum, and length, additional parameters in the pmd specify the computation to be performed. For a complete specification of the pmd conventions, please refer to the development tools user's guide (Intel 2004).

Table 11.1   Protocol Field Options

GUI dialog	Protocol Metadata File parameter	Format/Options
Common Protocol Field Name	name	String for GUI display, spaces between words
Packet Generator Name	alias	String for command line use, underscores between words
Width Type	widthType	FIXED. Width is specified by the width parameter.
		COMPUTED. This is a length field and its value is generated using an internal length algorithm.
		PADDING. Width is generated by an internal padding algorithm.
Width	width	Field size in bits
Description	description	String text describing the field
Display Format Type	displayFormat	HEX, DECIMAL, OCTAL, BINARY, IPV4ADDR, IPV6ADDR
Value Type	valueType	FIXED. Value is computed by the generator.
		LENGTH. Value is generated using an internal length calculation algorithm.
		CRC. Value is generated using an internal crc algorithm.
		CHECKSUM. Value is generated using an internal checksum algorithm.
		COMPUTED. Value is computed by a protocol support function provided in a DLL.
		SEQUENCE_NUMBER. Value increments with each successive PDU, starting with 0.
Value	value	Default value

For each field where you care about the value, enter default value and click OK. After all protocol layers have been defined, the last thing to define is the payload. If you check Simple Payload and Configure Payload, the Simple Payload dialog appears, as shown in Figure 11.10.

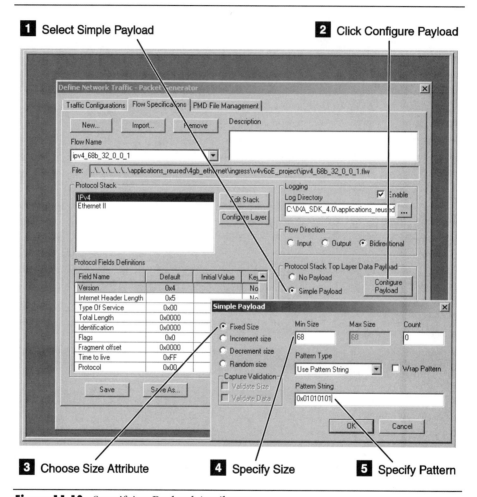

1 Select Simple Payload   **2** Click Configure Payload

3 Choose Size Attribute   **4** Specify Size   **5** Specify Pattern

Figure 11.10 Specifying Payload Attributes

Congratulations, you have one flow! Making more flows is simply a matter of changing a field, such as IPV4 destination address, and saving the flow as a different name, which automatically inserts the new flow in the project.

To load a custom protocol, use the PMD File Management tab of the Define Network Traffic dialog. As shown in Figure 11.11, import the Switch Fabric pmd example, as discussed previously in this chapter.

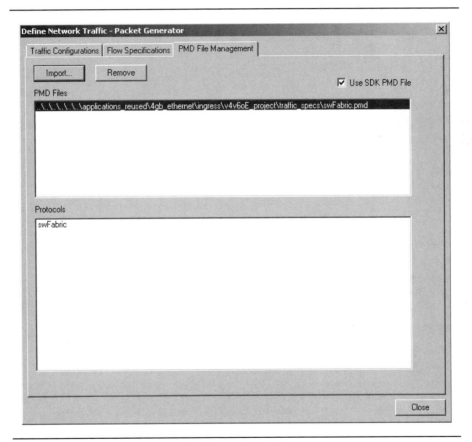

Figure 11.11 Importing a Custom Protocol

You now can create a flow with a custom header, as shown in Figure 11.12.

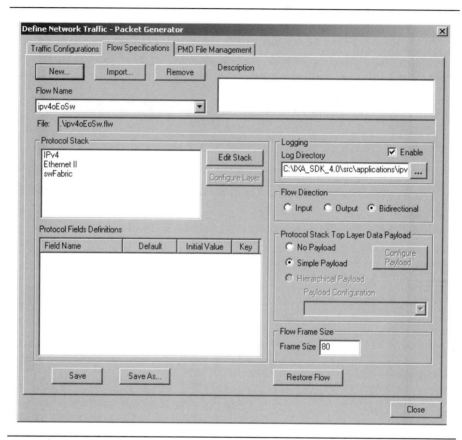

Figure 11.12 Adding Your Custom Header

Returning to the original IPV4 case, you have now saved four IPV4 Ethernet flows, with IP destination addresses 32.0.0.1, 32.0.0.2, 32.0.0.3, and 32.0.0.4, as shown in Figure 11.13.

1 After modifying the desired field, click Save As

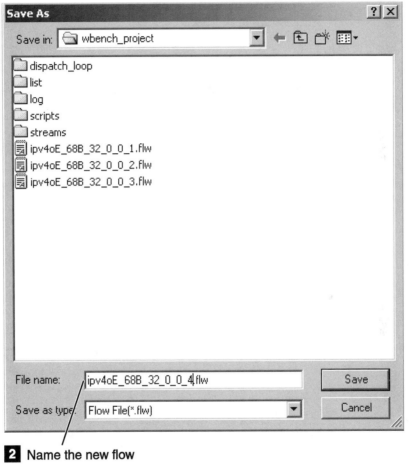

2 Name the new flow

Figure 11.13 Saving Flow Variations

Back in the Flows Specification dialog, under Flow Name, click the down arrow **1** to display the flows in the project, shown in Figure 11.14. If you have created flows in another project and saved them, you may also import the flows using the import button. If you would like to remove a flow from the current project, highlight the flow by first clicking the down arrow **2** and then dragging to the line of the desired flow. Then click Remove.

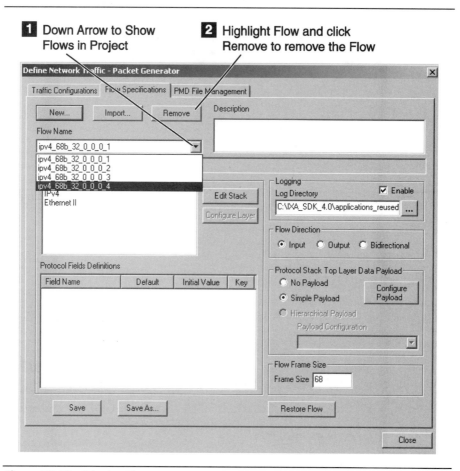

Figure 11.14 Display Flows in Project

When you have a set of flows, configure them into aggregates, known as traffic configurations. A traffic configuration can be at any level of the packet protocol stack hierarchy, as previously described. The most common—and required!—traffic configuration is at the device port. When you have put together a traffic configuration, you may later place it on a port or flow. Switch to the Traffic Configurations tab in the Define Network Traffic dialog. The top portion of the dialog is similar to the Flows Specification dialog. You can create new Traffic Configurations, import them, and remove them. As shown in Figure 11.15, click New ■, enter the Traffic Configuration Name, and choose a directory for it ■.

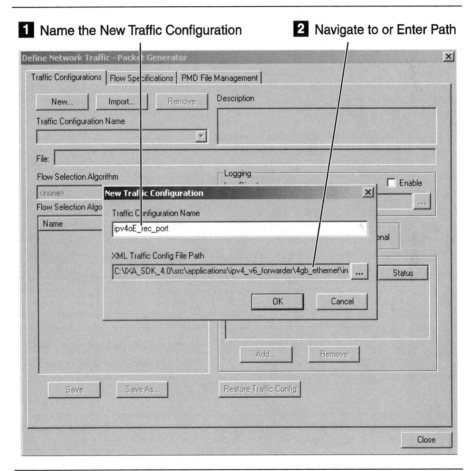

Figure 11.15 New Traffic Configuration

The name for this traffic configuration is ipv4oE_rec_port, to indicate the stack and the fact that the stack is designed to attach to a receive port on the IXP2XXX network processor. If you have a lot of flows, you might further qualify the name to indicate the test characteristics, such as min-size packet, token bucket, 1,000 queues, or other. When the name gets too long, putting it in the test directory is good enough. Whatever works for you. In the Traffic Configuration dialog, click Assign Flows to get the Flow Assignment dialog. Highlight the flow to add **1**, as shown in Figure 11.16. Do this for all the flows you want to add.

1 Select Flow to Add to Traffic Configuration

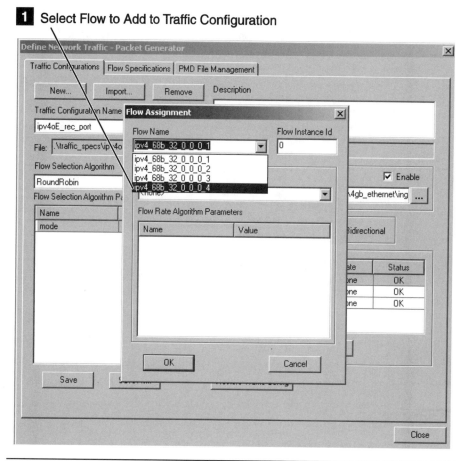

Figure 11.16 Flow Assignment

Now, just how would you like PacketGen to send them to the network processor, round robin, token bucket, or other? When you use the down arrow on the Flow Selection Algorithm **1**, shown in Figure 11.17, you see choices for distribution.

1 Choose the Packet Distribution Algorithm

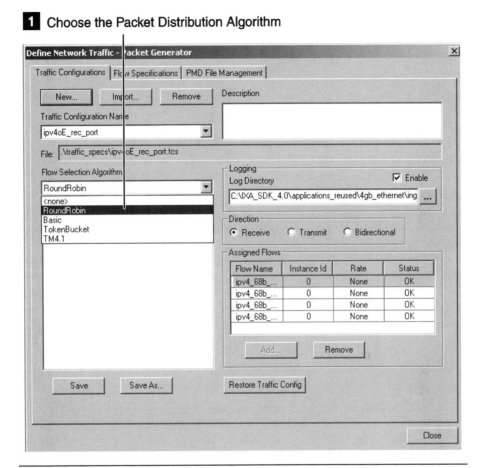

Figure 11.17 Flow Algorithm Selection

Early in the design, selecting round robin makes sense because you are debugging one packet at a time and you need some predictability. The round-robin selection causes PacketGen to send a packet from one flow, then a packet from the next flow, and so on, repeating from all flows in succession. Later, when the application seems to be functionally correct, you might try setting rates on individual flows, or using token-bucket distribution with over-subscription to see which packets get dropped.

The final step is to assign the traffic configurations to ports. From the top Simulation menu, choose Packet Simulation Options. Following the steps shown in Figure 11.18, click the Traffic Assignment tab **1** and click Assign Input **3**.

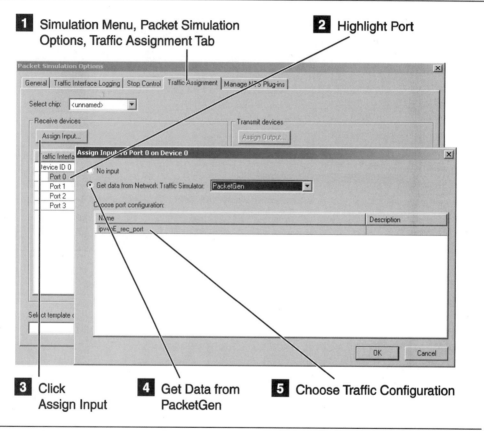

Figure 11.18 Assigning the Traffic Configuration to a Port

Previously, when reading the Developer Workbench chapter, you configured four ports. Well, here's your chance to feed them. The resulting traffic assignment for all receive ports is shown in Figure 11.19.

On the transmit side, you add expected Traffic Configurations to ports. Because these configurations are in the transmit direction of the IXP2XXX network processor, a flow algorithm is not needed. The protocol stacks in these flows are validated as PacketGen captures them. The validation consists of what was specified in the pmd file; for example, length, checksum, and crc.

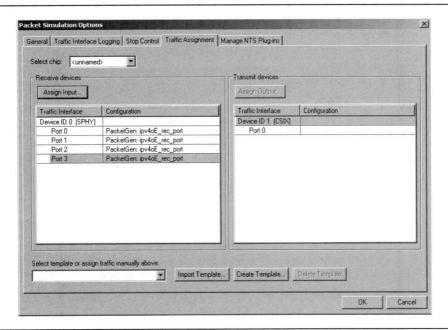

Figure 11.19 Assigned Network Traffic

Using Run-time Scripts For Initialization

The ME portion of the design handles packet forwarding but does not manage route lookup tables. That task is left to the route table manager in the Intel XScale® core. However, you would like to run your design without having to run the Intel XScale core simulation. Running it this way is like jumping into the middle of a working router with lookup tables already loaded. The initialization could be done by the MEs, but doing so would be writing duplicate temporary code because the actual code to do this is in the Intel XScale core and would take many simulation cycles to complete.

You can easily initialize the tables for simulation through the simulator command-line script using memory set functions. The command line can run in two modes:

1. *Ind mode, also known as the C-interpreter.* In this mode, the command line accepts a limited set of C function calls and syntax, plus basic transactor commands, which are not in C.

2. *Tcl shell mode.* In this mode, the command line executes Tcl scripts and interactive commands plus basic transactor commands in Tcl syntax.

Using C functions for initialization allows you to quickly port initialization code to the Intel XScale core. The transactor provides general set and get C support functions that take explicit address and data values. While not the most elegant C—pointers are not allowed—it does have that pleasing C syntax that everyone is familiar with. Here is a simple script example:

```
int some_dram_addr;
int i;
int table_base = 0x100;

set_dram(some_dram_addr, 42);

for (i= 0; i<0x1000; i++){
    set_sram(table_base+i, 0);
}
```

For simple linear tables, a `for() loop` works just fine. However, the IPV4 longest-prefix-match (LPM) lookup is much more complex. There are trees—also called tries—of pointers that are packed into fields of the lookups. A trie is a tree of tables used for fast route address matching. The trie lookup table is tailored to the network processor to achieve best possible performance for both packet forwarding lookups and route updates at runtime. Updating the pointers in the lookup trie can be tedious if you have to write each pointer with a separate script command. For more information about the data structures of the LPM, refer to the software building blocks manual (Intel 2004).

Here are ways you can load the route tries for simulation:

■ Create the lookup tree and route table using a command line initialization script. Insertion of trie pointers and packet fields is done through C-interpreted functions. Most of the applications in the Intel IXA Software Framework CD-ROM have examples of such scripts.

■ Invoke `ix_add_route()` through the Intel IXA SDK core components foreign model command line interface. By the time the book is out, this interface should be provided in the IXP2XXX Software Framework CD-ROM, cited in "References."

The preferred way to initialize the route tables is through Intel IXA SDK core components foreign model DLL. This DLL has the exact code that runs on the Intel XScale core. The DLL is loaded at run time and registers functions such as `ix_add_route()`. From the command line script, you can then create flows, configure your packets, and call `ix_add_route()` through the foreign model interface to the IPV4 forwarder core component.

Using Command Line Scripts to Configure Flows

You first run the design on the simulator, then on real network processor hardware. When sending test packets in the hardware environment, you are likely to use one of the popular test generators. These generators use Tcl scripts to configure packets. Here's an idea! Use the same script in simulation as in hardware testing. PacketGen provides a command line interface in both C and Tcl for configuring packets and flows plus translation wrappers to popular hardware test generator Tcl procedures. To run the Tcl shell from the simulation command line, just enter tclsh. To return to ind, enter exit. The following is a simple example that enters the Tcl shell, creates an IPV4 over Ethernet flow, and sets the IP destination address:

```
tclsh
set flow1 [PacketGen_FlowCreate "ipv4oE_32_0_0_1" 1 0]

set enet1 [PacketGen_AddStackElement ethernet flow1]

set ip1 [PacketGen_AddStackElement ipv4 flow1]

set ret [PacketGen_Set_FieldInt dest_addr 0x20000001 ip1]

if {(flow1 & enet1 & ip1 & ret) == 0} {
    puts "error, PacketGen flow creation failed"
exit
```

You can put the Tcl script in a separate file—for example, ipv4oe_flows.tcl —and execute it directly from the ind command line, as in the following examples. Notice the prompt in ind mode is >, and the prompt in Tcl shell mode is %:

```
>tclsh ipv4oe_flows.tcl
```

or

```
>tclsh
%source ipv4oe_flows.tcl
>exit
```

For each port, you must assign the traffic source. Previously, you assigned PacketGen as the traffic source. Now go to Packet Simulation Options, Traffic Assignment dialog **1** shown in Figure 11.20. Highlight the desired port **2**, click Assign Input **3** and in the Assign Input dialog, select PacketGen_CommandLine as the traffic source **4**.

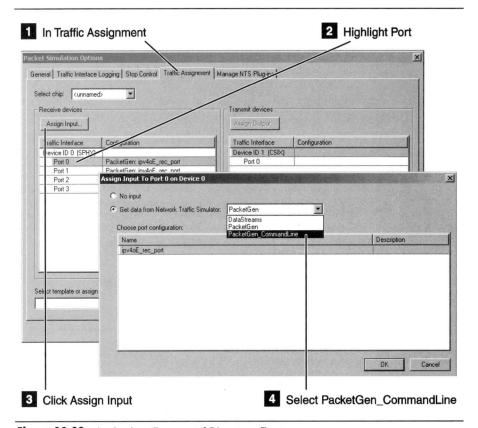

Figure 11.20 Assigning Command Line to a Port

Click OK. Now you are configured for command line packet generation.

Summary: Ready to Run

In this chapter, you learned how to configure packet flows for testing your design. The protocols are defined in an XML file format and loaded; packet-protocol editing GUI is created automatically. You placed protocol layers on stacks for each flow and defined the payload and size. You chose the distribution algorithm for aggregates of flows in traffic configurations and attached the aggregates to ports. You learned how to initialize memory and, more importantly, how to insert the correct IP destination addresses in the route lookup table. You learned the basics of configuring protocol stacks from command line scripts. Now it's time to run your design.

Chapter 12

Running the Simulation

The best way to escape from a problem is to solve it.

—Alan Saporta

The design is built. The packets are defined and ports are configured. So what are you waiting for? Click the Start Simulation button and go. No, wait! You should know just a few more things. In this chapter you will learn the options that need to be set up before simulation starts. You will learn how to increase simulation rate to run faster than the network wire rate, how to log simulation results, and how to use startup scripts. After starting simulation, you will learn the basic debug views and techniques for exploring the state of your application while it is simulating.

Example Design

For a simplified first simulation experience, let's take a look at another application, IPV4 ingress, in your SDK directory tree that you copied from the tools and applications CD-ROM. To get a copy, refer to this book's Web site, listed in "References."

```
\src\applications\ipv4forwarder\4gb_ethernet\ingress
```

This application handles IPV4 over Ethernet. No frills. No IPV6, tunneling, or extra decaps or encaps.

Simulation Options

You could start simulating now using the default settings. However, it is useful to control certain simulation settings before packets start to flow. For example, you can elect to save the packets received or transmitted by the network processor. You can send in a fixed number of packets, or you can stop the simulation after a fixed number of packets have been received or transmitted. You can automatically run initialization scripts as part of simulation startup. This section shows how to set simulation options before the fact; that is, before you discover you have wasted 15 minutes running a content-free simulation.

General

Figure 12.1 shows the general packet simulation options. You access options from the top Simulation menu, Packet Simulation Options, General dialog tab.

At some point you need to see how much headroom your design has. Can it just barely run at line rate? Can it run 10 percent faster than line rate? To find out, check Run Unbounded **1** and PacketSim force-feeds packet data to the network processor at full media switch fabric (MSF) rate. That is, every available bus cycle is used to receive packet data into the processor. The execution rate of the microengine code then becomes the limiting factor in packet-forwarding performance.

While simulation is running, you can view the receive and transmit speed in one of the debug views. You select units of measurement in the General Packet Simulation Options dialog **2**.

Statistics do not need to be collected every cycle to get an accurate performance measurement. You choose frequency of collection in this dialog, trading off accuracy for overall simulation performance **3**.

Random numbers are used for multiple purposes in simulation; for example, to create random packet sizes. By using the same random number seed for each simulation run, you can get deterministic results **4**. You can override this value by using `set_rand_seed(n)` in the simulation command-line script.

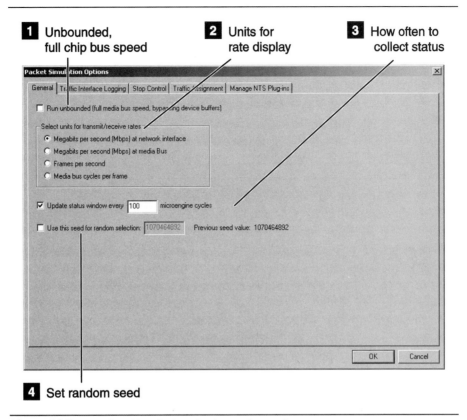

1 Unbounded, full chip bus speed

2 Units for rate display

3 How often to collect status

4 Set random seed

Figure 12.1   Packet Simulation Options, General

Logging

You can capture packet data in log files through the traffic interface logging feature. From the top Simulation menu, select Packet Simulation Options, Traffic Interface Logging, shown in Figure 12.2. To enable logging, check Enable logging. For selected devices and ports, you can separately log received or transmitted packets to files. Navigate as necessary to the directory where you want the files to be written.

You will likely choose one of the following three combinations for logging packet data:

■ *Raw data.* Raw packet data in ASCII form. Packets separated by linefeed. Enable logging and no other options produce this format.

■ *Frame numbers*. A sequence frame number is added and incremented for each packet. The frame number is written next to the packet data. Enable logging and log frame numbers produces this format. Frame numbers are helpful in identifying a failing packet from many packets.

■ *Log media bus cycles for SOP and EOP.* Add the MSF cycle time range from start-of-packet (SOP) to end-of-packet (EOP). Enable logging, log frame numbers, and log media bus cycles produces the detailed format. This type of log is for debugging purposes, enabling you to determine when the packet in question moved in or out of the processor in a very long simulation.

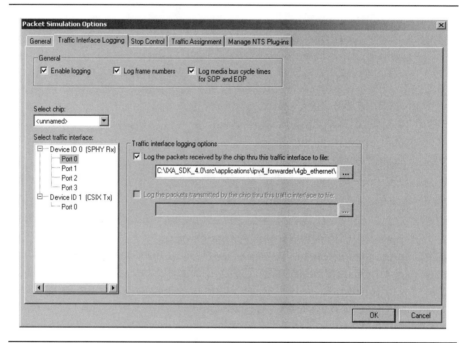

Figure 12.2   Packet Simulation Options, Traffic Interface Logging

Stop Control

Early in the debug process, you might want to send in just a few packets, then either stop simulation or stop sending packets from PacketGen. Stop control lets you do this. Go to Packet Simulation Options, Stop Control tab from the top Simulation menu, as shown in Figure 12.3.

MAC devices typically stop transmitting or receiving if an overflow or underflow occurs. In this dialog, you can model this behavior and stop simulation ■ to investigate the cause. On the network processor's receive-side, this condition indicates that the ME code's receive rate cannot keep up with the wire rate. If you check unbounded in the General settings, you cannot get receive overflow. If you are sending packets in at wire rate, it is possible to detect overflow. On the transmit side, the ME code is validating one TBUF element at a time, depending on the configuration, 64-256 bytes. If the packet is larger than this, successive TBUF elements must be written and validated for transmit at no less than the wire rate. If transmission is less than wire rate, the MAC device is starved, and underflow occurs. Select Stop on overflow or underflow if you want simulation to stop when either of these events occurs.

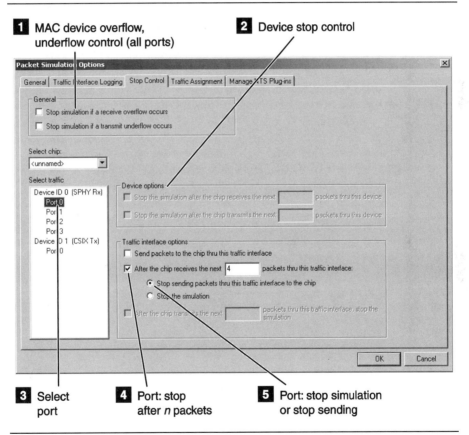

Figure 12.3   Stop Control

Stop control can be applied for the whole processor **2**. To do so for the receive side, check "Stop the simulation after the chip receives the next *n* packets through this interface" and enter the number of packets (*n*) in the box. For the transmit side, check "Stop the simulation after the chip transmits the next *n* packets through this interface" and enter the number of packets (*n*) in the box.

Stop control can also be applied to individual ports. Simply highlight the port ■3 and indicate packet count ■4 for the stop trigger, as was done for the whole processor. On the receive side of individual ports, you have the option to either stop sending packets or stop simulation ■5.

The Startup Script

The flow configuration in GUI can be exported to a script. Actually, the entire simulator startup sequence is exported from the top Simulation menu, Export Startup Script option, as shown in Figure 12.4.

The startup script is a command line script in ind format. The foreign model DLLs PhyDevice, CsixDevice, PacketSim, and PacketGen register C functions for configuring simulation devices, packets, and flows just as you did in this chapter with the GUI. If you check Enable Packet Simulation, packet simulation configuration commands are added to the project chip initialization startup script. These commands set the packet input source, output validation destination, output logging, and general port parameters for each port. In addition, depending on the device configuration in Simulation-System Configuration-MSF Devices, device simulation DLLs are loaded, and this script configures device simulators.

Take a look at the script. The following are always done:

- `path` declares directories to be searched for included files
- `foreign_model` loads other simulation DLLs, such as device simulators
- `inst` instantiates a chip simulator
- `init` initializes the simulator
- `set_clocks … tc*=` sets the simulator clocks
- `set_dram … set sram` sets memory parameters
- `load_ixc` loads microcode (.list files)
- `enable microengine` enables thread contexts and clocks for microengines

If Enable Packet Simulation is checked in the top Simulation menu these additional actions take place:

- `*_set_device_*` configures device simulators
- `*_set_port_*` configures device simulator port parameters
- `ps_set_port_input_nts_dll` attaches stream of packets to the network processor receive port to give the path to PacketGen,dll

■ `ps_set_port_output_nts_dll` attaches stream of packets to the network processor transmit port to give the path to PacketGen,dll

---

1 Top Simulation menu, Export Startup Script

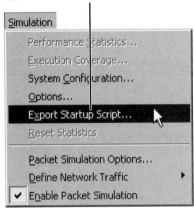

2 Default location is same directory as the project

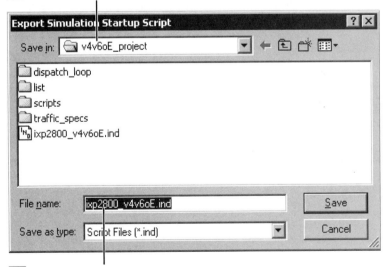

3 Default name is project name

Figure 12.4   Exporting the Startup Script

If Enable Logging options are checked in the Traffic Interface Logging tab of Packet Simulation Options dialog, these settings occur:

- `ps_set_port_input_logging` assigns log file for a network processor receive port. This logs all packets received by the network processor.

- `ps_set_port_output_logging` assigns log file for a network processor transmit port. This logs all packets transmitted by the network processor.

If additional scripts are specified in Simulation Options, Startup tab, this directive becomes active:

- `@*` includes another script file

Take a look at the Simulation > Options... > Startup dialog. In this dialog you can see a list of command line scripts. Insert your application-specific scripts, for example scripts that initialize data structures in SRAM and DRAM, here. All of these scripts are executed at startup in the order they appear in the list.

This cursory preview of the CLI shows some of the packet-related simulation commands. You can find much more detail on the command-line interface in Chapter 13.

Debug Views

During simulation, you can personalize the Developer Workbench to display multiple views of the processor and the ME application in progress. You can toggle the views on and off **2**, as shown in Figure 12.5. The view is enabled if you check the selection in the View > Debug Windows menu **1**. Your view preferences are saved when you save the project, either when exiting the project or at any time by choosing Save All from file menu.

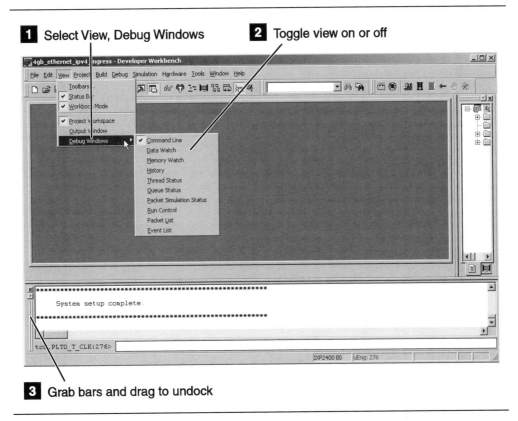

1 Select View, Debug Windows

2 Toggle view on or off

3 Grab bars and drag to undock

Figure 12.5 Debug Views

You can also use shortcut buttons to toggle debug views. If the view is active, the button is indented, as shown in Figure 12.6.

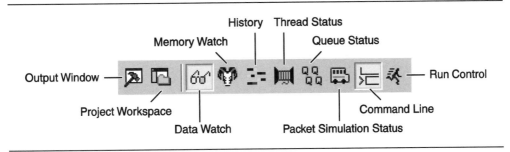

Figure 12.6 Debug View Shortcut Buttons

Docking

By default, the views are docked, or tiled, so that they fit neatly next to each other in the Developer Workbench window. Because there are so many views, you may want to undock them; make them a size that displays exactly what you want to see, no more, no less; overlap them; and then click the view you want to see to bring it to the front. To undock a view, grab the left window bars of the view and drag the window, as shown in Figure 12.7. To re-dock the window bars, grab the border and drag it back. If you have allowed docking and you bring the window edge near the Developer Workbench main window, that window tiles itself into the main window. Otherwise, you can keep the window free-standing.

Grab the border and drag

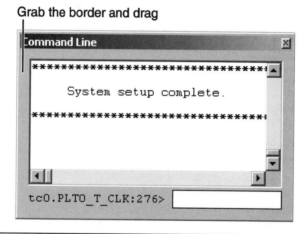

Figure 12.7   Moving the View Window

Command Line View

Enable the Command Line view from the View > Debug Windows menu or by clicking the Command Line button. With the command line view enabled, you can enter transactor, or simulator, commands and see detailed error messages interactively. In addition to transactor commands, the command offers an interactive C-interpreter. So whenever you feel rusty about your C programming skills, type some C into the command line and you'll be fine. If C isn't your preference, enter tclsh at the command line and then enter commands through the Tcl interpreter. You can find more detailed information about the command line in Chapter 13.

The command line prompt gives the chip name, followed by the clock base. If the chip has no name, none is shown. You can change the chip name when you are not in simulation by going to Chip Settings in the Project menu. Figure 12.8 shows the new chip name.

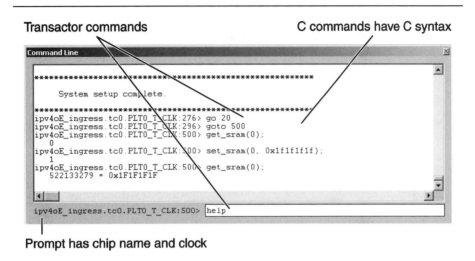

Transactor commands

C commands have C syntax

Prompt has chip name and clock

Figure 12.8 Using the Command Line

The default clock prompt tc0.PLT0_T_CLK is the cluster zero ME clock. Commonly used command-line features are go and goto, which advance the clock. A debug view for advanced clock stepping is covered later in this section.

A set of C support functions is also provided. You can use the C functions get/set/init/watch/check/dump <_memtype> for sram, dram, scratch, rbuf, tbuf, GPR, local memory, next neighbor, and transfer register access. Memory access uses byte addresses, so if you set to location three and get from location zero, you access the same 32-bit word.

Of course, when you feel like you don't know anything, enter help at the command line. The CLI displays a list of help topics. For any topic, enter help *topic_name*. For a complete description of all transactor commands and state access functions, refer to the development tools user's guide (Intel 2004).

Thread Status View

 Thread status view was the first GUI component of the Developer Workbench. In fact, before the Developer Workbench existed, the transactor command-line watch capability was used to print program counters and status for the Intel® IXP1200 Network Processor. As each screen rolled by, you would be mesmerized by the rippling program counter values. If a microengine stopped, the pattern would change noticeably. However, much has changed. By enabling Thread Status from View > Debug Windows or clicking the shortcut button, you get an interactive status window, as shown in Figure 12.9.

At the top left, you can choose which chip to display in the event you have a multichip simulation. The left column contains the ME and associated thread contexts. MEs are identified by cluster and ME within the cluster, separated by a colon. You may remember the balancing done in the Architecture Tool to ensure the bus bandwidths of the cluster are not exceeded. You can expand each ME to show individual threads by clicking on the ⊞ box at the left of the ME line.

Giving a meaningful name to the first thread of a group of threads that all do the same thing is a good practice. In this example, all threads of ME 0:0 are executing the rx_packet microblock, which receives packets from the MSF interface, reassembles them in DRAM, and assigns the packet to classification threads that are on other MEs. To rename the thread, right-click the thread line **1**, and select Rename Thread. Enter the new name in the dialog box **2**.

Thread status is given in the columns as follows:

- *Microengine:thread*. An arrow next to one of these threads indicates the currently executing thread context.

- *PC*. The program counter location last executed by the thread. Each thread has its own program counter. Only the active thread's program counter changes as simulation advances.

- *Condition codes*. Each microengine has one set of condition codes, used by the active thread. As a result of an operation that passes through the alu, certain instructions may set zero (Z); negative or bit 32 on (N); overflow (O); or carry out (C). Conditional branch instructions then use these to determine whether to branch to another PC or use PC+1 for the next instruction.

- *Signalled Events.* These signals have been received for this thread. Usually these signals indicate completion signals for I/O operations the thread itself requested. However, they could be signals from any source.

- *Wakeup Events.* These signals are required to be present for the thread to be eligible to run again. The keyword *voluntary* indicates the thread voluntarily swapped out to let other threads run and it has no wakeup dependencies, meaning it is eligible to run.

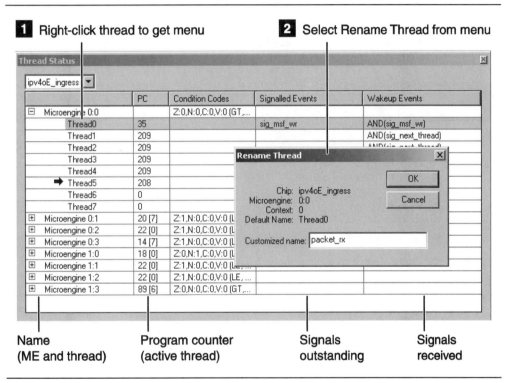

Figure 12.9 Thread Status, Renaming Thread

Thread List View

To see the currently executing code for a thread, right-click any thread line **1** of the Thread Status view and select Open Thread Window **2**, as shown in Figure 12.10.

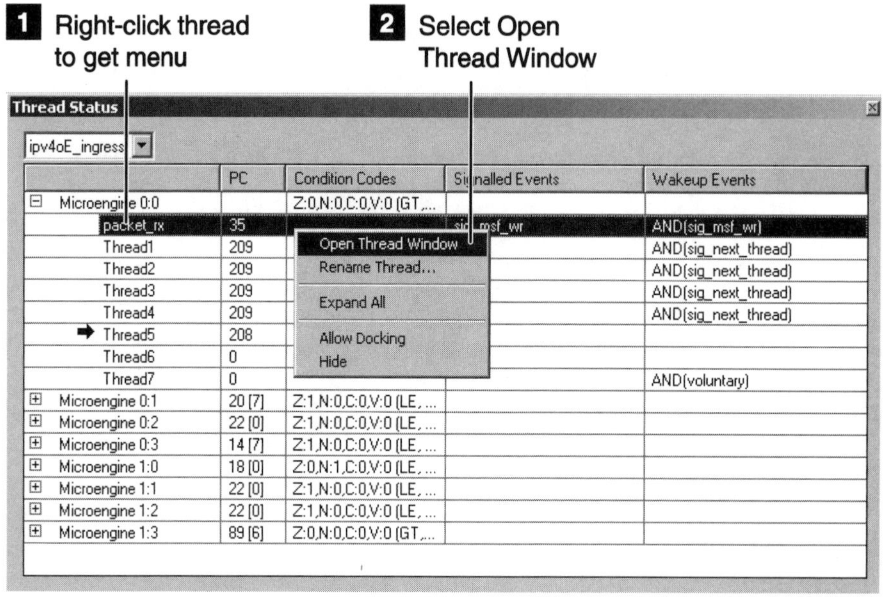

1 Right-click thread to get menu

2 Select Open Thread Window

Figure 12.10 Opening Thread List View

Thread 0 is executing the `rx_packet_init()` macro of the `rx_packet` microblock. Figure 12.11 shows the opened Thread List view, which is treated like an opened file, meaning you can close it from the top Workbench file menu. The left column has stacked arrows indicating the current code line in execution. When the thread list is first opened, you see the top level. If you have done a good job of partitioning your code, you should see the major code flow at this level.

What you see is what you wrote. Or is it? On close inspection, this code is not exactly what you entered. However, if you wrote your source in microcode, it is very close. If you wrote your source in C, the source C is shown above the microcode in the list.

Notice a prefix has been added to the variable names. This insertion is called "name mangling." Try to read it just with your right eye. Now it looks like the name you understand. Mangling is necessary inside macros to differentiate variables that might use the same name.

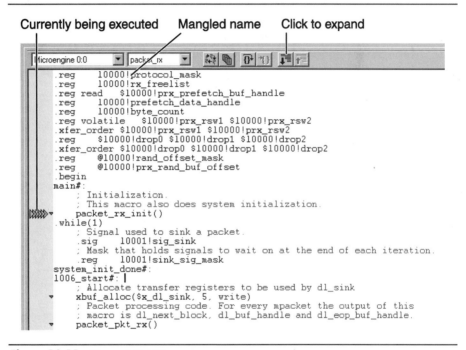

Figure 12.11 Thread List View

Right-click anywhere in the List view and select Display Instruction Addresses. The program counter values are displayed in the left border.

Expanding Macros

The following buttons can be used to expand and collapse macros:

 expand ▮▮ collapse

The location of your cursor determines which macros are expanded. For example, if the cursor is at the top level, not at or in a macro, all macros are expanded. If the cursor is on one macro, only that macro is expanded. Each time you click the macro expand button, another level is expanded, until it becomes gray. At this point, you have fully expanded the macro. Figure 12.12 shows the expanded list file.

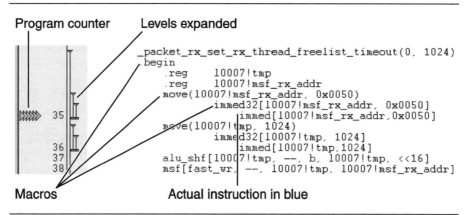

Figure 12.12 Thread List Expanded

With the list fully expanded, you see the microwords with instruction name highlighted in blue. This thread is not executing; its program counter is stopped at 35. Perhaps you really want to see the thread that is executing. That would be thread five. From thread status view, open the List view for thread five and expand the macros shown in Figure 12.13.

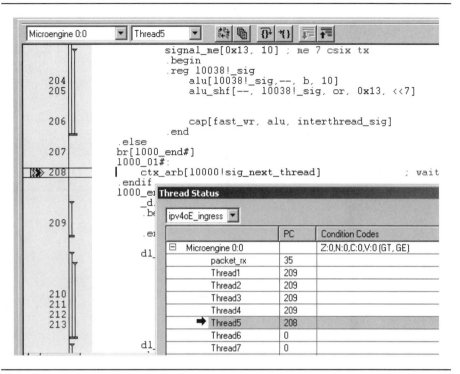

Figure 12.13 Thread Five List Expanded

 One of the program counter markers—called a "wedgie" just for fun—is now black. This thread is executing—but not for long! Step the simulation a few times by clicking the Cycle Step button in the Workbench top window and watch the wedgies advance. The black one turns yellow, meaning the instruction is aborting[1]. For several cycles, the program counter pointer has a yellow wedgie to indicate aborted instructions, then it reverts to a gray wedgie, pointing to the next instruction to execute when the thread swaps back in. Meanwhile, other threads are executing.

---

[1] Take my word for it, it was too expensive to put a color picture here.

From the List view, position the cursor inside some scope—in a macro or at the top window—then right-click ❶ to get the List view menu. Selecting Go To Source ❷, shown in Figure 12.14, brings up the source file for that scope. If you are in a macro, List view displays the file that has the macro definition. At the top level, List view displays the root source file for the microengine.

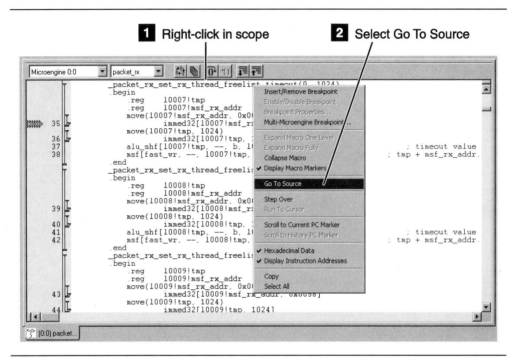

Figure 12.14 Go to Source

The source file displays. The list file is still there, under a thread tab. You can go back and forth between the two by clicking the desired tab.

Thread History

 So far you have command line, thread status, and thread list views. Now activate the History view from the Developer Workbench View > DebugWindows menu or click the History button. With this view, you can see at a glance what all of the threads have been doing for a range of simulation cycles.

Initially, History view displays each ME on a line. The bottom scroll spans the recent history, much like a logic analyzer. You previously specified the size of history collection in the Simulation > Options > History dialog. Hopefully, you also checked Collect Reference History in this dialog. If not, you have to start simulation all over again to see what you are about to see in this chapter. The ME cycle is shown along the top of the view. For each microengine, color-coded lines indicate execution activity. The following legend is used:

- *Black*—"thread executing."

- *Yellow*—Aborted, which occurs for defer shadows that were not filled with instructions. For example, if a branch was taken and no filler instruction follows it, the program counter enters a step rate, but the instructions abort and do not write results.

- *Red*—thread stalled. When the I/O command fifo is full, the cluster command bus bandwidth has been exceeded. Therefore, the bus cannot keep up with new I/O requests. If this condition persists for more than a few cycles, go back to the Architecture Tool and check your bandwidth utilizations.

- *Blue*—microengine idle. The microengine has nothing to do, usually because signals have not been received for I/O events, and all of the threads have not received their wakeup signals.

- *Dotted*—microengine disabled, which usually happens when the microengine is loaded without a list file.

If you want to confuse the other members of your team, click Customize and select the Colors dialog of the History view. Then swap the colors—not recommended. This is good for faking a demo for your boss to make a microengine that is idle appear to be executing.

Previously, you accessed the Thread List view from the Thread Status view. As shown in Figure 12.15, you can do the same from History view. To do so, position the cursor at the line and cycle of interest, and right-click **1** to get the menu. Then select Go To Instruction **2**.

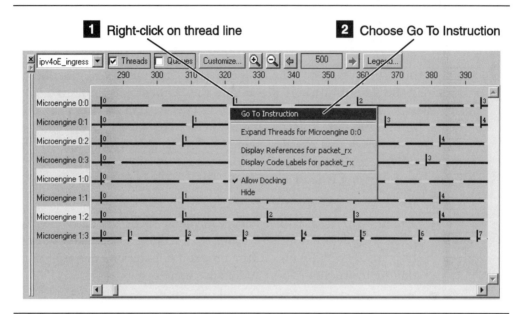

Figure 12.15 Thread History View, Go To Instruction

You can use the same menu to expand the ME thread line to display individual history lines for each thread context, as shown in Figure 12.16. Choose Expand Threads for Microengine 0:0 **1**. To show memory references, choose Display References for Packet_rx **2**, the thread we named previously.

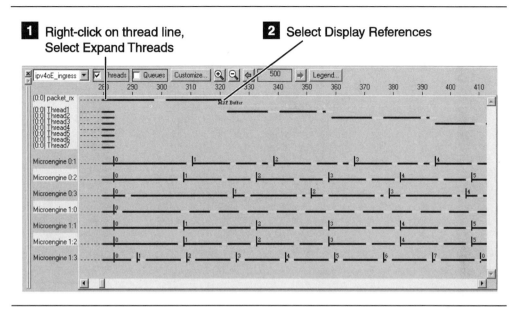

Figure 12.16 ME Threads Expanded Under Thread History View

I/O references are color coded as follows:

■ *Black*—DRAM

■ *White*—SRAM

■ *Magenta*—Scratch

■ *Yellow*—MSF

■ *Blue*—Hash

■ *Green*—CAP

Again, if you want to confuse the other members of your team, click Customize and select the Colors dialog of the History view. Then swap the colors—also not recommended.

The type of I/O reference is printed on the reference line, in case you are color-blind. The I/O Reference line, just below the thread line, shows the progress of your I/O operation. Clicking the legend button of the History view shows you the steps, as shown in Figure 12.17.

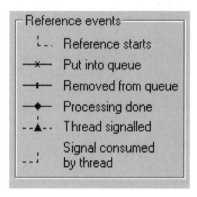

Figure 12.17 I/O Reference Legend

The steps are:

- *Reference starts.* I/O has executed, not stalled, and entered the ME command fifo.

- *Put into queue.* The I/O command has traversed the internal command bus and has entered the inlet fifo at the target unit. Target units such as memory controllers have fifos at their input to accumulate pending commands.

- *Remove from queue.* The target unit has started to execute the command.

- *Processing done.* The target unit has completed the I/O operation.

- *Thread signaled.* The I/O completion signal has been sent to the microengine.

- *Signal consumed by thread.* The thread has swapped in to execute again.

When you have thousands of cycles of history, the thread lines can begin to look as bare as your oldest clothes. Adding source code labels is a good way to know exactly where the thread is at any given cycle. To add labels, click Customize and select the Code Labels tab, as shown in Figure 12.18.

Left-click ME to list labels

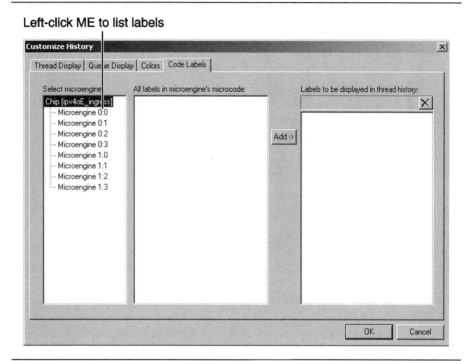

Figure 12.18 Customize History

Labels to be displayed are selected on a per-ME basis. Left-click the ME line in the left column to display all labels in the ME's code. Labels inside macros are mangled with a prefix in the same way variables are. Generally, you would choose to display major milestones, such as `system_init_complete#`, or start or completion of individual microblocks. However, when debugging a lengthy code block, you may want to display an intermediate step. Highlight the code label **1** and click Add **2** to move them to the display list, as shown in Figure 12.19.

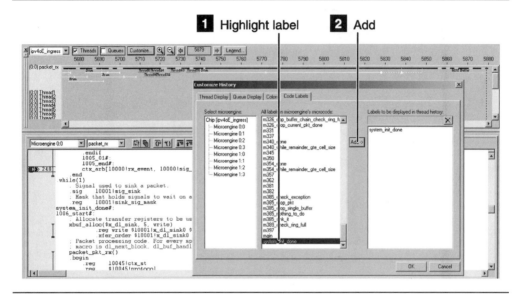

1 Highlight label   **2** Add

Figure 12.19   Add a Label to the History Line

When you have selected labels for all MEs, click OK. Set a breakpoint in the List view at `system_init_done#`. By default, this sets the breakpoint for all threads of the microengine. Click the Traffic Light button to resume the simulation. The traffic light is green when simulation is stopped and red while simulation is running. Simulation stops at `system_init_done#`. Your label is on thread line as shown in Figure 12.20.

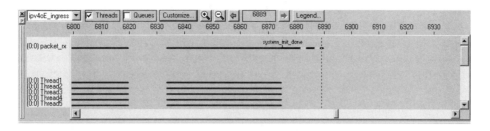

Figure 12.20 Resulting Label

Notice the vertical dotted line, which denotes the cycle of interest, which also happens to be the current cycle. You can move this line by dragging it horizontally or by clicking the left or right green arrows in the History view. When you change the cycle of interest, the program counter marker, or wedgie, moves in the List view accordingly. For example, if you move the cycle of interest back to the start of an I/O reference and right-click the thread line there to Go To Source, the List view for that thread is displayed with the program counter marker in the center and both List view and History view displayed, as illustrated in Figure 12.21.

Use the green arrows to walk through the history of your code execution. The value of the cycle of interest is shown between the arrows.

Use the magnifying glass buttons to zoom the history line. If you have labels too close together, you may have to zoom in (+). If you want to see the processing for a whole packet, zoom out (-).

Another feature of History view is queue history display. If you see thread stalls—red—for more than a few cycles, hardware queues could be backing up on you. Queue history provides queue fullness bar charts for the following hardware queues:

- *DRAM*—controller inlet FIFOs. One FIFO per channel
- *SRAM*—controller inlet FIFOs. One FIFO per channel
- *ME I/O command FIFOs*—I/O instruction commands not yet picked up by the target unit. One FIFO per ME
- *ShaC Command Inlet FIFO*—commands for accessing scratch, hash unit, and global CSRs
- *MSF Command Inlet FIFO*—commands for receive and transmit network interfaces

By default, queue history collection is normally not performed. The information is needed only if you have a performance problem due to a bus bandwidth bottleneck. If a memory access is taking too long, the cause could be a queue backup. For example, in the IXP28XX network processors, the DRAM address bits are swizzled at the controller to distribute commands across four internal queues within the controller. The Intel® Internet Exchange Architecture (Intel® IXA) framework applications allocate DRAM buffers so that proper distribution occurs. If all DRAM access addresses are the same, the commands create a bottleneck in one queue and latency greatly increases. As a result, your application performance may go down.

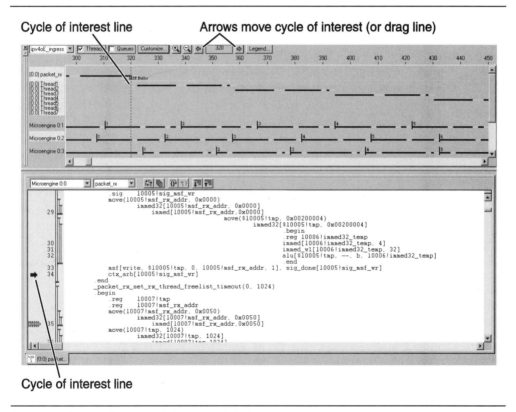

Figure 12.21 Walk Through History of Code Execution

ME command FIFOs can fill if too many I/O references are issued in a short period of time; for example, in four back-to-back cycles. When this occurs, the entire ME stalls, and no threads execute until I/O commands are taken by the target unit. Either the target unit inlet FIFOS are backed up, or the command bus bandwidth is exceeded. The command buses run at half the frequency of the ME, meaning one I/O command can be taken every two cycles from a cluster of MEs.

To enable queue history collection, you have to stop simulation—sigh!—and check Collect Queue History in the Simulation Options History dialog, as shown in Figure 12.22.

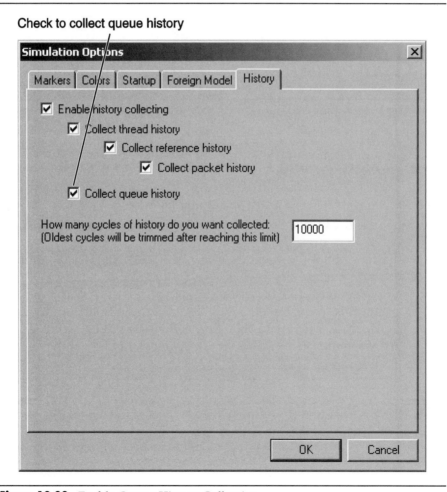

Figure 12.22 Enable Queue History Collection

Now run the simulation again—sigh again. Figure 12.23 shows what appears for queue history. You can scroll history horizontally to check for full queues, which are shown in red in the suspect cycles.

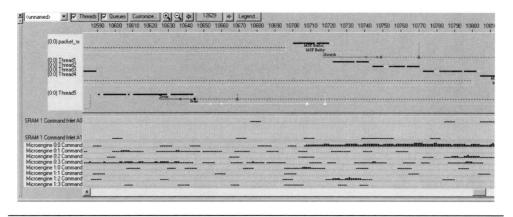

Figure 12.23 Queue History Display

Queue Status View

If you see a backed-up hardware queue in the queue history display, you can use the Queue Status view to find the exact cause. Enable the Queue Status view from the View > Debug Windows menu or by clicking the shortcut button. You get a display of DRAM, SRAM, ME command, Shac and MSF queues, as shown in Figure 12.24.

Depending on what history cycle you are in, you may or may not see commands in the queues. Slide the cycle of interest in the History view to the cycle where you want to see hardware queue contents or use the arrows in the Queue Status view to move the cycle of interest.

For each queue, the number of I/O command entries is shown. Expand the queue to show all entries by clicking the ⊞ on the queue line. The following I/O command parameters are displayed:

- *Command*—memory type and operation

- *Address*—starting address of a memory access

- *Thread*—ID of the thread that issues the command

- *PC*—program counter when the I/O instruction executed

- *Cycle*—ME cycle when the command was issued

- *#Lwords*—number of transfer registers read or written by the command

- *Sig Done*—whether the instruction requested a completion signal

Right-click any I/O command to display the Thread List view at the I/O instruction that issued the command.

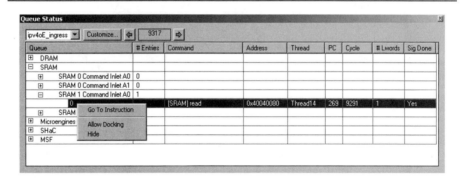

Figure 12.24 Queue Status View

Run Control View

Enable the Run Control view from the View > Debug Windows menu or by clicking the shortcut button. This dialog allows you to selectively step the simulator by choosing selected threads **1** and performing single cycle step, go, go to cycle, or go to label. The Run Control view is shown in Figure 12.25.

Instead of entering a breakpoint in the List view, you can go to a label **3**. Either enter a label name **2** or click the browse button at the right to display a list of valid labels.

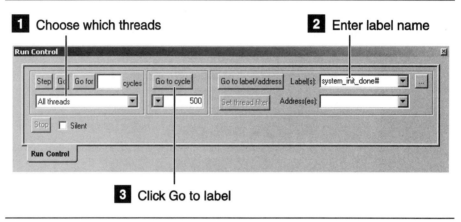

Figure 12.25 Run Control View

Selecting a single thread is useful if the thread is performing a set of tasks, swapping in and out. To single step a thread, you step one simulator cycle at a time while the thread is active. When the thread swaps out, a single step causes the simulator to run until that thread swaps back in. If you have List view for that thread displayed, you can easily follow the execution flow as the program counter marker advances.

Simulation Status View

How do you know if your application is really receiving and transmitting packets? Why, with Simulation Status view, of course!

 Enable the Simulation Status view from Developer Workbench View > DebugWindows menu or by clicking the shortcut button. Depending on the MAC devices and number of ports you have defined, the view will look more or less like Figure 12.26.

Number of packets received   Receive rate (all rx ports)

MAC buffer with packet data   Receive rate (each port)

Traffic Interface	Rx buffer fullness	Tx buffer fullness	Packets received	Receive rate	Packets sent	Transmit rate
Device ID 0 (SPHY Rx)			8	11024	n/a	n/a
● Port 0	178 [69%]	n/a	2	2755.952	n/a	n/a
● Port 1	178 [69%]	n/a	2	2755.952	n/a	n/a
● Port 2	178 [69%]	n/a	2	2755.952	n/a	n/a
● Port 3	178 [69%]	n/a	2	2755.952	n/a	n/a
Device ID 1 (CSIX Tx)			n/a	n/a	0	0.0000
● Port 0	n/a	0 [0%]	n/a	n/a	0	0.0000

Chip ipv4oE_ingress   Options...   Save Stats To File...

Packets received 8   Receive rate 11024   Mbps (at network)
Packets transmitted 0   Transmit rate 0.00   Mbps (at network)

For Help, select Help->Help Topics on the main menu   IXP2400 B0   uEng: 7637

Figure 12.26 Simulation Status

For the whole processor and for each port, Packet Simulation Status view displays the following:

■ Number of packets received and transmitted

■ Receive and transmit rates

■ MAC device buffer fullness. If your receive or transmit code cannot keep up with line rate, the MAC receive buffers will overflow.

Summary

In this chapter, you ran a simulation and achieved a basic understanding of the simulation options and debug views. But the best features have been saved for later. So read on!

Remember to click Save All periodically from the top File menu, which saves your personal preferences for the project in case your computer crashes.

Now try this on your IPV4V6 tunneling router design.

Chapter 13

Command Line, Watches, and Statistics

When the practised eye of the simple peasant sees the half of a frog projecting above the water, he unerringly infers the half of the frog which he does not see. To the expert student in our great science, history is a frog; half of it is submerged, but he knows it is there, and he knows the shape of it.

—Mark Twain

The Developer Workbench has additional features that could come in handy from time to time. These features include data watch, memory watch, Ind and Tcl command line scripts, creating and loading foreign models, performance statistics, and execution coverage.

Watches

Using Data Watch view and Memory Watch view, you can configure displays of GPRs, CSRs, pins, and memory arrays. You can set breakpoints on single addresses or a range of addresses to cause simulation to stop if the selected state value changes. The displays show data values for your selected simulation states when simulation is stopped. You can step back through history and view the data values at cycles of interest.

Data Watch

You can use Data Watch to set up and display watches for the following simulator states:

■ *Microengine Registers*—GPRs, transfer registers, next neighbor registers

■ *CAP CSRs*—self-destruct, thread message, scratch, hash

■ *Microengine CSRs*

■ *MSF (media switch fabric) CSRs*

■ *PCI CSRs*

■ *Intel XScale® core CSRs*

■ *Microengine Memory*—next neighbor, microcode storage, local memory, CAM

■ *MSF Buffers*—RBUF and TBUF

■ *Pins*. rx, tx, pci—watch raw packet data enter and leave the processor

 Enable the Data Watch display from the View > Debug Windows menu or by clicking the shortcut button. Figure 13.1 shows the selection of a watch for ME memory.

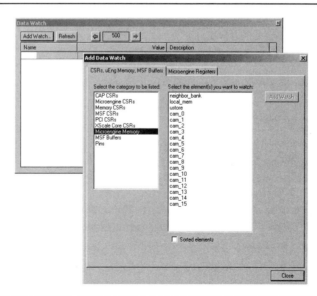

Figure 13.1   Data Watch Selection

Next, select local_mem, then the ME, as shown in Figure 13.2.

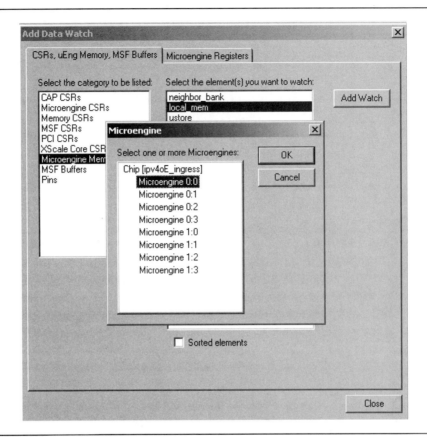

Figure 13.2 Data Watch Local Memory Selection

You must specify the address range for the watch. Memories are addressed with byte addresses. The local memory size is 640 32-bit words. If you specify a range of 0:639, as shown in Figure 13.3, you get exactly one quarter of local memory because you have specified 640 bytes, which is 160 32-bit words. At least all addresses in MEs and the Intel XScale core are consistent.

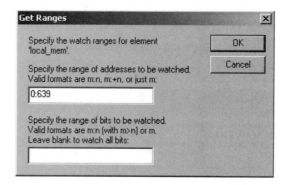

Figure 13.3   Data Watch in Local Memory, Specify Address Range

Finally, you can set a breakpoint on the data watch by right-clicking the watch item, as shown in Figure 13.4. For arrays, that is, for a range of addresses, you can set the breakpoint either on the entire range or on individual locations.

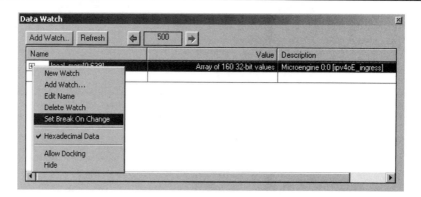

Figure 13.4   Data Watch in Local Memory, Set Breakpoint

Memory Watch

The Memory Watch view is similar to the Data Watch view. You can use it for DRAM, SRAM, or scratch watches. The locations are set in order in an array, left to right, top to bottom, for more compact display of very large arrays, as shown in Figure 13.5. As with Data Watch, you can also set breakpoints for the entire array or for individual locations.

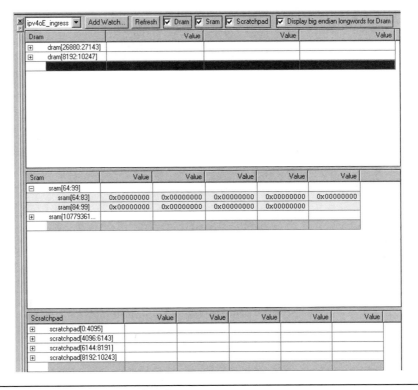

Figure 13.5   Memory Watch Selection

When a breakpoint occurs on a memory or data watch, the values that changed—caused the breakpoint—are highlighted in red.

Ind Command Line

Using the command line is like playing the blues on the guitar. As long as your fingers can keep up with your brain, there will be instant gratification.

—Don Hooper

The Ind command line, which consists of a transactor interface and a C-interpreter, is the most basic interface to the simulator. This section provides examples of commonly used commands and functions to help you get started with using the command line. You can find a complete list of command line features in the development tools user's guide (Intel 2004).

Running Standalone

You can run the transactor standalone without the workbench. Start up a command window from your system. A list of chip simulators is in the me_tools bin directory:

```
dir ixa_sdk_4.0\me_tools\bin\ixp*
```

The suffixes a1, a2, b0, and so on indicate the chip version. The highest suffix is the latest. You should be working in a test directory, where you have project-specific files such as startup ind from the Developer Workbench or list files produced by Assembler or Compiler. You might just create a work directory to play in. To run IXP2800 B0, enter:

```
ixa_sdk_4.0\me_tools\bin\ixp2800_b0
>>>
```

The Ind prompt is the greater-than sign (>). When the simulation first starts up, the simulation has no chip instance, so the prompt is (>>>). The path command shows the directories where the transactor looks for script files. Some of the directories are from system or environment settings, and the others are set up by the installation of the Intel® Internet Exchange Architecture (Intel® IXA) SDK.

```
>>> path
   Path search list for finding files
      1: .
      2:
```

For example, if you create a file hello.ind with the following statement:

```
printf("how did you do that?\n");
```

and place it in a directory listed in the path search list, you can run it with the @*file* command:

```
>>> @hello
Current working directory: C:\
how did you do that?
```

You can load the exported startup script of any workbench project in the same way. If you do, your prompt changes to reflect the processor and clock, as you saw in the Command Line view of the Developer Workbench project. A chip instance has been created, and the Transactor is now a Simulator.

You can navigate and view directories, starting with the directory you start simulation from, using standard DOS/UNIX commands:

- *dir*—lists the contents of the current directory
- *cd*—changes directories
- *pwd*—prints working directory

Running in the Workbench

The command line is the same when running from the Developer Workbench. However, when you start simulation from a project, the Workbench runs the startup script for you. Enable the Command Line view from the View > Debug Windows menu or by clicking the shortcut button. You can then use both GUI features and the command line.

The C-Interpreter

The C-interpreter supports a subset of C, only enough of the language to perform simple initializations and information capture during simulation.

The @filename command can be used to load common source header files (.h) used by the Assembler and the Compiler. Such definition files are used to define constants. Therefore, the C-interpreter supports the following basic preprocessor statements:

```
#define
#ifdef
#ifndef
#else
#endif
#include
#undef
```

The C-interpreter ignores C style comments. A common header file such as my_header.h typically looks like this:

```
#ifndef MY_HEADER_H
#define MY_HEADER_H

#define NOT_A_MAGIC_NUMBER 42
// rest of file

#endif // MY_HEADER_H
```

If this file is to be shared by the transactor, Assembler, and Compiler, be sure to use only supported preprocessor commands in the file. The example applications use `#ifdef IXP_MICROCODE` around Assembly-language preprocessor commands. IXP_MICROCODE is defined for the Assembler build settings, but not for simulation. To load header files into the C-interpreter use @filename.h. Also use the @filename form to load and run any ind script. The .ind file extension for a script may be omitted.

```
> @my_header.h
> @my_script.ind
> @my_other_script
```

The following data types are supported:

■ *int*—32 bit

■ *string*

■ *arrays*—int or string

The following conditional syntax is supported:

```
if
else
endif
for
while
```

As you have seen, printf can format information for log files or command-line notifications. A code block body can extend over multiple lines. The transactor changes the prompt to }> to indicate closing braces are outstanding.

```
> int a;
> for(a=0;a<8;a++){
}>    printf("a is %d\n", a);
}> }
>
```

You can create a log file using the log transactor command. The log file records everything that happens on the command line until the log is closed. Transactor commands and C can be used together. When using the log command, use the `responses` qualifier to record only simulator output, not command line input. The default is to record both commands and responses.

```
> string hw[2];
> hw[0] = "hello":
> hw[1] = "world";

> log mylog.log responses
> printf("%s %s\n", hw[0], hw[1]);
> close mylog.log
```

Of course, you will make typographical errors when interacting with the command line. The transactor counts your errors and continually reminds you of them in the prompt. However, it is easy to assign states in the transactor and in the chip simulator with C statements. Simply set the error count back to zero:

```
err=8> sim.error_count = 0;
>
```

The biggest problem usually is remembering what the state name is in the first place. Wildcards are helpful in finding and examining states. Be careful; you could be in for a very long printout if you make the wild card too simple. Use examine—ex for short—to examine a state.

```
> sim.error_count = 1;
err=1> ex sim.err*
sim.error_count<31:0> = 00000001    (1)    (Current Error Count)
sim.error_handle_mode<31:0> = 00000028(40)(Error Handle Mode
Switch)
```

You may see states that mean nothing to you. On the other hand, you could find the state you are looking for. Sorry, there is no state called bliss. The development tools user's guide (Intel 2004) provides a list of common state names.

You can create aliases for states that have lengthy names using the def_syn() transactor support function. Examine the new name first to make sure it does not already exist.

```
err=1> ex error_count
ERROR:  "error_count" not found
err=2> def_syn(error_count, sim.error_count);

err=2> int b;
err=2> b = error_count;
2
err=2> error_count = 0;
>
```

Occasionally, you need to invoke a transactor command from within a C statement. Do this with the cmd() function.

```
> cmd("ex error_count");
error_count<31:0> is a synonym state to sim.error_count<31:0>:
sim.error_count<31:0> = 00000000    (0)    (Current Error Count)
```

You can also define and use functions from the command line. The function declaration takes the normal C function definition form:

```
return_type function_name(type arg1, ..){body}
```

The return type for functions can be void or int. If the function returns an int, it can be used inside an expression. The function can be multiple lines. The transactor changes the prompt to }> to indicate closing braces are outstanding.

```
> int max(int a, int b){
}>   if (a > b) return(a);
}>   else return(b);
}> }
>
> int ans = 1 + max(5,6);
7
```

The transactor provides support functions for accessing well-known states such as DRAM, SRAM, and scratch.

```
> int data = 0;
> int addr = 0x100;
> set_sram(addr, data);
> printf("location %d has %d\n", addr, get_sram(addr));
```

You can use a watch definition to perform some action if the state being watched changes value. This definition takes the form:

watch*(watch_name, state1, state2, ..){C body}*

For example, place a watch on the MSF RX clock and print receive pin data to a log file every cycle. Checking the development tools user's guide (Intel 2004), you'll see that the MSF receive clock has the character string PLMS_MR01_CLK and MSF receive data 15:0 has PAMS_RX_DATA_RMR. Perform and examine at the command line to get the full name, including processor name prefix and cut and paste the full name into your watch.

```
> watch(mywatch2, ipv4oE_ingress.PLMS_MR01_CLK){
}>   printf("rxdata %d\n", ipv4oE_ingress.PAMS_RXDATA_D0_RMR01H);
}> }
>
```

The MSF clocks run at a different rate than the ME clocks. To change the command-line clock from the default ME clock to the MSF clock, use the set_default_go_clk command:

```
> set_default_go_clk ipv4oE_ingress.PLMS_MR01_CLK
> go 50
```

You can use the watch to print information to a log file as you did earlier. For very long simulations, capturing simulation information and formatting it to a file could just help you catch that bug.

Sometimes it is useful to stop simulation if an error condition is detected during a watch. The sim.halt transactor state can be set to nonzero to cause the simulator to halt. Interactively, you can reset it to zero again to resume simulation. Transactor states can be assigned with a simple C assignment:

```
> sim.halt = 0;
```

The transactor provides C functions for performing memory watches. Finding memory states in a network processor is difficult because usually the arrays comprising a memory have unrecognizable names and may be segmented. So it is best to use the C functions.

```
> watch_sram(addr);
>
> void stop_the_presses () {
}>   if ((get_sram(addr)) == 42) sim.halt = 1;
}>}
> watch sram_function("stop_the_presses", addr);
```

The previous watch is much like a conditional breakpoint. However, the breakpoint is performed only when the address in question changes value. You can use the breakpoint feature to associate a breakpoint with specific lines of code. You must first define the breakpoint function with exact arguments, whether you use them or not, that allow the simulator to invoke the function. If the return value is nonzero, the breakpoint halts the simulation. Therefore, you can convert the breakpoint to a conditional breakpoint by returning nonzero if a condition is satisfied. This functionality is the same as the conditional breakpoint in the Developer Workbench, which you will learn in the next chapter.

```
> int my_bp(string chip_name, int me_num, int ctx_num, int PC){
}>   printf("at bp\n");
}>   return(1);
}>}
>
```

Second, issue the ubreak command, referencing the breakpoint function. With this command, you give the individual breakpoint a name, reference a breakpoint function, provide a filter—in *microengines:threads* syntax—and provide a microengine instruction PC address or label.

```
> ubreak my_bp_inst "my_bp" ipv4oE_ingress(1:*) 267#
```

Note that, if the chip has a name, the name goes just before the filter. To better understand the filter, use the help command.

```
> help
> help ubreak
> help set_default_goto_filter
```

Here are some examples of filters and what they mean:

- (*) —apply to all MEs, all threads
- (1:*) —apply to ME 1, all thread contexts
- (2,1:*) —apply to MEs 2 and 1, all thread contexts
- (3-1:*) —apply to MEs 1–3, all thread contexts
- (0:2-1) —apply ME 0, thread contexts 1-2

At the command line, ME numbering is consecutive. In the Developer Workbench, you should see (Cluster:ME) as the notation to identify MEs. For the IXP24XX network processor, each cluster has four MEs. ME 1:0 in the Developer Workbench is ME 4 at the command line. For the IXP28XX network processor, each cluster has eight MEs. In that case, ME 1:0 in the Developer Workbench is ME 8 at the command line.

A goto_addr is similar to an unconditional breakpoint, where the simulator runs up to a PC. The argument is a label or PC address.

```
> goto_addr ipv4oE_ingress(*) system_init_done#
```

If your chip does not have a name, enter:

```
> goto_addr (*) system_init_done#
```

Foreign Model Interface

Running a system-level model with your MAC device simulators dynamically linked with the simulator is a good idea. To do so, you must create what is called a foreign model. A foreign model is a DLL that has a specific registration and callback API to the transactor. The complete API is specified in the development tools user's guide (Intel 2004). Table 13.1 lists the commonly used functions of foreign model APIs.

Table 13.1   Foreign Model API, Commonly Used Functions

Function	Description
`foreign_model_initialize()`	This function is called when the foreign model is loaded. In this function, initialize your foreign model and register console (command line) functions using XACT_register_console_function().
`XACT_register_console_function()`	This function registers a command-line function with the transactor. Following the console function registration, you can call this function from the command line as you would any C function.
`foreign_model_pre_sim()`	The transactor calls this function in your foreign model just prior to executing a simulation cycle.
`foreign_model_post_sim()`	The transactor calls this function in your foreign model just after executing a simulation cycle.
`foreign_model_exit()`	The transactor calls this function in your foreign model just prior to exiting.
`foreign_model_reset()`	The transactor calls this function in your foreign model just prior to the execution of a sim_reset command.
`foreign_model_delete()`	The transactor calls this function in your foreign model just after a chip instance is deleted.
`GetVmodForeignModelFunctions()`	This function is the sole entry point into the DLL. It provides required functions pointers to the Transactor.

The transactor API is specified in:

```
ixa_sdk_4.0\me_tools\include\xact_vmod.h
```

The XACT functions enable the foreign model to access the simulation state from a C interface. Although writing command-line functions is fun, if you really want them to run fast, define them in a foreign model, compile and load the foreign model, and call the functions as console functions. Some simple foreign model examples are provided in:

```
ixa_sdk_4.0\me_tools\samples\ForeignModelDLL\
```

Two ways to load a foreign model are:

1. From the Developer Workbench. At the Simulation > Options menu, use the Foreign Model dialog to name foreign models. When simulation starts, the foreign model is automatically loaded.

2. From the command line. The arguments are the name of the dll file, a unique instance name for the foreign model, and an optional initialization string to be passed to the function foreign_model_initialize().

```
> foreign_model my_foreign_model.dll unique_fm_1
```

Tcl Command Line

Enter the Tcl shell from the command line using the tclsh command. The Tcl shell supports complete industry standard Tcl functionality. To check the version, look for the Tcl library under me_tools\lib directory. The version is in the Tcl directory name; for example, me_tools\lib\tcl8.4.

The Tcl shell has a % prompt to distinguish it from the > prompt of the Ind. The Tcl shell may be entered from the Ind command line:

```
> tclsh
% set a 1
%
% # leave the Tcl shell
% exit
>
```

This tcl shell is global. Variables that are created in it are persistent even after you exit the Tcl shell. For example, you could create a simulation status array, leave and re-enter the Tcl shell during simulation, and continually add information to the status array. Enter the global simulation Tcl shell again:

```
> tclsh
% set b $a
% puts b
% exit
>
```

The variables of local Tcl shell do not exist after it is exited. To enter a local Tcl shell, use the /local qualifier:

```
> tclsh/local
```

You can run a Tcl script file from the ind. Enter the Tcl shell and source the filename as follows:

```
>...Ind commands ...
>
> tclsh
% source <filename>
% ...tcl commands ...
% exit
>
```

or

```
> ...Ind commands ...
>
> tclsh <filename>
>
```

A Tcl script may also be invoked from an ind file, using the *tclsh* command. This file may then be run in batch mode, as you might do to run regression tests. For example, the ind file could contain the following:

```
...Ind commands...

tclsh
source <filename>
...Tcl commands ...
exit

...Ind commands...
```

or

```
...Ind commands...
tclsh <filename>
...Ind commands...
```

Transactor commands and C function calls to the C-interpreter can be invoked from the Tcl shell, using cmd. For transactor commands, use cmd followed by the name of the transactor command and a variable number of arguments to the transactor command.

```
> tclsh
% cmd go 20
%
```

The transactor command `exit` cannot be invoked in this way. To exit the transactor, first exit the Tcl shell using Tcl exit, then exit from the command line.

```
> tclsh
% …Tcl commands…
% exit
> exit
```

Certain characters cannot be passed unguarded from the Tcl shell to the transactor. These characters include the following:

- #—interpreted as a Tcl comment

- ;—semicolon

- "—double-quotes

However, passing semicolon and quotes must be done in order to invoke a C function with a string argument. The two choices are:

- Encapsulate the entire statement in curly braces:

  ```
  > tclsh
  % set addr 20
  % cmd {get_sram(20);}
  ```

- Escape the offending character with a backslash:

  ```
  > tclsh
  % set addr 20
  % cmd get_sram(addr)\;
  ```

You can set simple transactor C variables and simulator states from the Tcl shell as well:

```
> string cvar;
> tclsh
% cmd cvar = \"hello\"\;
% cmd sim.error_count = 0\;
```

Setting Tcl variables from transactor states requires use of either get_state or get_string. The get procedures can either take a second argument, which is the Tcl variable to set, or return the value of the transactor state so that it can be used in a Tcl assignment. The following example initializes then gets int variables from the C-interpreter:

```
% cmd int xactint1 = 1\;
%# move it to Tcl shell environment
%# the return value is the state value
% set tclint1 [get_state xactint1]
```

```
%# alternate method, use second tclVar argument
% get_state xactint1 tclint1
%# examples of using index qualifier
% get_state command_bus<23:21> tclint1
% get_state {sram[0x100]} tclint2
% get_state {dram[0x200]<31:0>} tclint3
```

The following example initializes and then gets a string variable from the C-interpreter:

```
% cmd string xactstr1 = "abc"\;
# move it to Tcl shell environment
# the return value is the state value
%set tclstr1 [get_string xactstr1]
# tclstr1 is now "abc"
# alternate method, use second tclVar argument
%get_state xactstr1 tclstr1
```

Rather than escape characters such as semicolon and double-quote, use set_state and set_string. The following Tcl script declares two C-interpreter ints and sets them from the Tcl shell:

```
%# declare variables in the C-Interpreter environment
% cmd int xactint4\;
% cmd int xactint5\;
% set tclint4 0x1
%
% set_state xactint4 $tclint4
% set_state xactint5 0x1
```

The following Tcl script declares two C-interpreter strings and sets them from the Tcl shell:

```
% cmd string xactstr3\;
% cmd string xactstr4\;
% set tclstr "abc"
%
% set_string xactstr3 $tclstr
% set_string xactstr4 "cde"
```

If you have linked a foreign model DLL with the transactor, the toolkit provides the Tcl procedure `xact_register_tcl_proc` for converting registered foreign model functions to Tcl procedures. You can find this conversion explained in:

```
ixa_sdk_4.0\me_tools\lib\tcl8.4\
xact_register_tcl_proc.tcl
```

The syntax for this is:

```
xact_register_tcl_proc name numstrargs numintargs
```

where `name` is the function name, `numstrargs` is the number of string arguments, and `numintargs` is the number of `int` arguments. This syntax is used extensively in packet generation, where the same Tcl script for creating and configuring packets and flows can be used for simulation and hardware packet generation.

Performance Statistics

During simulation, performance statistics are collected for a variety of units and buses, such as the utilization of ME cycles, command buses, and FIFOs. Performance statistics are controlled from the top Simulation menu, as shown in Figure 13.6.

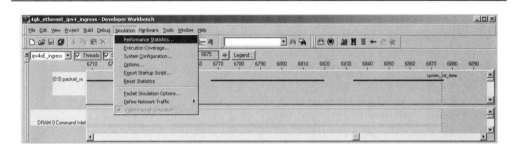

Figure 13.6   Setting Up to Collect Performance Statistics

You should first run simulation until the microengines are actually busy; for example:

- After initialization has been completed. In this example, go to `system_init_done#`, as described previously.

- When receive and transmit are at a steady state—running line rate. Use the Simulation Status window to run until transmit rate increases to approximately equal to the receive rate.

Now click Reset Statistics in the Simulation menu and run the simulation for a few thousand cycles.

The statistics show the activity when the chip is fully loaded. To display the dialog choose Performance Statistics from the Simulation menu, shown in Figure 13.7. As you can see, you can choose from a large selection. This should be roughly the same as the projections made in the Architecture Tool. If not, your architect has missed something.

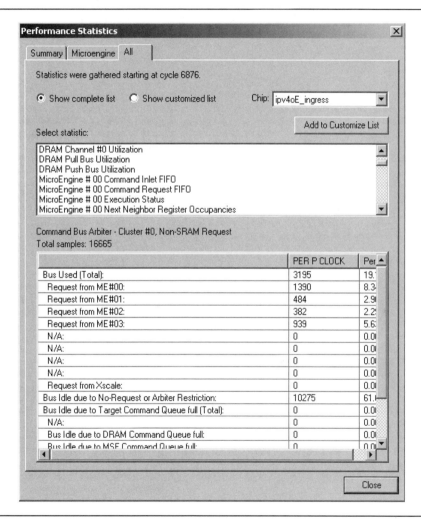

Figure 13.7   Performance Statistics

From the Simulation menu, choose execution coverage. This display, shown in Figure 13.8, provides a measurement of your code usage, including how many times each instruction, also identified by program counter value, executed.

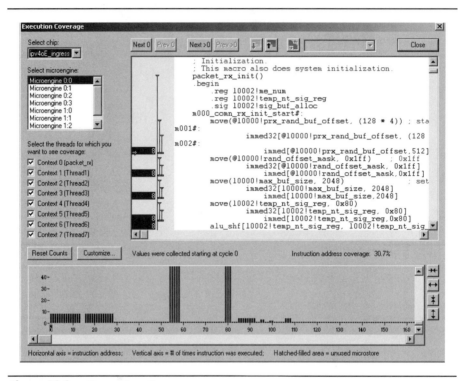

Figure 13.8   Execution Coverage

If a block of code was not executed at all, the bar graph stays at zero for a range of PCs for one of two reasons:

■ You did not run simulation long enough.

■ Your packet test cases were not rich enough to exercise all code paths. Your test engineer should write some more cases.

Summary

In this chapter, you have learned a number of useful features:

■ Use the data watch to capture and organize the values of selected hardware registers in one place. Set breakpoint on change.

■ Use the memory watch to capture and organize the values of memory address ranges in one place. Set breakpoint on change.

■ Through the C-interpreter and transactor command line interface, you have full access and control of the simulator.

■ Through Tcl command line scripts, you have full Tcl shell capabilities plus access to the C-interpreter and transactor command line.

■ By creating and loading foreign models, you can add functionality to the simulator.

■ Use performance statistics display to compare results with initial architecture unit and bus bandwidth utilization projections.

■ Use execution coverage to check test coverage.

## Chapter 14

Packet-Centric Debugging

*Finally, that fast packet quit ringing her bell, and started
down the river—but she hadn't gone mor'n a mile, till she
ran clean up on top of a sand-bar, whar she stuck till plum
one o'clock, spite of the Captain's swearin'.*

—Mark Twain

Now you have the simulation running. The packet generator is sending packets in to the Intel® IXP2800 Network Processor. You've established output log files to capture packets for each transmit port. You
look in the files, and what do you see? Mostly garbage and an occasional
packet! Or perhaps you have garbage in, packets out, as shown in Figure
14.1. This chaos is typical of the second microsecond in the life of packets that are thrust upon an untested design.

In the old days—that is, before you read this chapter—you had to
look in the output log file, scan through packet data, and when you
found something that was not right, you had to figure out which packet
contained the error and approximate the cycles in which the erroneous
packet went through the chip simulator. To do so, you probably re-
started the simulation and ran it until the packet appeared in the log file.
You subtracted about 1400 cycles from that time. Then you reran simulation again to the beginning of the 1400-cycle period. Then you had to
guess which code most probably had last touched the packet. It is even
worse if the same code is running on many microengines because you
have to look for the packet in all of them. Then you set breakpoints and
stepped through the code until you saw that packet, maybe a 1000 cycles

later. Only then could you begin tracing backward to the cause of the problem. You probably had to rerun the simulation a few more times because you could not determine a value that was in memory during an earlier cycle. So much for nostalgia! Let's get on to the new way.

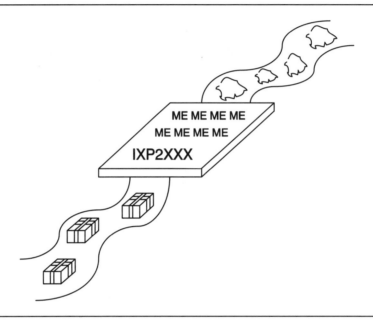

Figure 14.1   The Network Processor Validates, Modifies, Meters and Shapes Packets

This chapter describes new features that help you speed up the debugging process. The methodology of these new features is called *packet-centric debugging*. The name stems from the fact that in this debugging style, you start with tracing the packet, and the GUI presents the events and execution history of packets of interest as you select them. The tool in the Developer Workbench that traces the packets is called the packet profiler.

As you may recall in the previous debug session, you just knew where in the code to look for problems. With packet-centric debugging, feel free to forget how your code works; you can fill your brain with other things! Homework exercise: Repeat until memorized, "It's not about the thread, it's all about the packet."

The Enabler—Event History Collection

The Developer Workbench provides a collection of register write and memory reference events that have occurred during the simulation. To enable packet-centric debugging, the following types of events must be collected:

- *Thread program counter (PC)*. For each simulation cycle, thread PC history collection records each microengine's PC and execution state: that is, inactive, idle, executing, aborted, or stalled.

- *Register writes*. When microengine registers change in value, register history collection records the cycle, register type, address, and value. Information is collected for the following types of registers: general-purpose registers (GPRs), transfer registers, local memory, content addressable memory (CAM), next neighbor registers, and selected control status registers (CSRs).

- *Memory reads and writes*. For each read or write access, reference history collection records the command-issued cycle, the done cycle, any signaling information, the originating thread, and the identification of transfer registers used. This information is collected for DRAM, SRAM, Scratch, RBUF and TBUF.

- *Packet events*. The packet profiler saves packet-related events, having derived them from the other collected history events. A packet identifier is created and tagged on the events for a given packet. Also, you can specify certain packet events to be associated with specific lines of code. The packet profiler saves these events chronologically by simulation cycle, just like the other history events. Here is a brief summary of the types of packet-related events.

  - *Packet Generated*. PacketGen has generated a packet. Using the Packet ID, you can obtain system-level information about the packet, such as its flow and quality of service (QoS) parameters.

  - *Packet Receiving*. Packet data without end-of-packet (EOP) was stored in RBUF at the given cycle.

  - *Packet Received*. Packet data with EOP was stored in RBUF at the given cycle.

- *Associate Memory.* Packet data was stored in memory, such as DRAM, at the given cycle.
- *Disassociate Memory.* The packet was no longer associated with a memory location.
- *Processing Started.* An ME thread began processing the packet.
- *Processing Stopped.* An ME thread stopped working on a packet.
- *Packet Transmitting.* Packet data without EOP was validated for transmission from TBUF.
- *Packet Transmitted.* Packet data with EOP was validated for transmission from TBUF.
- *Tag with Packet or Tracepoint.* You can associate a packet with a code line or block of code, and you can cause a packet event to be generated when the code is executed. This associated code is called a tracepoint. You can place a tracepoint on an individual line of code, on macros, or on functions.
- *Packet Derived.* From a conditional breakpoint, you can indicate that a new packet has been derived from another packet.
- *Packet Dropped.* From a conditional breakpoint, you can indicate a packet has been dropped.

Setting History Collection Options

To set history collection options, from the Simulation menu on the Developer Workbench menu bar click Options **1**, as shown in Figure 14.2. Select the History tab to display the history dialog box.

To collect all the events needed for packet tracing, select all four options **2** on the History tab: Enable history collecting, Collect thread history, Collect reference history, and Collect packet history.

Queue history **3** is used for detailed debugging of unit queues, such as those in SRAM, DRAM and MSF (media switch fabric). It is not needed for tracing packets.

Next, you must decide how many cycles of history collection you need to capture enough debug information to trace from symptom to cause of failure. In your design, the time that a packet might spend inside the processor is approximately 5,000 cycles if it does not sit on a transmit queue too long. However, you many want to run a simulation with thousands of packets, then sift through them and debug the ones that are handled incorrectly. If the packet rate through the processor is one per 60 cycles, then 60,000 + 5,000 cycles are needed to record the events for 1,000 packets. In the box labeled "How many cycles of history do you want collected?" **4** enter 100,000.

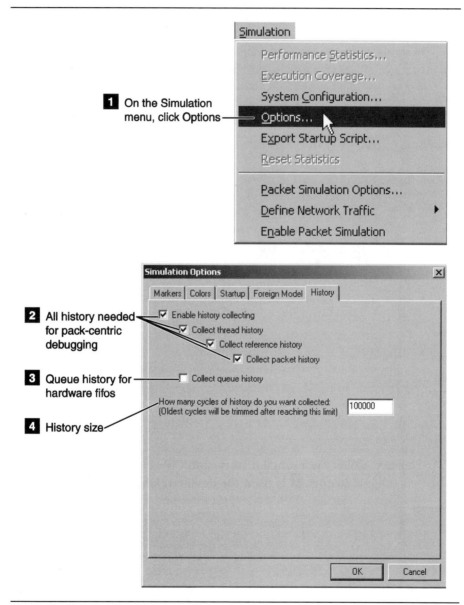

Figure 14.2 Selecting History Collection Options

Note

> The event history feature saves approximately 1,000 bytes per simulation cycle. Event history information includes address, data, initiator, and cycle information for register and memory events. Depending on the frequency and size of memory references, bytes per simulation cycle can vary.
>
> Make sure the history size fits within your system's virtual memory size. For example, 100,000 cycles could take 100 megabytes. You would set this limit even higher to allow for paging of the simulator itself—say 500 megabytes. You can adjust the virtual memory size (paging file size) in the system properties/performance options of your operating system.

ixp2800_v4v6oE Startup

Make sure you have copied the list of all startup scripts from the original 4gb_Ethernet_ipv6_ingress project into the new ixp2800_v4v6oE project's Simulation Options > Startup scripts. From the Options > Startup dialog, click Add Script(s) to add each script in its proper order. These scripts are important. They perform various initializations, including those normally done by the Intel XScale® architecture code. If you haven't noticed, this code is missing, but not needed, for the present microengine code debug. Among other initialization tasks, the startup scripts create route lookup tables for both IPV4 and IPV6.

Start the simulation. After chip initializations and startup scripts have run, open the Run Control view and browse the labels under goto label/ address. You see your new labels in the list. But for now, just select goto `system_init_done#`, as shown in Figure 14.3.

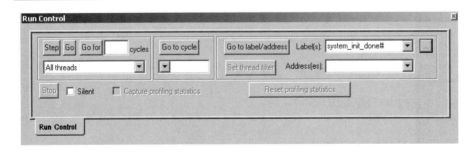

Figure 14.3   Simulation Started, Go to `system_init_done#`

Start the packet generation from the command line:

```
ps_start_packet_receive();
```

The generator begins sending packets when the console function `ps_start_packet_receive()` is called from the command line.

To automate these steps, put them in a simulation startup script. The script begins packet-based debugging after your code has completed initializations and is ready to accept packets. The next time you stop simulation take a few minutes to add another startup script to the project. Create the following script to do these two steps:

1. Run to the first occurrence of any thread reaching the `system_init_done#` label.

2. Start the packet generator.

```
// system_setup.ind

// Wait until Packet Rx microblock completes
// system initialization.

printf("Waiting for initialization ...\n");
cmd("set_default_goto_filter (*:*)");
goto_addr system_init_done#

// Start packet generation
ps_start_packet_receive();
printf("Packet generation started.\n\n");
```

Save system_setup.ind to the scripts subdirectory of your project and insert system_setup.ind into the project using Project > Insert Script Files. Finally add system_setup.ind to the startup list using the Options > startup dialog.

For a complete description of the transactor commands and command-line functions, refer to the development tool user's guide (Intel 2004).

Conditional Breakpoints

A conditional breakpoint lets you attach conditions to a normal break-point, thereby determining whether a break (simulation halt) actually should occur.

For example, let's say you want to stop simulation when your IPV4 forwarder code is just about to do a longest-prefix-match lookup for a range of IP destination addresses. As shown in Figure 14.4, go to the Thread List view of one of the packet processing microengines, ME0 in this case, and ▊ find the `ipv4_fwder` microblock in the dispatch loop. Then ▊ right-click on this line and select Expand Macro Fully from the drop-down menu. The macro expands several levels showing instructions for all program counters (PCs). The PCs are at the left. Assembly language notation (directives and instruction names) is shown in blue, your code is in black, and comments are in green.

Scanning down the microblock list code or clicking the Find button, you can see the macro `ipv4_route_lookup` ▊. It takes `da` as an argument. You want to put the breakpoint here. Well, not exactly here! Scan down a little further until you see the next instruction on the next line with a PC to the left. It is an `immed` instruction at PC 231. Right-click ▊ this instruction and select Insert/Remove Breakpoint on the drop-down menu. Now, you should see a red ball appear, just to the left of the PC, indicating that your breakpoint is set. However, you have not set any conditions, so this breakpoint is unconditional. It stops simulation any time this line of code executes.

Figure 14.4 Setting the Breakpoint on ipv4_route_lookup

To set a condition on this breakpoint, right-click again on the `immed` instruction and select Breakpoint Properties. The Breakpoint Properties dialog box appears, as shown in Figure 14.5.

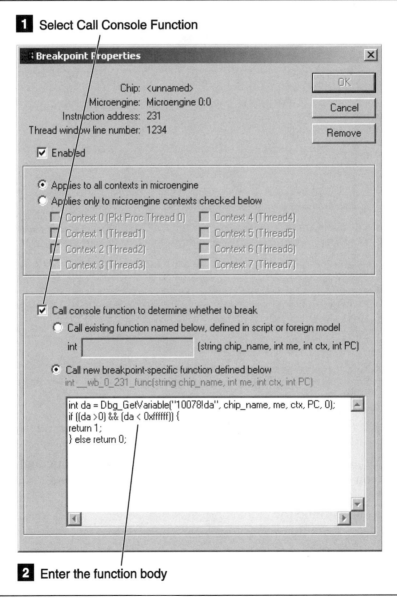

1 Select Call Console Function

2 Enter the function body

Figure 14.5 Adding the Breakpoint Condition

When you select Call console function to determine when to break ❶, you activate the breakpoint editor. The condition for the breakpoint is a normal C function body. You can then type the body of your breakpoint function ❷. In this function, you can do anything that you would normally do in a command-line C-Interpreter function. In fact, you can define a function in the command line and name it in the breakpoint properties dialog box instead of entering it here.

In the breakpoint function you can obtain register variables and other live simulation states from the Transactor and use them in a C expression. The return value of the function determines whether the simulation breaks (stops) or not. Return 1 to break or 0 to continue the simulation.

You still cannot catch all the occurrences of this condition in your code. Remember, you have four microengines executing the same IPV4 forwarder microblock. You can set the breakpoint on all threads of all of these microengines by right-clicking once again on the `immed` instruction and selecting MultiMicroengine Breakpoint. Then, highlight the six microengines and choose Insert Breakpoint.

If the code for the other microengines is not identical to this one, you get an error message. In such cases, you might need to enter the breakpoint separately on each microengine. At least you can select all threads of the microengine, so you don't need to enter it for every thread.

For a complete description of the Transactor command line and breakpoint features, refer to the development tool user's guide (Intel 2004).

Instruction Operand Trace

From the Event view, you have followed a packet event back to a line of code. By hovering over operand values, you see that a variable has the wrong value. This incorrect operand may still be a symptom and not the original cause of the error. Using the instruction operand trace feature, you can quickly follow this problem back to the cause.

After setting the conditional breakpoint on IP destination address, you continue the simulation. Sometime later, you get the break you have been waiting for. The Thread List view displays microengine 2, context 0 code. Figure 14.6 shows both the Thread List view and Thread History view for this case.

2 Right-click instruction PC224 and select "Trace PC 224, Previous Write..."

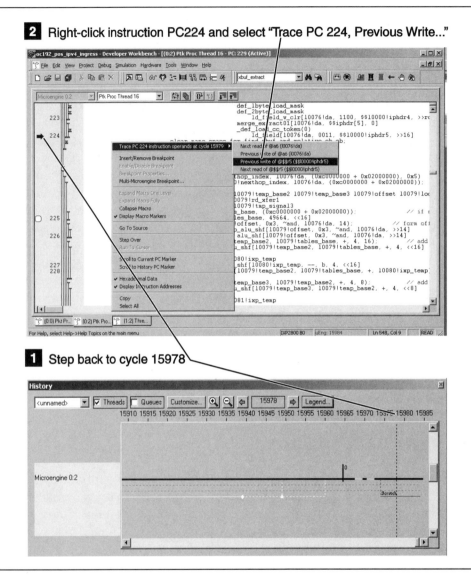

Figure 14.6 Instruction Operand Trace, After the Breakpoint

In the simulation history window, use the history back arrow to step the cycle of interest backward one cycle at a time **1**. As you do this, you see the Thread History "cycle of interest" decrement, and the Thread List "cycle of interest" arrow move up. A few cycles back from the breakpoint, you stop at the `ld_field` instruction that actually set `da`, the IP destination address.

From here you can go forward or backward tracing operands. Right-click **2** and select the previous write or next read of the operands of the instruction at your "cycle of interest."

You can jump hundreds of cycles instantly using operand tracing. Following the trail, you could even find yourself in a different thread or ME. For example, operand tracing traverses through next neighbor registers. Within seconds you can trace back to the RBUF status of the received packet. So, watch the ME and context number at the top of the active Thread List view and get ready to debug the fast way!

Automatic packet tracing uses the operand trace feature as well. When a packet has arrived in RBUF, it can trace forward to the thread that gets the autopush, set a Processing Started event, trace forward to a point where the thread writes memory, set an associate memory event, and so on.

Labeling the Application

In Assembly language, labels are the norm. They are needed to specify branch targets. However, labels have another purpose of marking Thread History segments in simulation. With a label strategically placed, you can easily tell what your threads are doing. In Microengine C, labels can be added in source code with the __global_label() directive. The following code is the dispatch loop of the packet header processing code in C. Labels have been added to mark the start of every microblock. The filename is:

IXA_SDK_4.0\applications_reused\4gb_ethernet\ingress\
wbench_c_project\dispatch_loop\ethernet_ipv6.c

```
while(1)
{

SIGNAL      scratch_put; // signal in scratch write
SIGNAL_MASK sig_mask;    // mask of signals to wait on

#ifdef ETHER_WITHOUT_L2
__global_label("ether_decap_classify");
ether_decap_classify(pkt_hdr, 0x0, DRAM_RD_REG);
#endif

dl_copy_iphdr_to_lmem();

/* IPv4 Forwarder */
__global_label("Ipv4Fwder");
```

```
        Ipv4Fwder(ipv4_hdr, 0, ipv4_hdr, 0, LOCALMEM, LOCALMEM);

        /* Tunnel decapsulation */
        __global_label("v6v4_tunnel_decap");
        v6v4_tunnel_decap(ipv6_hdr, ipv6_hdr, ipv4_hdr, 0, 0, 0,
                            LOCALMEM, LOCALMEM, LOCALMEM);

        /* IPv6 Forwarder */
        __global_label("ipv6Forwarder");
        ipv6Forwarder(ipv6_hdr, 0, ipv6_hdr, 0,
                    LOCALMEM, LOCALMEM);

        /* Tunnel encapsulation */
        __global_label("v6v4_tunnel_encap");
        v6v4_tunnel_encap(ipv4_hdr, ipv6_hdr, 0, 0,
                            LOCALMEM, LOCALMEM);

        /* IPv4 Forwarder */
        __global_label("IPv4Fwder");
        Ipv4Fwder(ipv4_hdr, 0, ipv4_hdr, 0, LOCALMEM, LOCALMEM);

        if (dlNextBlock == IPV4_NEXT1)
        {
                dlNextBlock = BID_NEXT_BLOCK;
        }

        __implicit_read(&scratch_put);
        sig_mask = 0;

        __global_label("dl_qm_sink");
        dl_qm_sink(&sig_mask,&scratch_put); // dispose the packet

        // source next packet
        __global_label("dl_source");
        dl_source(DL_THREAD_NO_ORDER,sig_mask);

} // end while
```

In a future version of the Developer Workbench, the microblock boundaries will be automatically recognized and identified in the Thread History window. However, there may still be places within the microblock that you will want to label.

Start the simulation for the v4v6 router. Remember, you have four flows with four different IPV4 packets. Keep it simple at first. To place breakpoints at these labels, from the Run Control Go to Labels dialog, add your labels to the go to list, as shown in Figure 14.7.

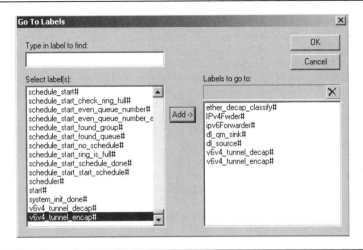

Figure 14.7   Setup to Go to Microblock Labels

Just because you have set breakpoints on these labels doesn't mean Thread History will display them. To select them for display on the thread line, select Customize in the Thread History dialog and the Customize History dialog displays, as shown in Figure 14.8.

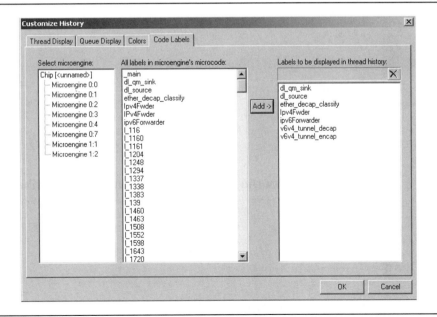

Figure 14.8   Customize Which Labels to Display

On the Code Labels tab, select the microengines that have packet header processing and move the microblock labels to the display list on the right.

Using the Run Control window, click Go to label/address. Do it again several times. You see your microblocks, as shown in Figure 14.9.

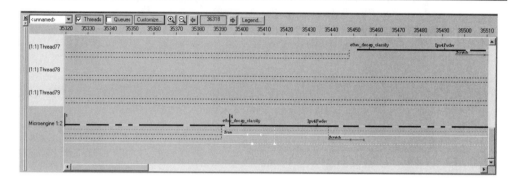

Figure 14.9   Microblock Labels in Thread History

As you learned before, it is a simple matter of right-clicking on any thread at your cycle of interest, now marked by a label, and you are transported to the Thread List view where you can step through the code.

Packet Status and Events

In the ixp2800_v4v6oE project simulation, you ask the generator to send packets in through the simulated MAC device and MSF interface. You expect the packets to be forwarded, that is, the network processor receives them, processes, classifies, slices, dices, and transmits the packets. Now, you really want to debug with a packet focus.

Using Conditional Breakpoints to Set Packet Events

You can insert packet profiler calls into the conditional breakpoint function. You can use these to augment the automatic packet tracking events with your own packet events. Here is a list of packet profiler calls you can use:

- *PacketTrack_Create* creates a derived packet.

- *PacketTrack_GetPacketHandle* gets the packet identifier this thread is working on.

- *PacketTrack_TagThreadWithPacket* marks a milestone in the code; that is, it sets a tracepoint.

- *PacketTrack_ProcessingStarted* tells you when the thread is starting to work on this packet.

- *PacketTrack_ProcessingStopped* tells you when the thread is stopping work on this packet.

- *PacketTrack_Receiving* tells you that the RBUF has received a partial packet.

- *PacketTrack_Received* tells you when the RBUF has received the entire packet.

- *PacketTrack_Transmitting* tells you that the TBUF has transmitted a partial packet.

- *PacketTrack_Transmitted* tells you that the TBUF has transmitted the entire packet.

- *PacketTrack_AssociateMemory* associates the packet with the memory location referenced by this instruction.

- *PacketTrack_DisassociateMemory* removes the packet ID association at the memory location referenced by this instruction.

- *PacketTrack_GetInputDevice* gets the number of the device that sent this packet in.

- *PacketTrack_GetInputPort* gets the number of the port that sent this packet in.

For a complete description of the packetTrack functions, refer to the development tool user's guide (Intel 2004).

As this book goes to press, packet tracing has not yet been fully automated. However, packet transmitting and packet transmitted events are automated. In this section, you will learn how to manually instrument the design to supplement the automated events.

Note | While printfs to the command line are helpful, they slow the simulation run rate considerably. You could encapsulate them in #ifdef DEBUG_VERBOSE to call the printfs only when you need the additional information.

Restart simulation. When it gets to the initialization complete point, open the thread 0 list view Thread status, Thread 0, right-click, and select Open Thread Window. Right-click the line with packet_pkt_rx() and select Expand Macro Fully. Find the instruction that extracts the port number from the receive status word. It should be the second instruction in packet_pkt_rx(). Set a conditional breakpoint there with this function body.

Conditional Breakpoint Example

```
1    int packetHandle = 0;
2    int rsw1 = Dbg_GetXferReg("$10000!prx_rsw1", chip_name,
     me, ctx, PC, 0);
3    printf("---conditional breakpoint---\nCtx %d on me %d  PC
     %d\n", ctx, me, PC);
4    if (0 == (rsw1 & 0x200))
5    {
6    int port = rsw1 & 0xff;
7    printf("RX1 %d:%d rsw1 = %X\tPort = %d\n", me, ctx, rsw1,
     port);
8    int RbufElem = 0x7F && (rsw1 >> 24);
9    printf("RX1 %d:%d rbuf elem is: %d\n", me, ctx,
     RbufElem);
10   packetHandle = PacketTrack_Received(chip_name, me, ctx,
     PC, port);
11   printf("PacketTrack_Received packet ID: %X\n\n",
     packetHandle);
12   PacketTrack_TagThreadWithPacket(chip_name, me, ctx, PC,
     packetHandle);
13   PacketTrack_ProcessingStarted(chip_name, me, ctx, PC,
     packetHandle );
14   return 0;
15   }
16   else
17   {
18   printf("Ctx %d received a NULL packet\n\n", ctx);
19   }
20   return 0;
```

Line 2

Get the value of the receive status word. This is in a read transfer register. When packet data is received and an RBUF element is filled, the hardware autopush mechanism loads this transfer register.

Line 4, 18

If this is a NULL packet, ignore it.

Lines 8–9

> Extract and print the RBUF element number.

Lines 10–11

> Issue the Received event and print the packet handle.

Line 12

> Tag the thread with the packet handle obtained at line 11.

Line 13

> Issue the ProcessingStarted event.

Line 14, 20

> Return 0 to allow simulation to continue after this breakpoint.

Note | Save your conditional breakpoint function bodies in a text file. If breakpoints are inadvertently removed, you will be able to quickly recover and reinsert them using copy and paste. The breakpoint function bodies for your router project are in the file IPv4v6oE_breakpoints.txt, in your project directory.

Find all of the dram[rbuf_rd...] instructions. At the instruction following each of these, place a conditional breakpoint with this function body.

Conditional Breakpoint After dram[rbuf_rd...] Example

```
1    int packetHandle = PacketTrack_GetPacketHandle(chip_name,
     me, ctx, PC-1);
2    printf("---conditional breakpoint---associate memory,
     packet %x\nctx %d on me %d  PC %d\n\n", packetHandle,
     ctx, me, PC);
3    PacketTrack_AssociateMemory(chip_name, me, ctx, PC-1,
     packetHandle);
4    return 0;
```

Line 1

> Get the packet handle. This is the same packet handle previously tagged on this thread at the last breakpoint.

Line 3

> Issue the AssociateMemory event for the `dram[rbuf_rd...]` instruction. Note that the breakpoint must occur after the dram instruction has been executed, and the AssociateMemory refers to the dram instruction using PC-1.

Line 4

Return 0, allowing simulation to continue after the breakpoint.

The Packet List View

At any point after these initializations, choose View from the Developer Workbench menu bar and under Debug Windows click the Packet List checkbox, as shown in Figure 14.10.

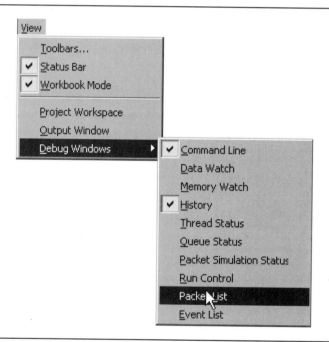

Figure 14.10 Selecting Packet List View

This selection opens the Packet List window, which presents the status of all generated packets as a list of packets ordered by packet ID. Figure 14.11 shows the Packet List window after simulation has completed initializations, started packet generation, and run several thousand more cycles. The information in this window is for the current "cycle of interest," which if you have not yet gone back in history, is the current simulation cycle.

Packet ID	Type	Status	Disposition
00000005	received-manual	active	---
01000006	received-manual	active	---
02000007	received-manual	active	---
03000008	received-manual	active	---
00000009	received-manual	active	---
0100000A	received-manual	active	---
0200000B	received-manual	active	---
0300000C	received-manual	active	---
0000000D	received-manual	active	---
0100000E	received-manual	active	---
0200000F	received-manual	active	---
03000010	received-manual	active	---
00000011	received-manual	active	---
01000012	received-manual	active	---
02000013	received-manual	active	---
00800001	transmitted-auto	transmitted	---
00800002	transmitted-auto	transmitting	---

Figure 14.11 Packet List View

The first column has the packet ID. Note that the ID is in hexadecimal the left digits identify the port (receive or transmit) and the right digits contain the sequence number. The sequence number is the order in which the packet was received or transmitted. The second column shows the type of packet. The type field also indicates whether the packet was automatically or manually detected.

■ *Received*. A received packet is a packet received through the MSF and placed in RBUF. If the whole packet does not fit in an RBUF element, the partial packet the mpacket is received, and the packet receiving status is given in the Packet List view. When end-of-packet is received, the packet received status is given. As of the printing of this book, received packet events are manually instrumented as you did earlier in this chapter. However, future versions of the Developer Workbench will automatically detect received packets and generate receiving and received events. If you see these events, you must remove the manual instrumentation, or your receive events will be double-counted.

■ *Derived*. When you create a new packet in your microengine application, you can send a profiler command in a conditional breakpoint to create a new derived packet. The derived packet is related to an original packet in some way. This relationship gives the validator the necessary clue for obtaining expected results associated with the original packet.

◼ *Transmitted.* When the profiler detects a transmitted packet, it automatically creates a transmitted packet with its own ID and generates transmitting and transmitted events.

The third column in Figure 14.11 shows the status. The profiler records the following packet events as major status changes in the packet:

◼ *Generated.* The packet generator has begun sending the packet to the MAC device.

◼ *Receiving.* Some of the data for the packet has been received.

◼ *Received.* All data for the packet has been received.

◼ *Active.* A thread has started processing on this packet.

◼ *Dropped.* The packet was dropped. This event must be sent from a conditional breakpoint profiler call.

◼ *Transmitting.* Some of the data of the packet is transmitting out of the processor.

◼ *Transmitted.* All of the data for a packet has transmitted.

◼ *Validated.* The validator has checked the packet.

The fourth column contains an explanation of the status, such as the reason that it was dropped or that the validation failed.

Additional column(s) may contain other information about this packet, such as: the flow it belongs to, its quality of service (QoS) parameters, and so on.

Notice your hand accidentally dragged the cursor down and highlighted packet 7 (well, if you didn't, do that now). The line with packet 7 is shaded, as shown in Figure 14.12.

Go to code line that created the status-changing event. Right-click **1**, select Go To Packet Event and Go to Received Event.

Shazam! You are instantly transported into the code **2**. The history cycle of interest is now set to the cycle of the event, the Thread List window appears, and the cycle arrow on the left points to the PC and instruction that created the event.

1 Right-click on "packet of interest"

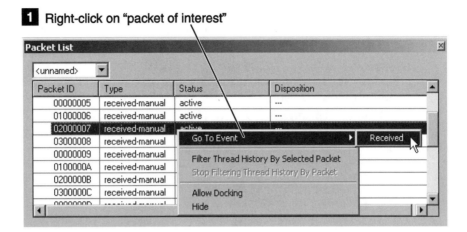

2 Cycle of Interest

Figure 14.12 Go to Code Associated With the Event

The Event List

Of course, a program can have many more packet events than just the major status changes. What about Processing Started, Associate Memory, and Tracepoint? You can display the complete packet event list by choosing the View menu from the Developer Workbench menu bar and click Debug Windows > Event List, in the same way that you did for Packet List.

Figure 14.13 shows the Event List.

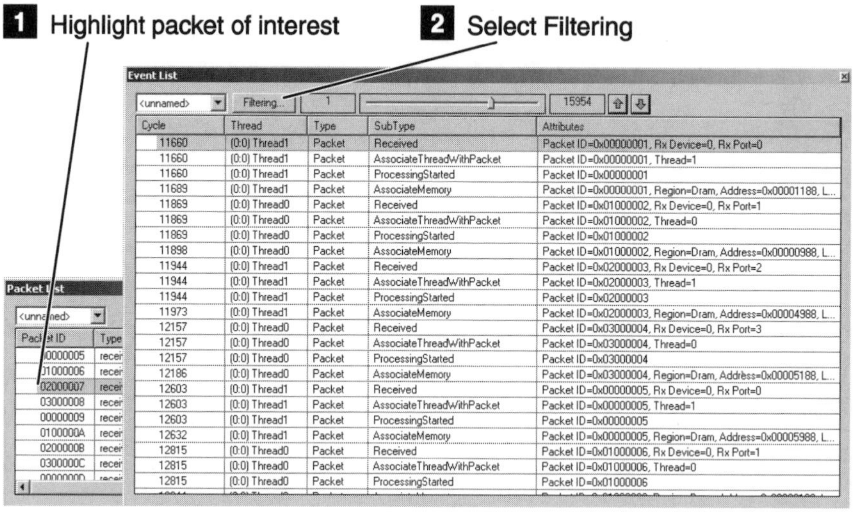

Figure 14.13 The Event List

When you **1** highlight a line in the Event List, the packet profiler sets parameters that can then be used to enable synchronization of the Developer Workbench simulation windows and filtering of information for display.

- *Cycle of interest.* You can set the cycle of interest while in Thread History, Packet List, or Event List views. Thread History and Thread List correspondingly scroll and center on the new cycle of interest.

- *Packet of interest.* A filter may be applied to show only events of the same packet id as a highlighted event.

You can **2** select filtering to open the Event List Filtering dialog, as shown in Figure 14.14.

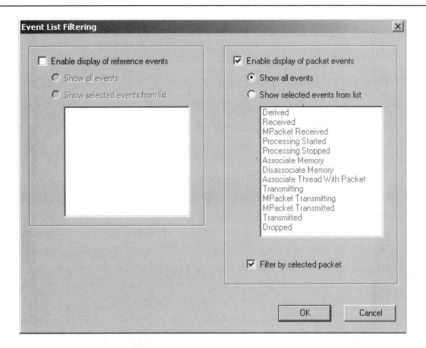

Figure 14.14 Filtered List of All Events for Packet 7

With this dialog, you can filter the collected history events several ways:

■ *Packet Events.* In the right side of the dialog, you can select filtering for all packet events or specific packet events. Most importantly, you can filter by the packet that is highlighted in the Packet List or the Event List.

■ *IO Reference Events.* In the left side of the Event List filtering dialog, you can select filtering for all or selected I/O reference events.

Figure 14.14 shows what you get if you select Filter by packet, a great way to focus on one packet. In the filtered events list of the events window, you can change the highlighted event, and go to the code that caused the event, just the way you did in the Packet List window. These two windows are very good ones to keep around.

Thread History Filtered by Packet

By now, you can envision all the key events in the life of your little packet. It is no longer lost in a forest of threads and references that span thousands of cycles. Now that you mention it, Thread History also supports filtering by packet.

Normally in Thread History you see 128 threads operating over many thousands of cycles. Finding your packet by hand would be difficult indeed. Instead, select a packet of interest in the Packet List view and take a look at Thread History. While the cursor is in the Packet List or Thread History view, right-click and select Filter Thread History by Selected Packet. The entire history view collapses to show just that one packet. The threads that were not working on that packet are gone. Figure 14.15 shows the filtered history of packet 0x02000013.

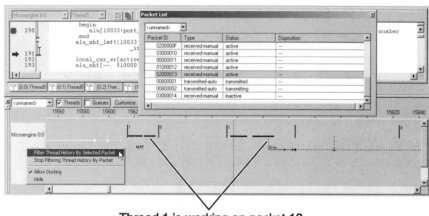

Thread 1 is working on packet 13

Figure 14.15 The History of a Packet

You can scroll horizontally backward and forward in history to follow that packet while other threads work on it. At any cycle you can right-click and select Go To Instruction to see the code that was executing at that time.

In each of the history views—Thread History, Packet List, Event List, Thread List—you can change the cycle of interest by simple navigation. In Thread History, you can drag the vertical dotted line to change the cycle of interest. You can click the left and right arrows in Thread History to step cycle of interest forward or backward in time. Stepping forward or backward also changes the cycle of interest in the Thread List. For Packet List and Event List, the cycle of interest is changed when you right-click on a packet or event and select Go To Event. When you change the cycle of interest, all of the other history views are automatically updated. This capability allows you to go back and forth, or look at them all simultaneously, while remaining at the same cycle. Just a hint: try a two-monitor setup to display all of these views.

Scenario: Unknown Protocol

To test the design more thoroughly, you want to add some bad packets to the mix of good packets in your network traffic configuration, just to see whether they are handled properly. If you want a true debugging experience, have someone else do this next step. Then see if you can discover what happened to your packets.

In the Flow Specification tab of the Define Network Traffic dialog, modify the IP version field of one of the flows to 0x5. You know, that's the non-standard version with source and destination address larger than 32 bits, but less than 128 bits, as shown in Figure 14.16.

Modify the name of the flow to ipv4oE_68B_32_0_0_V5 and save it. Add the new ipv4oE_68B_32_0_0_V5 flow to the ipv4oE_rec_port traffic configuration, so that the traffic generator sends the following flows, round-robin, to the four receive ports:

```
ipv4oE_68B_32_0_0_1.flw
ipv4oE_68B_32_0_0_V5.flw
ipv4oE_68B_32_0_0_2.flw
ipv4oE_68B_32_0_0_3.flw
```

Because ipv4oE_rec_port is connected to all four receive ports, the packet generator sends the first flow to each port, then the second flow to each port, and so on. Therefore, the unknown protocol is the fifth packet sent in. The unknown protocol results in a dropped packet. There is no way for packet tracing to determine whether a packet has been dropped. It simply does not show up as transmitted in the Event List. To account for this packet you must instrument a packet dropped event.

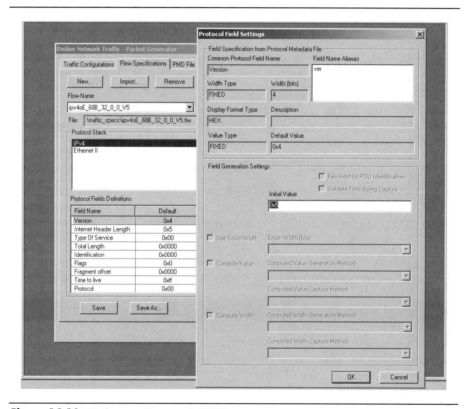

Figure 14.16 Unknown Protocol: IPV5

MEs 0:1, 0:2, 1:1 and 1:2 have the packet header processing code used to detect packet header errors. Code for each of these MEs is the same, except for a few additional instructions in ME0:0. You will be setting conditional breakpoints in these MEs.

 Start the simulation and run to the initialization complete point. Open the thread window for Microengine 0:1, thread 8. Click the Toggle View button to display the microcode instructions and their PCs.

Now set a conditional breakpoint that gets the packet handle and associates the thread with the corresponding packet. Find the `dl_source#` label. Just after this, find the `dram[read...]` instruction. Set a breakpoint at the instruction just after the `ctx_arb` that follows the two `dram[read...]` instructions. Add the following function body in the breakpoint properties dialog.

Breakpoint After ctx_arb Example

```
1    int packetHandle = PacketTrack_GetPacketHandle(chip_name,
     me, ctx, PC-4);
2    printf("---conditional breakpoint---dram read packet
     header completed, packet %x\n", packetHandle);
3
4    int dram_addr = Dbg_GetVariable("b3", chip_name, me, ctx,
     PC);
5    printf("packet buffer address: %x\n", dram_addr-32);
6
7    int ip0 = Dbg_GetXferReg("$$3", chip_name, me, ctx, PC,
     0);
8    int ip1 = Dbg_GetXferReg("$$4", chip_name, me, ctx, PC,
     0);
9    int ip2 = Dbg_GetXferReg("$$5", chip_name, me, ctx, PC,
     0);
10   int ip3 = Dbg_GetXferReg("$$6", chip_name, me, ctx, PC,
     0);
11   int ip4 = Dbg_GetXferReg("$$7", chip_name, me, ctx, PC,
     0);
12   int ip5 = Dbg_GetXferReg("$$8", chip_name, me, ctx, PC,
     0);
13   printf("packet ip header: %x %x %x %x %x %x\n\n", (ip0 &
     0xFFFF), ip1, ip2, ip3, ip4, ip5>>16);
14
15   PacketTrack_TagThreadWithPacket(chip_name, me, ctx, PC,
     packetHandle);
16   return 0;
```

Line 1

Get the packet handle. This is the packet handle associated with the memory location of the dram reference at PC-4.

Line 4–5

Get and print the address of the dram reference.

Line 7–13

Get and print the IP header obtained by the dram reference.

Line 15

> Tag the thread with this packet. This allows other breakpoints on this thread to get the packet handle.

Line 16

> Return 0, allowing simulation to continue after the breakpoint.

Find the scratch[incr ...] instruction just after

```
if (result != IPV4_FAILURE)
```

This is the point where the error counter for dropped packets is incremented. Because the IPV4 microblock is called twice in this code, this scratch increment occurs twice in the code. However, with your current packet mix of just IPV4 packets, only the first one is executed. The first one is for packets that are received as IPV4. The second one is for packets that were IPV4 tunneled inside IPV6. Set a conditional breakpoint on the scratch[incr ...] instruction with the following breakpoint function body.

Breakpoint on scratch[incr ...] Example

```
1    int packetHandle = PacketTrack_GetPacketHandle(chip_name,
     me, ctx, PC-1);
2    printf("---conditional breakpoint--- packet %x dropped,
     ctx %d on me %d  PC %d\n---\n", packetHandle, ctx, me,
     PC);
3    PacketTrack_Dropped(chip_name, me, ctx, PC,
     packetHandle);
4    return 0;
```

Line 1

> Get the packet handle. This is the packet handle previously tagged on this thread.

Line 3

> Issue the dropped event.

Line 4

> Return 0, allowing simulation to continue after the breakpoint.

Run the simulation watching the command line scroll. You see the printfs from your breakpoints. Stop simulation when you see a packet dropped notification. Figure 14.17 shows the resulting Packet List.

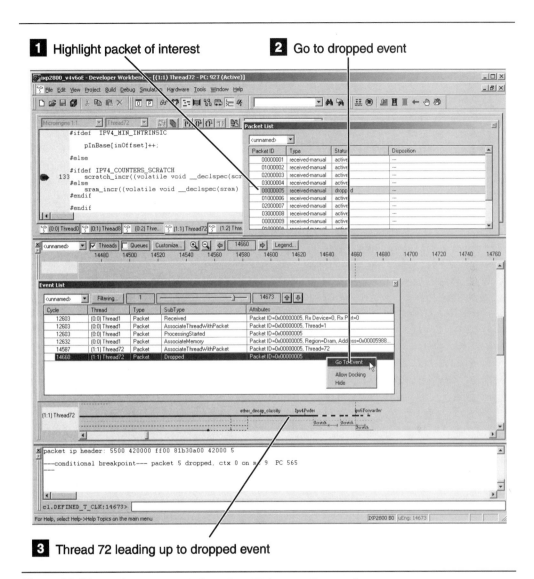

Figure 14.17 Packet-Centric Debugging: Unknown Protocol

Highlight the dropped packet in the Packet List **1**. Because you pre-viously selected filter by packet, the Event List now shows only those events for the dropped packet. Right-click while on the event, select Go To Packet Event **2**, and the Thread List view displays the code where the drop occurred. Thread History for this packet shows thread 72 execution line leading up to the drop **3**. You can step back through the Thread List using the Thread History back arrow to the point of failure. You can also right-click anywhere on thread 72 to go to the Thread List location corresponding to that cycle. You can also look in your command line to see the IP header for the failing packet. You should be able to find the bug in seconds!

Scenario: Illegal Destination Address

Stop the simulation. Modify one of the flows to have an IP destination address of zero as shown in Figure 14.18.

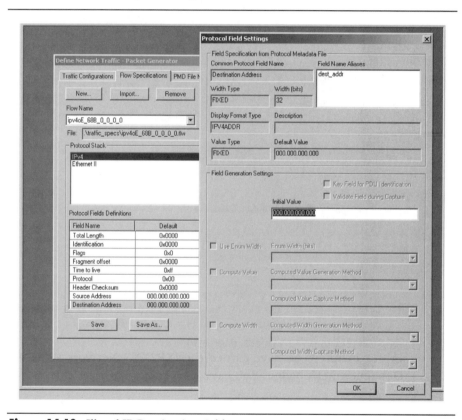

Figure 14.18 Illegal IP Destination Address

According to RFC1812, zero is an illegal destination address and should not be forwarded by your router. Be sure to change the name of the flow before saving it or you will overwrite your previous good flow. Add the illegal destination address flow to the traffic configuration ipv4oE_rec_port. Rerun the simulation.

Figure 14.19 shows the resulting Packet List and filtered Event List for the dropped packet.

Right-click on the event to go to the code that resulted in the dropped packet. Awesome! You are now officially dangerous!

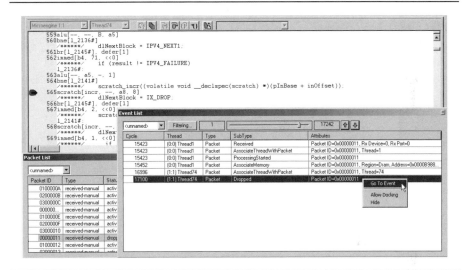

Figure 14.19 Packet, Event, and Thread Lists, Illegal IP Destination

Summary

In this chapter you have earned the IXP2XXX Network Processor Expert Debugger merit badge. You have learned about these features:

- ■ History collection

- ■ Conditional breakpoint

- ■ Instruction operand tracing

- Thread History labeling
- Packet view
- Event List view
- Packet-filtered Thread History view

You have also run some real-life debug scenarios on your IPV4V6 router, including unknown protocol and illegal IP destination address.

Application-specific debugging is the future of Intel® Internet Exchange Architecture (Intel® IXA) SDK tools. The tools will continue to improve in this area, providing the information in a familiar setting, the context of your design!

Appendix **A**

MEv2 Instruction Set Syntax

Table A.1 lists the syntax for the microengine version 2 instruction set.

Table A.1   MEv2 Instruction Set Syntax

Instruction type	Syntax Example	Description
Alu	alu[dest, a, op, b] op: +, +16, +8, +carry, -carry, -, B-A, B, ~B, AND, ~AND, AND~, OR, XOR	Perform alu operation using a, b sources, result to dest.
Alu Shift	alu_shf[dest, a, op, b, bshf_op] alu_shf[res, a, AND, b, <<rot4] bshf_op: >>n, <<n, >>indirect, <<indirect, >>rotn, <<rotn	Shift b, then perform alu operation using a, b sources, result to dest.
Byte field insert	ld_field[a, 1001, b] ld_field_w_clr[a, 1001, b]	Insert bytes into a from b. w_clr: clear a first
Branch	br[label#], opt_tok	Go to instruction after label#: Optional token defer[max 2]
Branch on condition	bcc[label#], opt_tok bcc: beq, bne, bmi, bpl, bcs, bhs, bcc, blo, bvs, bvc, bge, blt, bgt, ble	If condition code true, go to instruction after label#: Optional token defer[max 3]

Table A.1   MEv2 Instruction Set Syntax *(continued)*

Instruction type	Syntax Example	Description
Branch on bit	br_bclr[reg, bit_pos, label#] br_bset	If bit clr or set, go to label#.
Branch on byte	br=byte[reg, byte_pos, val, label#] br!=byte	If byte compare to value, go to label#.
Branch on state	br_inp_state[state_name, label#] br!_!inp_state br_signal br_!signal	If ME or signal state true, go to label#.
immed	immed[dest, const] immed[dest, const, shf_op] immed_b0, immed_b1, immed_b2, immed_b3, immed_w0, immed_w1	Load a literal value.
Jump	jump[src, label#]opt_tok	Go to label# + GPR offset.
Context Swap	ctx_arb[op], opt_tok op: sig_list, voluntary, bpt, kill, --	Thread context voluntary swap.
Nop	nop	No operation.
I/O	unit[op, xfer, a1, a2, count], tok unit: dram, sram, msf, cap, scratch, pci, crypto op: read, write	Send I/O instruction to unit. Read to or write from xfer, address = a1+a2, num words= count.
Byte align	byte_align_be[dest, src] byte_align_le	Use residue from previous align in dbl shift.
CAM	cam_clear cam_lookup[dest, src], opt_tok cam_read_tag[dest, reg, entry] cam_read_state[dest, reg, entry] cam_write[entry, src, state] cam_write_state[entry, state]	Cam write and lookup.
CRC	crc_be[crc_type, dest, src], opt_tok crc_le opt_tok: crc_ccit, crc_32, crc_iscsi, crc_10, crc_5	Perform CRC calculation with previous crc residue.

Table A.1   MEv2 Instruction Set Syntax *(continued)*

Instruction type	Syntax Example	Description
CSR	local_csr_rd[csr_name] local_csr_wr[csr_name]	Access ME CSR. Result in next instruction's b operand.
Double shift	dbl_shf[dest, a, b, shf_op], opt_tok shf_op: <<n, >>n opt_tok: indirect	Right shift 64 bits a/b into dest. If indirect, shift amount from prev A operand.
Find first set	ffs[dest, src]	Find first bit set.
Halt	halt	Put thread to sleep, breakpoint.
Hash	hash_48[xfer, ref_count]opt_tok hash_64, hash_128	I/O type instruction to hash unit.
Load PC address	load_addr[reg, label#]	Load address of PC to reg.
Return	rtn[reg],tok	Return to a PC, reg previously loaded by load_addr.
Multiply	mul_step[a, b], tok tok: 24x8_start, 16x16_start, 32x32_start, 24x8_step1, 16x16_step1, 16x16_step2, 32x32_step1. 32x32_step2, 32x32_step3, 32x32_step4, 24x8_last, 16x16_last, 32x32_last, 32x32_last2	Multiply series of instructions.
Count bits	pop_count1[src], pop_count2[src] pop_count3[dest, src]	Count number of bits on in a register.

Appendix **B**

What's Next

There comes a time in the history of any project when it be-comes necessary to shoot the engineers and begin production.

—MacUser Magazine

The tools and example code are continually improving. This section describes some of the new features under development.

Application-based Debugging

Instead of a packet event list, wouldn't it be nice to also see code task execution and data structures, like you drew in the IXP2XXX Product Line Architecture Tool? The Developer Workbench is expected to have a view for this called the packet dataflow view.

You will display the packet dataflow window by choosing the View menu from the Developer Workbench menu bar and clicking the Debug Windows / Packet Dataflow checkbox, in the same way that you did for packet list. Figure B.1 shows the concept of the packet dataflow window.

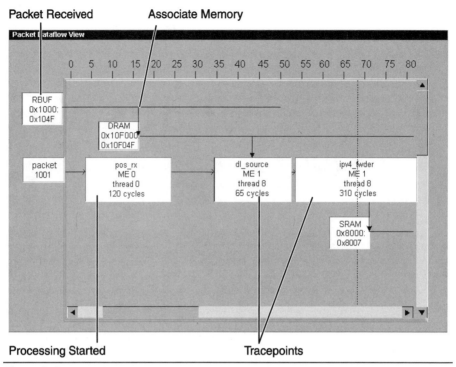

Figure B.1   Packet Dataflow Window

Like the thread history view, the packet dataflow view presents horizontal lines along a timeline. The timeline is your history size, up to the maximum limit you selected in the history options dialog. However, instead of threads, you see packet code and data flow along the horizontal lines. In addition, you can select data to be presented for references of selected memory types, such as DRAM, SRAM, and local memory.

You can scroll horizontally backward and forward in history. You can also select more than one packet and scroll vertically through packets and data structures.

By attaching tracepoints to your macros, functions, or code, you can mark the entry into important sections of code. The Intel® Internet Exchange Architecture (Intel® IXA) Software Framework sets up the tracepoints for the standard microblocks. Thus, if you build a design mostly with microblocks, you get most of your tracepoints without penalty.

Open Developer Workbench

If you use a UNIX or Linux system, you probably wish that all of this fancy GUI would run on your non-Microsoft workstation.

Currently under development is a conversion of the Architecture Tool and Developer Workbench to an open software platform. This software platform is expected to run on Windows, UNIX and Linux systems. The GUI look and feel should be substantially the same. As shown in Figure B.2, this platform will be a multiple-tool platform allowing microengine, Intel XScale® technology, Windows, Intel Architecture and other tools to work as plug-ins in one common environment.

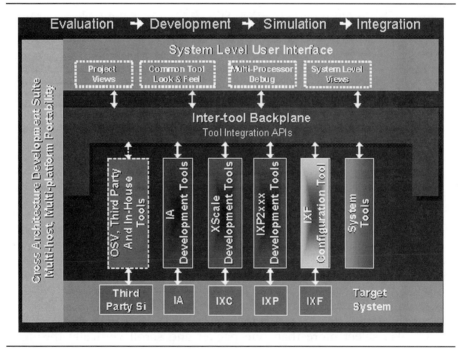

Figure B.2   Cross-Architecture Development Tool Suite

Autopartitioning Compiler Code

This book uses software building blocks from the Intel IXA Software Framework to create a new design quickly. As this book goes to press, most of the microblocks are in microcode or Microengine C. New microblocks and PPSs are being developed for the autopartitioning C compiler. In future Intel IXA Software Framework releases, look for these in the C subdirectory of the microengine building blocks library. The three coding styles will be found in:

- *autopartitioning C*—IXA_SDK_4.0\src\building_blocks\...\c\
- *microcode*—IXA_SDK_4.0\src\building_blocks\...\microcode\
- *microengine C*—IXA_SDK_4.0\src\building_blocks\...\microc\

Glossary

API is an applications programming interface. APIs enable programmers to work in parallel to a common interface or to use tested and released product libraries.

CCI is the Intel XScale® core component interface. In the Intel® Internet Exchange Architecture (Intel® IXA) software framework, management and exception code blocks reside on the Intel XScale core and are called core components. The portable API for these is the CCI.

CSR is a control status register. This hardware register is used to control hardware behavior. It holds hardware configuration parameters and other states.

Console function is a function available for calling on the transactor command line by the C interpreter. The function can be defined interactively, in a script file, or by a foreign model through the transactor console function registration interface.

Context is a hardware-supported execution thread of a single microengine. Contexts are numbered from 0 through 7 for microengine version 2 (MEv2).

Defer shadow is the dead cycles that may occur in a microengine following a branch taken or context swap.

Developer Workbench is the graphics user interface framework for the Intel IXA toolkit.

DLL is Dynamic Link Library. This separately compiled program is linked in at run time with the main program.

DRAM is dynamic random access memory. DRAM is cheaper than SRAM, but DRAM access time (latency) is more than twice that of SRAM. In IXP2XXX network processors, DRAM is typically used to hold packet data, and SRAM is used to hold packet descriptors.

Fast path is also known as the data plane forwarding code path. On the "fast path," the microengines process the bulk of packet data at full line rate. Packets that cannot be processed at line rate follow the exception code path and are handed off to other processing units, such as the Intel XScale core or a PCI host.

Foreign model is a simulation model linked with the transactor, such as a MAC device simulator or packet generator.

GUI is a graphical user interface.

HAL is hardware abstraction layer, a low-level library that insulates the programmer from hardware specifics.

IPV4 refers to Internet Protocol, version 4.

IPV6 refers to Internet Protocol, version 6.

IXA refers to the Intel Internet Exchange Architecture.

IXP refers to the Intel Internet Exchange Processor.

Longword is a 32-bit word, 4 bytes long.

LPM is the standard longest-prefix-match lookup used in IPV4 or IPV6 route lookups.

MAC is a media access carrier device. This data framer is on the physical network interface.

MEv2 refers to microengine, version 2. This microengine is used in the IXP2XXX network processors.

MSF refers to the Media Switch Fabric of the IXP2XXX network processor. Depending on the processor type, this interface has a Utopia, SPI-4, CSIX or other physical layer interface. MSF is the primary packet interface between the network processor and the network or the switch fabric.

Microblock is a discrete unit of microcode or C code that is written according to the guidelines specified in the Intel IXA portability framework. Microblocks are coarse-grain building blocks of tested code that can be reused in new designs. Microblocks conform to one of several types: driver, transform, source, or sink.

NAT is network address translation. Using NAT, the packet destination layer 3 address is modified when packets traverse from one network domain to another.

Next neighbor registers are microengine registers to be used for passing data directly from one microengine to an adjacent microengine.

OK stands for okey-dokey. You say this to your manager to answer any question.

Packet-centric debugging is a method of debugging where the GUI shows events and execution history of packets of interest as you select them.

PacketGen is the packet generation and validation tool of the Developer Workbench.

Packet profiler provides packet event collection and tracing capabilities for the Developer Workbench. It uses the packet list, the event list, and the packet dataflow views to display packet-related information.

PC is a program counter, not to be confused with a personal computer. The PC is the value of the instruction storage address that identifies which instruction is executing in a processor.

Quadword is a 64-bit word, 8 bytes long.

RBUF is the receive buffer in the MSF unit.

RFC is a Request For Comments specification for Internet-related standards.

SDK is a Software Development Toolkit.

Slow path is the execution path of packets that require exception handling. This category consists of error packets or packets that need to be handled differently than the vast majority of "normal" packets. The exception path is performed on nonmicroengine processing units, such as the Intel XScale core or a PCI host.

SRAM is static random access memory. SRAM is more expensive than DRAM, but SRAM data width is narrower, and access time (latency) is much less. In IXP2XXX network processors, SRAM is typically used to hold packet descriptors, queue data, and other information that needs to be accessed quickly.

TBUF is the transmit buffer in the MSF unit.

Thread is a hardware-supported execution thread of the microengines of a network processor. Threads are numbered globally across all microengines. Depending on the processor, they may have a microengine cluster prefix.

Traffic configuration is the ability to group flows and set their characteristics in PacketGen.

Transactor is the processor simulator in the Intel IXA SDK.

Transfer Registers (also called Xfer Registers) are I/O registers in the microengine that hold data for transfer to or from other units in the processor.

Intel XScale core is a processing unit core based the V5TE instruction set of the Intel® StrongARM* technology. It is a processing unit in the IXP2XXX network processor. The Intel IXA tools use the Intel XScale core to configure and debug the microengines.

References

Carlson, Bill, *Intel Internet Exchange Architecture and Applications: A Practical Guide to IXP2XXX Network Processors*. Hillsboro: Intel Press, 2003.

Johnson, Erik J and Aaron Kunze, *IXP2400/2800 Programming: The Complete Microengine Coding Guide*. Hillsboro: Intel Press, 2003.

Intel® Internet Exchange Architecture (Intel® IXA) Software Development Toolkit (SDK) CD-ROM, *Intel® IXP2400 Hardware Reference Manual*, Intel Corporation, October 2002.

Intel® IXA Software Development Toolkit (SDK) CD-ROM, *Intel® IXP2800 Hardware Reference Manual*, Intel Corporation, January 2003.

Intel® IXA Software Development Toolkit (SDK) CD-ROM, *Intel® IXP2XXX Product Line Architecture Tool User's Guide*, Intel Corporation, 2004.

Intel® IXA Software Development Toolkit (SDK) CD-ROM, *Intel® IXP2400/IXP2800 Network Processor Programmer's Reference Manual*, Intel Corporation, 2004.

Intel® IXA Software Development Toolkit (SDK) CD-ROM, *Intel® IXP2400/IXP2800 Network Processors Development Tools User's Guide*, Intel Corporation, 2004.

Intel® IXA Software Development Toolkit (SDK) CD-ROM, *Intel® IXP2400/IXP2800 Network Processors Microengine C Language Reference Support Manual*, Intel Corporation, 2004.

Intel® IXA Software Development Toolkit (SDK) CD-ROM, *Intel® C Compiler for Intel® Network Processors: Autopartitioning Mode User's Guide*, Intel Corporation, 2004.

Intel® IXA Software Framework and Applications CD-ROM, *Intel® Internet Exchange Architecture (IXA) Software Building Blocks Applications Design Guide*, Intel Corporation, 2004.

Intel® IXA Software Framework and Applications CD-ROM, *Intel® Internet Exchange Architecture (IXA) Portability Framework Developer's Manual*, Intel Corporation, 2004.

Intel® IXA Software Framework and Applications CD-ROM, *Intel® Internet Exchange Architecture (IXA) Software Building Blocks Developer's Manual*, Intel Corporation, 2004.

Using IXP2400/2800 Development Tools page on the Intel Press Web site, www.intel.com/intelpress/sum_ixpt.htm

Index

❝As the pace of technology introduction increases, it's difficult to keep up. Intel Press has established an impressive portfolio. The breadth of topics is a reflection of both Intel's diversity as well as our commitment to serve a broad technical community.

I hope you will take advantage of these products to further your technical education.❞

Patrick Gelsinger
Senior Vice President and Chief Technology Officer
Intel Corporation

**Turn the page to learn about titles
from Intel Press for system developers**

IXP2400/2800 Application Design
Best Known Methods for Intel's Network Processors
By Uday Naik and Prashant Chandra
ISBN 0-9743649-8-3

Software architects and network system engineers will appreciate this nuts-and-bolts explanation from senior architects of the Intel® Internet Exchange Architecture (Intel® IXA). Many adopters of this new technology struggle with perforance analysis and software reuse for network applications, so this book shows you how to get the most benefit from these methods. Case studies of applications in defined market segments show you how to use the microblock framework of Intel IXA to build specifically targeted data plane applications and how to use proven analysis methodology to estimate performance before you build the application.

Know the best methods before you start...

Intel® Internet Exchange Architecture and Applications
A Practical Guide to Intel's Network Processors
By Bill Carlson
ISBN 0-9702846-3-2

In this invaluable developer resource, Bill Carlson provides an overview of the Intel® Internet Exchange Architecture (Intel® IXA) and an in-depth technical view of the standards required by hardware and software developers of next-generation OEM networking equipment. This book is not only for hardware and software engineers; it also explains to support professionals, management, and salespersons how the IXP2XXX processors are replacing ASICs. *Intel® Internet Exchange Architecture and Applications* describes a typical network processor architecture and provides a detailed example of a DSLAM using the multi-protocol software framework.

66 Engineers should read this book then use it for a reference to streamline the coding process. 99
Douglas A. Palmer, PhD

About Intel Press

Intel Press is the authoritative source of timely, highly relevant, and innovative books to help software and hardware developers speed up their development process. We collaborate only with leading industry experts to deliver reliable, first-to-market information about the latest technologies, processes, and strategies.

Our products are planned with the help of many people in the developer community and we encourage you to consider becoming a customer advisor. If you would like to help us and gain additional advance insight to the latest technologies, we encourage you to consider the Intel Press Customer Advisor Program. You can **register** here:

www.intel.com/intelpress/register.htm

For information about bulk orders or corporate sales, please send email to
bulkbooksales@intel.com

Other Developer Resources from Intel

At these Web sites you can also find valuable technical information and resources for developers:

developer.intel.com	general information for developers
www.intel.com/IDS	content, tools, training, and the Early Access Program for software developers
www.intel.com/netcomms	solutions and resources for developers of networking and communications products
www.intel.com/software/products	programming tools to help you develop high-performance applications
www.intel.com/idf	worldwide technical conference, the Intel Developer Forum

INTEL
PRESS

Special Deals, Special Prices!

To ensure you have all the latest books
and enjoy aggressively priced discounts,
please go to this Web site:

www.intel.com/intelpress/bookbundles.htm

Bundles of our books are available,
selected especially to address the needs
of the developer. The bundles place
place important complementary
topics at your fingertips, and the
price for a bundle is substantially less
than buying all the books individually.